The Hedge Tree

By Laura J Merrell

Black & White Press

For Hazel Emma Sintz Merrell, naturally

Chapter One

The yellow poplar is the state tree of Indiana. Also known as the tulip tree, it produced the logs used to make the Lincoln family cabin in the early nineteenth century. In addition to building the homes of future presidents who have yet to outgrow their humble origins, the tulip tree also produces a distinctive blossom that once served as Indiana's official state flower until being replaced by the zinnia in 1931 and the peony in 1957. The tulip tree can be an unpredictable bloomer.

My younger brother Trilby weighed ten pounds when he was born in 1971. I was only three then and he seemed relatively close to my size, or at least closer than anyone else I knew. I could tell from all the fuss being made over Trilby that he was different from me in some fundamental way and people often found me staring at him through the bars of his crib, my face puckered into a worried frown that amused my parents and gave the impression that mischief was the last thing on my mind; an anxious child was supposed to be a trustworthy child. Sometimes I proved otherwise, which made me look dishonest for failing to meet expectations.

"Now your mommy and daddy have a boy," our neighbor Ethel Gabbard said to me during a new-baby visit to our house, where she'd arrived with a box of Pampers and a Raggedy Andy doll pillow, a gift I was allowed to unwrap for my brother. Ethel said 'boy' like it was a synonym for happiness. It probably is in some languages.

I must have decided that I didn't much care for it— the difference or the fuss—and when no one was looking I basted Trilby's face and head in Vaseline from a jar left sitting on top of the diaper bucket. My father caught me in the act and from that moment on I was officially the Jealous Type, not a good thing for a little girl to be. Jealousy, an upshot of envy, vanity, and wrath that could easily merge into greed and lust, the last stops before gluttony and sloth. Deadly sins all and unfeminine to boot. Being jealous meant admitting you wanted or needed something that no one liked you enough to offer of their own accord.

What I remember most about my mother is how much she loved trees. She even sang hymns to the ones she planted in order to help them grow. Our family's corner-shaped ranch house already sat on a miniature two-acre forest of maples, sycamores, oaks, and walnuts in the southeast heel corner of Indiana but my mother kept planting more trees in the front of the house, first to line the driveway and then to fill in the yard. Scotch pine saplings were placed in strategic locations to serve as Christmas trees once they matured. I don't remember if my mother sang to me or not.

Besides the trees, my mother also planted peppermint roses, evergreen shrubs, and a collection of perennials inside the rock gardens she designed in the front yard and around the sides of the house with natural flagstones that my father pried from a riverbed off of Green Creek Road and carried home in the back of his Ford F-250. Unless the ground was frozen, my mother could usually be seen outside, gloved hands in a pile of mulch or pushing a wheelbarrow full of humus. I could usually be seen tagging after her, mimicking her movements or trying to distract her from the job at hand.

"Go play with Deborah," my mother would say. "You always get underfoot whenever I'm trying to get some work done."

Deborah was my doll, a blue-eyed blond like me who came out of her box wearing a pink sleeper with white polka dots. Deborah laughed, cried, or babbled in random order whenever the string at her hip was pulled. A third birthday gift from Grandma East, my paternal grandmother, Deborah probably wasn't the only doll I had but she was the only one I could ever remember, permanently lost several months later when I misplaced her at the Cincinnati Zoo. The zoo was more than an hour's drive away and even at that age I knew there was no possibility of my parents going back to retrieve her. As I bawled that I couldn't live without Deborah, Grandma East did her best to help me through the mourning process.

"Now simmer down," she said as she wiped my eyes and nose with a fistful of pistachio-colored Kleenex. "All you need to do is wait till you're sixteen and then you can learn to drive and go back and get Deborah yourself."

"Girls don't drive," I hedged; any type of machinery made me nervous.

"Why, yes they do," Grandma East said. "Just about every lady I know can drive a car nowadays. Your mommy drives a car."

"You don't," I said.

"That's just on account of the one time your grandpa tried to teach me, I went and knocked down a tree in the front yard. It was a peach tree that always gave me a lot of good fruit, too. I was so mad. And then your grandpa went and said, 'Why couldn't you of at least

8

knocked down one of the hedge trees?' I tell you, I wanted to smack him."

"Really?" This sounded exciting.

"Yes, ma'am. And all those trees are all still out there," Grandma East said, pointing out the living room window towards the edge of her front yard. "They just drop those nasty apples in the yard all the time and you can't hardly cut them down without a stick of dynamite. People used to cut them up to make fence posts and sometimes even the fence posts would turn back into trees."

I looked out at the trees, which always produced a bumper crop of the inedible, pebble-skinned green apples that looked like mutant grapefruits. Helping to gather them each fall would become one of my regular chores when I was older. After a storm there were usually loose branches to be picked up, with thorns that pricked my hands and arms in a way that felt vaguely threatening, like an insect's bite. Everything had to be disposed of to prevent more of the trees from taking root; it was a fecund species.

Grandma East's real name was Esther. As a two-year-old I called her Grandma Easter and the name stuck, gradually shortening itself from a holy day to a holy direction. She didn't mind.

My mother's parents were Grandma and Grandpa O'Bryan, who lived an hour's drive northeast in Ohio. Both were from the eastern Kentucky Appalachia region and both had left home at the age of fifteen, two of a stream of hungry teenagers crossing the Ohio River during the Great Depression to stay with relatives and look for work. In the 1930s Grandma and Grandpa O'Bryan were known as Sue Marge and Malachi. Sue Marge stayed with her older sister and brother-in-law on their farm in Indiana to attend the local high school since there weren't any within walking distance of her parents' house. When she wasn't at school, Sue Marge kept busy helping her sister on the farm or handling assignments from a dressmaker in Cincinnati who sometimes needed extra help.

Malachi lived in a rented room at a house in Cincinnati where some of his relatives were staying, working as a day laborer and going to school when no jobs were available. He and Sue Marge met for the first time at the library in Cincinnati after a brief squabble over the only available copy of *The Grapes of Wrath*. One year later Pearl Harbor was bombed and Malachi joined the Army Air Corps after a quick City Hall marriage to Sue Marge, who wore a dark red dress that she'd made from an old church curtain and a black wool Sunday coat borrowed from her sister. The Greatest Generation could scrape a living off a corncob and let no spoiled, soft-handed grandchild forget that for a minute.

"Have you been good?" Grandpa O'Bryan would ask me whenever they came to visit.

"Yes . . . I guess?" I might say cautiously; my parents didn't like it if I showed off.

"Are you sure about that?" Grandma O'Bryan would smile sideways to suggest that she and Grandpa knew something I didn't, some mistake unintentionally made that I was liable to get spanked for if they told my parents, which I always began to wish they'd do and put an end to the suspense. To the O'Bryans it was friendly ribbing; to me it was another case in point of adults taking their laughs at the expense of befuddled, anxiety-ridden children. Since adults were always right, I never thought they could be befuddled.

It was Grandma East who wanted to name me Charity; Corinthians 13 was her favorite chapter in the King James Bible that she read from each day. The only other Charity I ever saw was a Puritan girl on an episode of *The Twilight Zone* who was being accused of witchcraft in seventeenth-century Salem. All hope appeared to be lost until the girl learned through a source in the T-Zone that her accuser had robbed and murdered two other men a year earlier, handily stashing their corpses in a nearby forest. And so my namesake literally knew where the bodies were buried and wasn't too polite to blackmail ye olde bastarde into staying on her good side. I liked that.

We never used the Scotch pines that my mother planted since she died less than two years after the house was built, when Trilby was six months old and I'd just turned four. A buildup of fat deposits had grown on her liver during the pregnancy and went unnoticed until she silently hit the floor during a ladies' auxiliary meeting at church one night just before Christmas. Fainting wasn't something the women did much of in Roosevelt County and that alone would have had people talking.

"Like a puppet strings with its strings cut," Ethel Gabbard said to Bonnie Cooper at a gathering the night before my mother's funeral, arms held limply in the air to better illustrate her point. Bonnie clucked her tongue and murmured nothing in particular to be sociable.

I was standing only a few feet away from the two women and giving them my full attention but they took no notice of me. Had they looked closely, they would have seen that I was the child of the deceased and the conversation might have shifted but most people didn't look closely at children during public gatherings. Attention was for adults, although one of the unwritten rules of polite society in Roosevelt County, Indiana was that nice children played Helen Keller if they happened to catch a grownup saying or doing anything inappropriate, like flatulating in public or leaking the fact that little Jimmy McKenzie's parents were actually his grandparents. It was a rule that everyone was born knowing except me, according to my father.

"Now that poor baby doesn't have a mother." I could hear Bonnie saying to Ethel. "And Charity's too little to be any help with him. Victor says she's not all that bright anyway."

Being called too little was a slap to my vanity. I stepped up and pushed my way between Ethel and Bonnie, giving them no choice but to acknowledge me.

Once I had their full attention, I gave each lady the skunk eye and ran from the room. The sound of vacuous laughter followed me into the hallway, which meant Ethel and Bonnie had no idea that I'd just made an obscene gesture at them in the only way I knew how.

Grown-ups laughed for strange and sometimes cruel reasons, especially the older ones like Ethel who always asked me what I wanted to be when I was Big and who always responded with the same anemic chuckle whether I was opting to be a nurse, a mommy, or a missionary. I probably could have said brothel keeper or bounty hunter and reactions would have been the same. The only point of being asked was to provide a vocal response to external stimuli, like Deborah when her string was pulled. What I actually said was only static.

Some of the older folks also had a habit of laughing when they saw me or another child being yelled at or smacked by their parents. It was probably what they thought children were meant for in the modern age, to be entertaining like small, clumsy puppies that needed housebreaking, or to pick up the tab for a joke. Infuriating but a good Christian child never showed or even felt anger towards an elder, regardless of the provocation. Aside from the occasional lucky day, I was not a good Christian child and it was almost a foregone conclusion in my mind that one day the goblins would probably come for me.

People usually become honorary saints if they manage to die young, attractive, and free of any sociopathic tendencies. My mother qualified on all counts, which meant at the age of four I suddenly became the child of a saint and was expected to play the part. My birthday would have been one month before the funeral and there might have been a party but the only thing I could ever remember was the cake, a lush devil's food covered with a cloud of sugary snow-white frosting. The last cake my mother would bake for me and it was painfully delicious. Always leave them wanting more.

Morris and Saurland's was one of the two funeral parlors operating in Hazelwood, the Roosevelt County seat, and it was there that I was presented to my mother for the viewing in her open casket. She was wearing a yellow dress that looked like a nightgown and her thick, dark auburn hair was arranged in the curls of a 1940s pinup, just like she would have wanted it for a special occasion. I had my father's hair, ash blond with textures running the gamut from corn silk to armpit. It was also curly, which meant having it combed was usually an exercise in torture endurance.

A homespun eulogy for my mother was delivered by Reverend Johanson, our minister from the Presbyterian church in Mount Olive. He recited from the book of Acts 9:36-41, the story of Dorcas the seamstress who died young and was much mourned for her generosity and her sewing skills, both of which she used to help clothe the poor. Her friends asked the future Saint Peter for an intervention, which he provided. *Tabitha, exsurge in nomine jeiu Christi.* Dorcas was up and threading her needle in no time.

"Dorcas rose, not only to live another day, but to live forever in Christ, just as our beloved young sister Eleanor will," said Reverend Johanson in his somnolent bass voice that made him sound like God's direct mouthpiece even when he was talking about the toilet being stopped up in the men's restroom.

For me the choice of scriptures sent a mixed message. Since no one had tried explaining to me what death meant to the living, I must have supposed that my mother was playing a joke of questionable taste and would get up before long, like Dorcas. Reverend Johanson was the bookish and brooding type of clergyman who'd never married or had a family and he was too settled in his own sphere to take the imagination of a preschooler into consideration.

"Say good-bye to your mommy," Grandma East said as we walked by the casket. She'd told me earlier that my mother had gone to heaven but obviously she hadn't if she was right there in front of us.

"I can't, she's asleep," I replied. "She'll get mad if I wake her up."

Scandalized hisses came from a clutch of elderly kinfolk who were already provoked by the vivid red and purple colors of my plaid flannel dress, a birthday present made by my mother and the only winter dress in my closet that still fit me, something everyone was too preoccupied to notice until the day of the funeral. My wool coat with the rabbit fur collar—also my mother's work—was an equally vibrant shade of turquoise, which didn't help. I looked like I'd gotten dressed in the dark and was on my way to a Christmas party.

"That's an unusual dress," Ethel Gabbard said to me at the funeral, although the words were meant for my father.

"It's what she wanted to wear," my father said carelessly. He was probably afraid that telling the truth would have Ethel spreading the word that he couldn't afford to buy me any winter clothes. Instead Ethel told everyone that I'd insisted on wearing the dress and was behaving like a brat on the day of my mother's funeral. Embellishing stories to put someone in the worst possible light was Ethel's hobby.

My father walked behind me in the leave-taking procession, his grief kept in check with a tranquilizer and a quick swig of vodka in the car. It was unthinkable for a man to fall apart, even a 24-year-old man who had just lost the love of his simple life and now faced the prospect of raising two children on his own. An adult man in full-blown despair would embarrass everyone; the funeral guests would have to mill around self-consciously and pretend not to notice while Grandma East helped my father pull himself together.

As for me, it was my dry eyes that offended the older folks even more than the words I said or the clothes I wore. Presumably in the world according to the golden age of Hollywood and *The Saturday Evening Post*, funeral etiquette for the younger offspring of the deceased called for angelic, quietly shed tears—minus the nasty nose—like Oliver Twist or Blessed Little Eva.

I couldn't cry without becoming red-eyed, slushy, and loud, which was probably why my father hadn't explained anything to me beforehand. He was never the explaining type anyway.

When it was time to go to the cemetery, Trilby and I were driven home with Grandma East, who made hot chocolate for me and warmed a bottle for my brother. "Your mommy's gone with the angels now," she said, settling herself at the kitchen table after putting Trilby in his cradle. "And if you keep on being a good girl, you'll see her again when it's time for you to go live with Jesus."

It sounded like a piecemeal family move. "When do I go?" I asked.

"Not for a long, long, long time." Grandma East wrapped her arms around me and refused to give further specifics.

So it was possible for a mother to be at home one day, sewing a dress for her daughter—like Dorcas, skilled with her needle—giving her baby a bottle, or serving her husband something in a cold can and the next day for her to flounce off with the angels without so much as a farewell or eat my dust. By the time my new reality began to appear in sharp focus, the wake was over and I was sitting on the living room floor while my father and Grandma East sat on the couch and spoke quietly with Grandma and Grandpa O'Bryan. My mother's seventeen-year-old sister Una reclined in our rocking chair without saying a word.

"Are you my aunt?" I asked Una, hoping to start a dialogue.

"Don't call me aunt," she said, her eyes pale pink from crying.

"So you're not my aunt?"

"Can't you be quiet for five minutes?"

I waited for what I thought was five minutes and then asked to watch TV since no one wanted to talk to me. The request triggered a moan of grief from my father, who began to sob. The O'Bryans stared at me as if I'd grown a third eye and a tail. They'd lost their oldest child and her oldest child wanted to watch TV. This they could never forget.

"Victor, she's little, she hasn't got everything figured out yet," Grandma East said softly to my father as she rocked Trilby's cradle with one arm.

"She's big enough to figure out the TV," Grandma O'Bryan snapped, her thin voice like a china cup spattering to the floor. Once again I'd managed to push the applecart straight off a cliff. There was never any way of knowing ahead of time what should and shouldn't be said or why. It didn't help that I was big for my age, which made me look like an immature six-year-old instead of an ordinary four-year-old.

Nothing more was said to me and the menacing vibes dissipated, leaving the adults limp with misery again. I maneuvered my way into my blue coat and went outside to play, a sense of dread beginning to manifest itself as a twinge of cold pain in my right hand. It was frosty and still outside; the first snow hadn't come yet. The yard and surrounding fields were a blur of frozen greens, browns, and grays that were blurring into the early twilight of mid-December. I wanted snow to fall and cover the dull colors like a coat of clean white paint. That might solve the strange, unnamable problem that was keeping my mother away, a problem I must have played a part in to judge from everyone's behavior.

By this time it was four days since I'd seen my mother living and the pieces of the puzzle were coming together in my mind, the beginning of understanding in the conventional sense. By bedtime I was smarting all over as if I'd been smacked by a single giant hand. I went to sleep with a fading hope that my mother would be back by morning.

We moved in with Grandma East after the funeral. I spent my first few weeks in her house trying to imagine different ways that I might facilitate my mother's return, a necessary diversion as I absorbed the void caused by her disappearance. I could see her in my mind, standing at Grandma's front door with a ghost of a smile on her face as she explained that there'd been a change of plans. The angels had made a mistake, failing to realize that my mother was a fruit-bearing tree who was needed at home. My father's walk would lose its defeated shuffle and he'd be back to making jokes and letting me sit on the floor between his feet once again, rocking me from side to side with his knees like a carnival ride while I laughed and turned dizzy.

Chapter Two

My family didn't celebrate Christmas the year my mother died but the one after that marked my first appearance in the children's choir for the Christmas Eve service at the Presbyterian church. The appointment came complete with a light blue robe neatly sewn up by Grandma East from an old bed sheet, a pair of aluminum-covered cardboard wings, and a matching halo. They were worth the evenings spent in rehearsal with Heloise Getz, the Presbyterian Sunday school commandant who threatened to have my father whip me when I refused to make the cloying hand gestures she wanted to accompany our rendition of "Away in a Manger." I wore the costume at home after the holidays were over, which annoyed my practical father.

"Why don't you take that thing off?" he asked. "It's not even Christmas anymore."

"I'm pretending."

"You need to stop pretending so much. It'll make you tell lies and if you tell lies all the time you'll go Down There," my father said, pointing to the floor for emphasis.

Oh, the irony.

The house that we shared with Grandma East was a white clapboard Shaker built in the late Victorian period by her father-in-law's parents, descendants of pilgrim immigrants who came as a group out of Württemberg, Germany in 1803. The pilgrims were led by George Rapp, a sect leader and excommunicated Lutheran who would go on to establish an ambitious commune known as Harmony in the central part of Pennsylvania, followed by a duplicate commune in the southwestern toe of Indiana. Somewhere between Harmony I and Harmony II, my ancestors decided that communal living and celibacy weren't conducive to their own harmony, or possibly that harmony was overrated. According to the genealogy book kept by great-grandma Gertrude Sintz when she was alive, the family broke ranks with the Rappists and struck out on their own after crossing the state line from Ohio into Indiana.

Great-grandma Gertrude was remembered by everyone who knew her as a Teutonic and uncompromising woman who kept the white clapboard house spotless. She was also conscientious about family history and the genealogy book was one of her better legacies, an account of the Sintz family tree that went back to the Rappists and included photos that were carefully labeled in Gertrude's firm handwriting. The book was a frequent bedtime reading request from me and Trilby since Grandma East was liable to start sharing family gossip whenever she opened it, telling stories about which branch of the family was renegade Amish or who among her female cousins had decided to try their luck in the world instead of staying in the county, which usually meant starting out as a maid for one of the rich Jewish families in Cincinnati. Being a maid for a rich Jewish family sounded exotic to me, like working for Queen Esther in the Old Testament. I imagined myself in a white dress and gold headband with matching bangle bracelets, beseeching Esther not to risk her life by approaching the king uninvited.

The Sintz house was two stories plus the attic. The first floor held the oversized kitchen and its butcher block table where we ate our meals, a living room with a pot-bellied stove, a master bedroom, and a full bathroom with a tub and shower. There was a European-style water closet on the second floor, along with the three bedrooms where my father and brother and I slept. I liked Grandma's house better than my parents' newer one, which was sold after my mother's funeral.

Grandma's house had a round, stained-glass window at the top of the stairs that discreetly faced the side yard. It was supposed to be the sort of accessory women wanted in the days that the house was built, like the skylights in homes designed a century later. There were other houses like ours all over the county, some with their own small window. Maybe the stained glass was meant to instill a reminder of Sunday manners and mindset on the weekdays. Or maybe the small splash of color was the only vanity that the homebuilders of the time would allow themselves. Our window was relatively plain, a blue circle wrapped with curved bars of red, green, and yellow.

Sometimes I stood on tiptoe to look through the blue window, my hands pressing the top of the bannister, not understanding the melancholy, unformed thoughts that came to me as I told stories to myself and stared through the watery colors without focusing to hypnotize myself, channeling or recreating the emotions of others who must have stood in front of that window over the years to pray, fume, or daydream.

I knew from watching TV and then from reading books that parties could be held where people sang or danced and drank wine or cocktails instead of sitting and talking with Pepsi, lemonade, and beer for the men if the gathering wasn't church-related but such parties could never have been held in our awkward old house with its spinster face and incompatible front porch. The porch was an oversized, concrete monstrosity, added on to the house by my paternal-paternal great-grandfather Ansgar Sintz in 1937, forty years after the house was originally built by his own father.

As might be expected for someone with such a name—German for Spear of God—Ansgar was unhinged. Or notoriously undiplomatic, as Reverend Johanson once tactfully put it when he, Grandma, and Dad were discussing local history. My father had been more direct.

"Bats in the belfry," he said of his late grandfather.

"Now, don't be talking like that," Grandma shushed him. It was only for appearances; Ansgar and Gertrude had been a joint thorn in her side as in-laws.

For reasons unknown to anyone, at the age of forty Ansgar became obsessed with the idea that there was gold buried in the front yard and he dug a swimming pool-sized hole trying to find it, according to Grandma. She believed this was how the house came by the ugly front porch; it was probably easier than waiting for the front yard to grow back. My father demurred, saying the hole was more along the lines of a septic tank and the ugly porch was built to show off Ansgar's new Nash 400 and allow him to keep an eye on it from the living room window, which was called the parlor window in those days.

"So did great-grandpa Ansgar ever find the gold?" I asked once.

"There wasn't any gold out there," my father said, displeased by the small vein of greed he heard in my voice. "And don't you get any smart ideas about looking for it unless you want your butt whipped."

For my first day of school I was kitted out in a rose-colored dirndl with a white underskirt to match the puffed sleeves and wide, rounded collar. The dress was made for me by Grandma East, who alternately ordered and begged me to stand still on the appointed morning as she patiently lassoed my hair into a pair of old-fashioned French braids to complete the Gretel Von Trapp look that she was aiming for. To ensure that none of her handiwork was compromised, a bath towel was spread over the passenger seat in my father's already clean truck, where he was waiting to drive me to the recreation hall of the Methodist church in Mount Olive for kindergarten since the elementary school was too small and below code to handle any more groups. I curled up with my feet on the towel, under strict orders to keep my new black and white Oxfords unblemished until I could be seen by the teacher and hopefully some of the other children's parents.

"And don't tell the teacher you have to pee or you have to poop," Grandma East called from the yard as we pulled out of the driveway. "Just say you have to go to the bathroom."

"You'll to need be a big girl now that you're going to school," Dad said as he wrestled the truck's obstinate gearshift into third. "You can't be acting bad."

Having been a mischievous child himself—a topic Grandma was always happy to snack on—my father kept alert for any misdemeanors that Trilby and I might be contemplating. His manner and mien were usually solemn with a hint of suspicion to keep the two of us from getting any clever ideas. With me it was effective; I rarely got clever ideas and I could feel guilty about something even if it happened in New Zealand. There was always the possibility, I believed, that an inadvertent act of mine could somehow trigger a reaction somewhere else, like an accidental spell being cast. Had I not helped to cause my mother's disappearance merely by being a pest? No one ever thought to tell me otherwise.

"Will we read books at school?" I asked my father.

"I expect so." His generation hadn't gone to kindergarten.

Miss Sizemore was young and pretty, with college graduation confetti still clinging to her shiny dark hair, which was long and fashionably lank with pixie bangs. Her flowered polyester mini-dress was the latest in what the Sears catalog advertised as a nifty knit. Miss Sizemore was probably the type of young woman who got a teaching degree because she thought she loved children.

"That's an awfully pretty dress you're wearing," Miss Sizemore said after my father made the introductions.

"Say thank you," Dad said curtly, as if I were planning to blow a raspberry instead. I flinched and turned away from him.

"Your hair looks really pretty too," Miss Sizemore continued. "But you need a smile on that face."

My father gave his dry laugh and I felt twice stung; this kindergarten business was already looking bleak. No one had warned me that a special expression was required for school, which meant I'd have to be careful not to let too many people look me in the face in case it wasn't set right. I didn't know why anyone wanted to stare at it in the first place.

The day didn't get any better; I came back from the bathroom to find my seat taken by a little boy named Jerry Corbett, even though my white sweater was hanging on the back of the chair in plain sight. During the after-lunch recess Jerry jumped in front of the swing set on the playground just as I was flying forward in my swing. "Fall off and die, ugly girl!" he shouted jubilantly. We collided and he fell backwards in the dirt.

"You did that on purpose," he cried before running to Miss Sizemore for succor.

"You need to be more careful," Miss Sizemore said to me as she helped Jerry brush the dirt off his pants. The mild rebuke left me assuming that I was at fault somehow, even if it was only meant as a sop for Jerry. Had I been swinging too hard, trying to fly too high? Was it my fault because I'd provoked Jerry with my ugliness? I didn't tell Miss Sizemore about that part since it might make her take a second look at me and decide that Jerry was right to call me ugly, in which case the blame would be mine by default.

But after a few days I adjusted well enough and even began to enjoy kindergarten from time to time. Some of the toys were impressive, like the miniature kitchen appliances for pretend cooking and the hollow cardboard blocks used for building forts. There were also girls to play with for the first time in my memory, girls with smooth, straight hair who laughed and wore bright pastel outfits from JC Penney's that I would admire and describe to Grandma at suppertime.

Miss Sizemore remained a puzzle that I never quite solved. She came to return my sentiments, not realizing that as the newest principal adult in my world, I assumed she exercised the power of life and death. With my father's orders to behave weighing on me—he didn't believe in accidents—I asked endless questions about assignments, playtime rules, show-and-tell rules, chair-folding rules, dodging mistakes of any kind and taking as few chances as possible. Miss Sizemore didn't really play favorites but she did play least favorites and I knew I was on the list.

In addition to the futility exercises, I learned the usual secrets. The alphabet had twenty-six letters, five vowels—with 'y' and 'w' occasionally serving as auxiliary vowels—and twenty-one consonants. I learned to write my name, noting that it had five consonants and two vowels in the first name and one vowel and four consonants in the last name. My middle name, Eleanor, had a bonanza of four vowels if I counted both e's but Miss Sizemore only allowed me to use the initial for signing my papers.

"How come your middle name is Eleanor?" asked a girl named Katie Morgan, who watched with disapproval as I printed the 'e' on my finished assignment. "My middle name is Ann and my older sister's middle name is Jean. Middle names aren't supposed to be long."

Katie's voice was confidant and matter-of-fact and since I knew nothing about the rules for middle names, or even that there were any, I took her word for it and began to worry. If I asked Miss Sizemore whether or not it was permitted to have a middle name with more than one syllable, it could lead to trouble. If I kept quiet, Miss Sizemore might realize eventually that my name was too long and give me grief for not speaking up about it sooner. She might even complain to my father and then I'd be in the soup for sure.

Concluding that uncertainty was the worst of all possible worlds, I took the plunge and walked up to Miss Sizemore's desk. "You know, my middle name is Eleanor," I whispered to her as I handed over my drawing.

"Yes, I know," Miss Sizemore said with the beginning of a frown, another one of my bids for attention that I didn't need.

"Is that okay?" I asked. That the matter could be resolved so easily was too good to be true.

"What do you mean, is it okay?"

I pointed to my opinionated classmate. "Katie said middle names have to be short."

"Why would they have to be short?"

"I don't know," I said, feeling stupid and desperately wishing that Miss Sizemore could just give a simple yes or no without asking me to explain the wiring of Katie Ann Morgan's pea-picking mind.

"So what's this?" Miss Sizemore held up the picture I'd drawn of a white cat. "I told you to draw a pretend animal that you wanted for a pet," she sighed. "A pretend animal is like a horse with wings, or a dragon."

"This cat has purple eyes." I quickly pointed to the picture, my stomach knotting up tighter. "That makes her pretend."

To my happy surprise, Miss Sizemore agreed and placed my picture in a stack with the others. I went back to my seat flush with triumph and eager to rub

Katie's nose in the dirt after all the stress she'd caused me. It was the best day of kindergarten ever.

There weren't any books in kindergarten, only the *Weekly Readers*, small newsletters no bigger than a grocery store circular. Barely aware of any desire to learn, I still wanted real books in my hands, as if the mere act of holding them would make me wiser. Grandma laughed when I tried to explain this to her.

"I think you're putting the cart in front of the horse, doll," she said.

"What's a horse got to do with that?" I asked.

"Well, if you want to ride somewhere, do you put the horse in front of your cart or in back of it?"

"You put him in the back, inside," I said, mystified. "Then you tie the cart to your truck."

Grandma took my answer as proof that I was adorable beyond belief and saw fit to share it with everyone at church the following Sunday. By the time Sunday school was over, half the congregation was favoring me with condescending smiles and clichéd remarks about the mouths of babes while the other half thought I was a smart-aleck who needed a swat. Those were the ones who believed that wit was the domain of boys, while the girls were supposed to stand primly to one side and serve as an audience, approving or disapproving as the case might merit.

Being in first grade meant catching the yellow school bus that stopped on the road at the end of our driveway and riding to the narrow red brick building on Hillman

Road with the bigger kids. Mrs. Huber, the first grade teacher, was a harridan of the old school in her sixties whose long years of working with small children had left her with a permanent grudge against the species. A Dexamyl addiction that predated the Kennedy era made the picture complete.

From a six-year-old's eye-level, Mrs. Huber was like an unstable Doberman who never got quite enough to eat. It was her habit to walk up and down the rows of old-fashioned, inkwell-holed desks with ruler in hand, ready to slap it down on the head, hand, or shoulder of anyone who swung their feet too much or used their eraser too frequently. Mrs. Huber openly disparaged the kids who qualified for free lunches and reserved special torment for Russell Jones, the only left-handed child in our class.

"You'd do better work if you used your right hand," Mrs. Huber complained when it was Russell's turn to recite the list of vocabulary words on the blackboard. He was one of the slower learners who always mixed up 'come' with 'go' and 'like' with 'lake.' Mrs. Huber ignored the illustration of the left-handed writer on page two of our penmanship books, saying she was older than the person who wrote the book and knew better.

Once at reading time I furtively held the book in my left hand to see if it was harder to recognize the letters that way. It wasn't. Literacy had kicked in for me, a magic moment. At home that night I tried holding the book between my toes, marveling that even then the words were legible.

Some days I was the goat. Mrs. Huber might catch me with dirty shoes or forgotten lunch money and could be counted on to sniff about my not having a mother to keep me from being such a mess. She might have meant it as a criticism of my father for not remarrying since it was her custom to bullyrag the child if the parents were in her bad books, either for past misconduct or some more recent waywardness. Mrs. Huber knew most of our parents from their grade school days and once scandalized the class with a narrative about my ten-year-old father being physically thrown off the school bus for his rowdy behavior.

"And there was a winter storm going on too," Mrs. Huber added, gripping me with a freezing stare of accusation, caught in one of her time warps where my father was still in trouble but it was me taking the rap in his place. "With snow coming down and the road was covered with ice. So when Charity's father got thrown off the bus, he cut his head on the ice. That's what can happen to you when you're bad."

Everyone nodded soberly except me; I was frozen with mortification and waiting for Mrs. Huber to start quoting threats from the Book of Exodus. Possibly afraid that she'd gone overboard, Mrs. Huber quickly added, "Your mommy was such a sweet little girl," in the voice she used for playing nice, which sounded like a bad imitation of a parakeet.

My father always reminded me to use caution with Mrs. Huber since getting on her bad side meant she'd be that much harder on Trilby in three years. The thought of my heedless little brother being at the mercy of Mrs. Huber kept me awake at night, although Grandma told me there was nothing to worry about. "Trilby's so sweet, there's nobody in the world that could be mean to him," she promised.

"People are mean to me sometimes, even when I try to be nice to them."

"Well . . ." Grandma hemmed, looking for a save. "Maybe you're just a little too sensitive sometimes."

She probably said this to protect me from the fact that the world had its unfair sides and worse. Instead I took it as evidence that any complaint I might have was only from my natural inclination to be tetchy or overly demanding. It was up to me to keep bad things from happening and if they happened anyway, I'd have to pretend they were good or accept them as just desserts.

Chapter Three

There weren't any other children within walking distance of our house, which meant my brother was my only regular playmate until I was eight. We spent hours by the creek that ran through a wooded acre of Grandma East's property, sometimes playing cowboys and Indians or semi drivers and Smokey Bears. There was never a shortage of ideas.

"Do you want to hunt crawdads?" Trilby might ask on a Saturday morning after our favorite cartoons were over, our beds made, and any small jobs that Grandma East assigned were finished.

"No, let's go look for puffballs in the woods. Elvin Witt said he'd give us fifty cents for each one we bring him." Depending on what time of year it was, I might alternatively suggest hunting for June roses, rabbits' nests, or building a replica of our house with snow. Sometimes I read books to Trilby but he was easily distracted and thought nothing of taking a bathroom break and then wandering off to look for a snack or watch TV when I was in the middle of a story, leaving me hanging until it was obvious that I was on my own.

Our neighbor Abigail Irwin's son Adam was shot down somewhere over Haiphong in North Vietnam in late 1972—the Christmas bombings, they called them in the news—and she refused to change his room or go through his things for three years. When Saigon fell in 1975, Abigail crumbled and asked some of the other women at church to stop by and take anything they wanted from Adam's room. Grandma was the only one to accept the offer; the others were probably afraid that Abigail might start crying on them. This meant most of Adam's old toys, books, Penncrest record player, and album collection were loaded onto Dad's truck, making it Christmas in April at our house. At Grandma's insistence, I carefully penned a formal thank-you note to Abigail and signed it with my name and Trilby's.

"You didn't need to put your whole middle name on that," Grandma said. "There's hardly any room left for your brother."

Once the thank-you note was written, Trilby and I were free to plug in the record player. We immediately got to work memorizing nearly every song ever recorded by the Beatles, whose albums made up the bulk of Adam's record collection. The books were less interesting; we were only allowed access to a single box of *Hardy Boys* mysteries that were illustrated with characters dressed in the buttoned-down fashions of the early fifties whose bland, unlined faces reminded me of the mannequins at the Sears store in Cincinnati where we'd gone to buy my Brownie uniform.

Roosevelt County was patently nostalgic for the years following the end of the Second World War, ridiculous clothes or not. To hear people talk, life had been near to perfect then, even with polio and Khrushchev to worry about. The seventies might have brought automatic transmissions and color TV for the working man but anarchy was the byproduct. People could see more of what they were missing and like Grandma said, more women were behind the wheel, driving away from disagreeable situations or into a tree after some elbow-bending at the newly coed White Light Tavern in Hazelwood.

The family farms were disappearing too, which meant social order was going out the window. Maybe this was why so many people didn't know what to do with children besides asking them hackneyed questions about school and what they wanted to do when they were big. Without having any kind of hand in a family enterprise, children were now more parasitical by definition, their overall standing reduced like a fallen stock price even as taxpayers were being expected to lay out ever-increasing sums of money and energy to subsidize them.

We didn't have many books in the house besides Grandma's King James Bible and a set of Funk & Wagnalls from 1960, although there were a few remnants from my father's busy childhood. Trilby's favorite of these was *The Little House*, a story about a small pink house built in the country that was gradually squeezed in on all sides by a sprawling monster of a city filled with skyscrapers. The little house was rescued in the end by the granddaughter of the original owners, who arranged to have it moved out of the city and into a more pastoral setting, where it was lovingly restored to its former state of Hummel figurine adorability.

"This little house shall never be sold for gold or silver and she will live to see our great-great grandchildren's great-great grandchildren living in her," said Grandma as she read the story to Trilby for the wazillionth time. She turned to my father, who was watching TV with me. "Can you imagine having a pink house? I'd feel like I was living in a cathouse."

"Can we get a pink house for our cats?" I asked.

"No," my father said. He laughed hard, surprising me.

"Grandma, the little house was very happy as she sat on the hill," Trilby prompted impatiently.

"Keep your britches on, junior. The little house was very happy as she sat on the hill and watched the countryside around her . . ."

Grandma knew a lot of stories. She told us fables about why the sea had salt in it, a fisherman catching a magic fish that gave him three wishes, and a sad little pine tree that wished for leaves instead of needles. There were also some nonfiction gems—Grandma at the age of nine taunting her best friend Junie Applegate with a captured garter snake as they picked green beans for Junie's mother. And Junie consequently screaming, peeing her drawers, and chasing Grandma all over

37

Mount Olive with a hoe, in that order. Our favorite was the pig story, Grandma aged five standing outside her uncle's barn one day when her fifteen-year-old cousin Josiah grabbed her and plopped her onto the back of a small pig that was in the vicinity.

"I don't know who was scareder, me or that pig," Grandma always said. The animal took off in a nervous sprint, running around in circles and squealing like a tornado siren while Josiah ran alongside of them and held on to her. Grandma's brothers and sisters called her Demon for a while.

There were eight children in Grandma East's family and six in Grandpa East's—Trilby and I always forgot his name was Reuben—but together they had only one child survive to voting age. Besides four miscarriages, there were two daughters named Alice and Henrietta who died from diphtheria in the spring of 1941. Grandpa East was drafted in 1942 since his father was still alive and able to run the farm with his daughter and some of the younger local women replacing the male hired hands who were serving in the Army. My father didn't have a chance to arrive until the post-war boom of 1948.

Owing to their ability to speak German, Grandpa East and some of the other young men from the county were sent to the European theater of the war instead of the Pacific. His best war story took place one night in the French countryside after a shellacking from the Luftwaffe. A young private in his unit opened fire without warning and killed a soldier wearing an

American uniform who was approaching them on foot from a forest.

"Private, what the Sam Hill did you do that for?" the sergeant demanded. He probably said hell instead of Sam Hill but Grandma East wouldn't have repeated that.

"I couldn't make out his uniform," the trigger-happy private allegedly said. "I just saw him walking stick-legged like my pap so I figured he was a Kraut."

A search of the dead man revealed that he was a German spy and it was noted for the record that American soldiers did tend to slouch and saunter in random patterns when they walked, a perfect display of the slapdash individualism that da Furor saw as evidence of genetic inferiority. The private was complimented on his observation skills, for which he received a commendation and a bottle of good cognac that he and his best friend drank at once and immediately regurgitated. All this for shooting someone who reminded him of his father.

Grandma East grew up in Roosevelt County, a farm girl turned wife for years but after Grandpa East died when I was two she began renting her land to Elvin Witt, whose acreage bordered hers on the eastern side. There were three fields facing our house, each one growing corn, wheat, or soybeans, depending on the rotation schedule. Each field was always planted like the others.

"Why don't they plant something different in each field?" I asked my father once when it was soybean year.

"What for?" he asked, his eyes on the issue of *Farm Journal* in front of him.

"So it'd be something different," I said lamely, not knowing the word for variety. My ideas never made sense when I sounded them out. "Why don't they ever plant strawberries or tomatoes or potatoes?"

"We got all those things in the garden," Dad said, missing my point. "More than we need."

He was right about Grandma's garden. It was a cornucopia of Silver Queen and popcorn, bib lettuce, cucumbers, three kinds of tomatoes, pole beans, russet potatoes, sweet onions, green peppers, and cucumbers in one half and strawberries, cantaloupe, watermelon, and pumpkins in the other. Strawberries were the nearest thing to a guilty pleasure that Grandma had; their plot was the largest and my father always said she ate half as many as she picked each summer. Any excess from the garden always went to Reverend Johanson or one of the neighbors.

We kept a few chickens in an indoor coop for eggs and the occasional fryer; other than that, our barn was empty. The hatching of baby chicks was always a red-letter day for Trilby and me, though we were forbidden to hold them unsupervised. Most of them went to the sale barn in Hazelwood once they grew feathers. There was always a cat or two around the house and Herman, our basset hound. Grandma liked animals and had a knack for choosing names that suited them. My father could take the cats or leave them but he enjoyed Herman's company and sometimes offered him table scraps or a handful of crushed red peppers.

"Here you go, Smoky Link," Dad would say with his hand out, which was Herman's cue to scarf down the peppers and immediately run straight to the bathroom for a long drink from the toilet while everyone laughed. Herman's credulity made it hard to feel sorry for him although Grandma at least made sure the toilet was flushed first.

Grandma spoke to the cats the same way she spoke to the rest of us. "Lana, you need to eat more," she would scold the blue-eyed, ginger-on-white female whose markings suggested a blonde mink cape and matching hat. "You worry too much about keeping your figure." "Now George, you need to go and give Pearlie a hand with those kittens. You're the one that got her in the family way in the first place and all you ever do around here is sit on top of that TV set."

On a rainy fall day I got off the school bus and came into the house to find Grandma and Trilby sitting by the screen door to the back porch, where they were paying homage to a large, ungainly black cat with a white jabot who'd arrived earlier in the day with dripping wet fur and limp ears. Settling himself on the mat lying in front of the back door, he meowed for service until Grandma and Trilby brought him into the house for a dish of milk and a slice of stale Swiss cheese. Once his stomach was full, the weary traveler favored us with an occasional half-nod as he gave himself a wash.

"His name is Thomas," Trilby said. My brother was nothing if not a traditionalist.

"Are you sure he's a boy?" Grandma asked.

"Yep," Trilby said confidently. At four he believed that gender was optional. Thomas settled well into our irregular household, immediately making friends with Lana and the snowball-colored Pearlie but taking no interest in George.

Five months later Thomas gave birth to a litter of six.

"He didn't like being a boy so he changed into a girl," I teased Trilby. My brother cried, possibly afraid the same could happen to him if he wasn't careful. But the kittens served as a consolation prize and we changed the cat's name to Mrs. Thomas while Grandma shook her head and searched for good homes. Most of our neighbors drowned unwanted kittens but Grandma always said she could never face the mother cat afterwards. Lana was always on hand to help with the bathing and babysitting.

"Dyke cats," said my father's cousin Luther when he saw Lana and Mrs. Thomas snuggling by the pot-bellied stove while the kittens played tag in front of them. "Now I seen everything." I'd never heard the word 'dyke' before and thought it meant two women sharing the same children.

Grandma baked white bread each week and only used the store-bought kind to make sandwiches. She also made our birthday cakes, neatly decorating them with a frosting pump that was won in a game at Ellen Beasley's bridal shower. Grandma always promised that I could learn to decorate cakes when I was ten but in the meantime I was trusted with simpler things, like mixing cookie dough, washing dishes, or helping in the garden.

My father ran the farm supply store in Mount Olive, selling everything from alfalfa seed to Ziram with Luther, who was the son of our great-aunt Louise Sintz and who had to be called Uncle Luther by me and my brother even though he was only our second cousin. Uncle Luther was childless and divorced. He never spoke directly to Trilby or me, nor did he ever look us in the face.

My father showed no interest in courting or marrying anyone. With Grandma to cook and housekeep for him, two children to favor with his attention if he was bored, and Herman for laughs, he appeared to be satisfied or at least mollified with his life. Some nights after coming home he did projects around the house like putting a new rail on the staircase wall or replacing tiles on the kitchen floor. On Friday nights he went into town after work to visit the bank and the White Light, following up with a stop at Patty's Pizza for takeout. We all loved a pizza, even though Grandma was afraid to try such an alien-looking dish at first. We usually ate and went to bed early, like the farmers.

After supper my father usually did some paperwork or accounting from the store before settling into his favorite TV chair, where he sometimes drank one can of Pabst after another until his thoughts became like Cheerios left to sit in the milk for too long and Grandma and I would have to help him to bed. He drank less on Saturday nights to avoid falling asleep before *Hee Haw* came on TV, which we never missed. Sometimes to tease me out of a sour mood, my father would sing "Doom, Despair, and Agony on Me," a signature number from the show, or Trilby and I might yell, "Grandma, what's for supper?" and she would imitate Grandpa Jones to make us laugh.

"I'd give the brats something to holler about if they was mine for five minutes," Uncle Luther said after one of our performances. He was smiling to give his words a veneer of jocularity but Grandma wasn't fooled. She whacked Uncle Luther on the elbow and told him to stop being such a snot-nose, saying he wouldn't know a good child from a groundhog.

Each weekday morning I stood at the edge of our driveway to catch the yellow bus that went by our house and was usually nauseous by the time it pulled into the graveled school parking lot, especially when cold weather kept the windows shut and everyone huffed and sweated in their winter coats. I usually sat alone or with the boys. The girls on my bus ignored me under orders from Jodie Hampson, a strident little creature on the bus route who confidently barked out orders on the school playground and who always dictated the choice of games for any group of girls she happened to be favoring with her presence. Jodie also took dancing and gymnastics lessons in Hazelwood and each year there were new photos of her and other girls in their glittering recital costumes displayed in the front window of Dixie's School of Dancing Dolls on Main Street.

"You can't play with us, Charity," Jodie said to me in the first grade when I tried to join her and two other girls who were dancing on the sidewalk at recess on the first day of school. "We're starting a club for girls that are going to be on TV."

"Yeah, we're going to dance on TV and our moms are going to make us purple dresses with silver stuff on them," added Jenny Strohmeier.

"You don't even have a mom," Brittany Burke said to me in an accusing way, as if this made me an imposter of some sort.

Sometimes children could be even more mystifying than grown-ups with their need to flaunt feathers and throw gauntlets. I walked away, wondering how someone went about getting on TV. As for dancing, it was something I did only at home with the record player; Grandma had already told me there was no room in the budget for lessons at Dixie's. She suggested that Trilby and I try to teach ourselves, which became a good way to keep us busy on rainy days.

My social life gained some traction in the second grade when I met Veronica Hall, a girl with gray eyes, light brown curls, and a severe stammer that charmed me. Mrs. Landers, the second grade teacher, was more flexible than Mrs. Huber and we were allowed to sit next to our friends at lunchtime instead of being lined up in alphabetical order. I always took the bee's route to Veronica.

"Wh-wh-what did you b-b-bring for lunch, Ch-ch-charity?"

"Why don't you just call me 'Chair'?" I offered. "That way you won't get all tangled up."

"Th-thanks." She offered me a bite of her Dolly Madison lemon pie.

People were quieter than usual at church on the Sunday before my seventh birthday and I was let down when no one seemed interested in the small party that Grandma was planning for me and Veronica. The only thing the grownups wanted to talk about was someone I'd never heard of called Edmund Fitzgerald. I didn't realize they were talking about a freight ship that had sunk in Lake Superior a few days earlier with all twenty-nine crew members lost after being caught in the kind of storm known by sailors as a November witch.

"That one of mine is a November witch all right," my father said to Reverend Johanson as he gestured towards me. "A ship sinks and all she's thinking about is what she's going to get for her birthday."

My right hand hurt and tears came to my eyes. My father's voice was a flat monotone like mine and sometimes his jokes went over my head. When it was obvious that my feelings were injured, he told everyone I was a Wednesday's child and they laughed.

"What's a Wednesday's child?" I asked Grandma after church.

"Someone born on a Wednesday," she said. "There's an old poem that says 'a Wednesday's child is full of woe' so that means if you were born on a Wednesday you're going to be sad a lot. I guess that's why you always look so serious." Grandma smiled at me, the only person in the world who could love my cloudy face exactly the way it was.

"What day was Trilby born on?" I asked.

"A Thursday, so that means he has far to go. Maybe he'll be a trucker."

Grandma never said what happened to children born on other days of the week but I found the rhyme she was quoting in an old copy of *Mother Goose* and saw that she wasn't kidding. I was jinxed, predestined to be moody and morose while my brother would be sailing down I-75 in a Peterbilt. It rankled.

Veronica started speech therapy after Thanksgiving. By Easter the words were rolling off her tongue like water down Niagara and I was selfish enough to be disappointed. With her stammer gone, Veronica was able to befriend girls with more conventional standards than my own.

"You can't play with us, Charity," Veronica told me the first Monday we were back in school after Easter break, her words cool and clipped. "Me and Jodie and Jenny and Libby are going to play four square and you can't have five for that."

"Yeah, we played four square at my house last week and I taught them dancing lessons in my bedroom with the eight-track player I got for my birthday," Jodie said self-righteously, her toys and finery serving as indisputable proof that Jesus was in her corner and her piss didn't stink.

I ate lunch by myself. Not that I was jealous. There was no reason to be now that Veronica was ordinary. Besides which, Jodie and her toadies had yet to make good on the TV appearance boast and I'd noticed that they no longer brought it up.

Chapter Four

I came home from third grade on a Friday afternoon to find a suitcase packed with clothes for me and my brother and the news that the two of us were spending the weekend at Grandma and Grandpa O'Bryan's house in Ohio, our first visit to their home since before our mother's funeral. Trilby couldn't remember them and began to cry when he realized our father was leaving us overnight. I kept silent and allowed my brother to act out for both of us; he was younger and could pull it off better.

The O'Bryans also lived in a farmhouse but theirs was new, a modern ranch with a garbage disposal in the kitchen and a finished basement instead of a cellar. They had a color TV and a stereo with more records than I could count. A tall walnut bookcase in the living room was filled with paperbacks and a shiny new set of 1975 Encyclopedias Britannica. The bedroom we were put in had twin beds and a glass-fronted case that held Aunt Una's doll collection, along with a stack of board games tucked on a shelf in the closet. An imitation antique gumball machine filled with M&M's stood in the living room and a two-month-old litter of barn kittens played in the backyard near the woods.

We weren't allowed to touch anything. The M&M's would spoil our dinner, breakfast, or lunch. The kittens wouldn't let us anywhere near them and anything else might get damaged or lost if we were given access to it. The O'Bryans' fears were justified; Trilby dropped and broke one of Aunt Una's dolls after forcing the case open and I tore a page in one of the encyclopedias after Grandma O'Bryan walked up behind me on small, determined feet and startled me with a shoulder tap.

"I'm sorry," I said, looking from Grandma O'Bryan's disbelieving face to the torn page and back again. "It was an accident." I tensed, waiting to see if she would slap me.

"Don't whine about it; that's childish."

Trilby was ridiculed by the O'Bryans for his homesick tears and I was taken to task for laughing too loudly at *The Carol Burnett Show* in an effort to cheer him up.

"Anyone who goes around laughing like a halfwit isn't going to get anywhere in life," Grandpa O'Bryan told me. He smiled when he said such things, like Uncle Luther.

"She never could live without her TV," Grandma O'Bryan said.

From then on I was careful to keep my face in a grim set like my father's. Soon I could overhear complaints from the O'Bryans that that my attitude was bad, whatever this was supposed to mean. And Trilby was without self-discipline, unable to keep himself still or his hands off of small, damageable objects. Late on

Saturday afternoon he and I began running races in the front yard to relieve our boredom. Aunt Una came outside to watch us and my hopes briefly rose that we'd finally found a way to capture her interest.

"Come race with us, Aunt Una," Trilby called to her.

"You two aren't using your free time very productively," she said before going back into the house. "And don't call me aunt."

Trilby and I were waiting at the door with our suitcase on Sunday evening but the O'Bryans urged our father to come in and sit for a while. Over RCs they tattled on me and my brother for every misstep we'd made over the weekend and every personality flaw we possessed. I had a face like a rock and was giving them the evil eye all weekend. Trilby had the worst case of ham fists they'd ever seen; the final count wasn't in on the number of items he'd managed to leave his mark on.

"They must keep you pretty busy," Grandma O'Bryan said to my father. "I can see why you're not thinking of getting married any time soon." Thin, dry laughter all around, the kind that came from people who didn't waste excess energy on anything unproductive or unedifying. Just hearing it made me feel lazy and worthless.

My father had no trouble understanding their subtext: the brats needed work. I knew Trilby and I would both get spanked later and the O'Bryans would probably spend their evening toasting each other with RC and congratulating themselves for giving me and my brother the most miserable weekend of our lives. I assumed the weekend itself had been meant as a punishment of some sort for our imperfections.

"How come they was so mean?" Trilby whispered to me as we climbed into the truck.

"I guess because our mom died." I said, not entirely sure what I meant by this but my gut told me that the O'Bryans resented us for being such a poor substitute for their daughter.

"You both better keep quiet if you don't want a broken arm," Dad said as he started the truck. "I have never been more ashamed in my life."

Grandma East was on hand to make a fuss over us when we returned home that night and I felt a quick flash of contempt for her naivety in failing to realize what a substandard pair of crumb crushers she had on her hands. As she welcomed us back with hugs and wet kisses, Dad filled her in on the poor showing we'd made with the O'Bryans. He followed up by grabbing my arm and whacking my backside as hard as he could until I cried and Grandma made him stop, the usual routine. Trilby he left alone. Unfair but I was too prudent to complain. My brother had suffered enough anyway.

"Well, I just don't know what to say," Grandma said as she weighed her own instincts against her regard for the O'Bryans, whom she'd always admired for their industry.

"They didn't like us," Trilby said, making me cringe as he dug our hole even deeper. "They was mean."

"I'm not surprised. You both acted bad all weekend and then you complain about them not liking you." My father glared at me as he spoke; I was the oldest and ought to have managed things better. Exactly how he didn't specify. It was a familiar story: common knowledge everywhere but not much of it was floating my way.

Grandma East spent the rest of the evening with a worried face as she prepared supper in silence. Something was expected of me but I had no idea what it might be. I also had no idea why grownups couldn't just say what was on their minds instead of leaving me to guess and then becoming outraged or heartbroken if I was wrong.

After supper I took an old brown shag rug from the attic and went outside to play. It was March and the weather was more erratic than usual. Wearing only a t-shirt and Wranglers, I wrapped the rug around me like a cape and ran into the barn when it began to rain. Settling myself up in the loft where the chattering hens wouldn't get on my nerves, I pretended that the rug was a bearskin and I was a pioneer girl waiting for my parents to return from the trading post with a wagonload of supplies and some horehound candy for me. Then I fell asleep and dreamed that I was riding a camel in a desert somewhere with a group of other kids I'd never seen before.

Grandma came looking for me. "I was afraid the gypsies got you or something," she said, parroting the old wives' tale. Gypsies and Roma have almost certainly never been in the habit of stealing children from outsiders. An unjust myth from the fifteenth or sixteenth century, it was probably revived after Victor Hugo published *The Hunchback of Notre Dame* in 1831. It has no basis in fact since both groups tend to view outsiders as agents of pollution. Too bad for me.

One month after our visit to the O'Bryans, it was angels who came around to snatch a body, not gypsies. Again the stupid angels who were supposed to be so wonderful. I was in school but Trilby was home from morning kindergarten and learning how to count in Spanish by watching *Villa Allegre* on TV when he saw Grandma East slide a coffee cake into the oven and then buckle sideways like an accordion before collapsing to the kitchen floor. Instead of Spanish, my brother learned how someone might behave in the process of having a fatal stroke that was aggravated by an undiagnosed case of type 2 diabetes.

Grandma's over-anxious lectures on fire safety were effective and Trilby had the presence of mind to turn off the oven before calling our father at the store. He had to call back twice since Uncle Luther kept answering and hanging up after warning my brother that he wasn't allowed to play on the phone. Uncle Luther never apologized to Trilby later on for being such a 110-proof jackass, any more than he would have said sorry to a glass of milk for spilling it.

Chapter Five

An urban legend about a woman who buys a sapling rubber tree from a nursery and places it in her living room to get it started before moving it outdoors: the next day she notices the tree tilted over in its pot like the Tower of Pisa. She straightens it up and pats the dirt back into place. A few hours later the tree is lopsided again, this time in a different direction. The woman calls the nursery to explain the problem and asks if the tree might have diseased roots. According to one version of the story, the woman is told to leave her house immediately and a team in Hazmat gear arrives shortly to remove the tree and inspect the premises. The shifting is being caused not by diseased roots but by a very healthy family of black widow spiders unintentionally brought along for the ride when the sapling was uprooted from its original spot in South America.

I learned several years after Grandma East's funeral that the number four is considered bad luck in some East Asian countries because its sound or written appearance invokes the word for death. My mother dying when I was four and Grandma East following when I was eight might have led the neighbors to start throwing rocks at me if we'd lived in such a country. The quick, guarded looks coming my way from so many of the visitors at the wake led me to believe that I was in trouble again; they probably knew I wasn't supposed to let bad things happen.

Grandma and Grandpa O'Bryan stayed only long enough to have a short, private conversation with my father and say hello to a few of their friends. There was always the same whispering and eye-shifting in my direction whenever the O'Bryans spoke to someone and I knew that they were probably telling everyone how my brother and I must have tormented our grandmother into her grave. I wanted to defend myself but I didn't know how so I sat on the living room sofa with my knees drawn beneath my chin and buried my face in my arms, ostrich-style.

"Charity, get your feet off the couch," I could hear my father saying. "Say hi to Mr. and Mrs. Holmes."

I looked up and saw him standing with Bud and Hattie Holmes, a couple who lived a few miles away in Mount Olive with their three daughters. They belonged to the Methodist church where the kindergarten class still met on weekdays and our families had never socialized although their daughter Carrie was in my

Brownie troop. Mr. Holmes worked at the roofing factory in Hazelwood and rented the family's house from Dorothy White, who also owned the service station and the general store in Mount Olive. Mr. Holmes had no business, land, or skilled trade of his own, which marked the family as below average in the county.

"Aren't you going to say hello?" Mrs. Holmes asked with a nervous giggle. She giggled a lot. Mr. Holmes said nothing. He said nothing a lot.

"Her manners haven't been the best today," my father said, his voice unexpectedly tender. "I reckon she really loved her grandma and now she's being a wounded tiger."

Being likened to a tiger didn't sound too demeaning, wounded or not. I resisted the urge to take my father's hand; he would probably make fun of me and I'd lose what little face I had. Mrs. Holmes giggled again and said something halfwit about a tiger needing to be big and brave. Mr. Holmes said nothing. They left us and went to the kitchen, where people were serving themselves from the pitch-in offerings.

My father sat down next to me and explained that I would be going to visit with the Holmeses for a few days while he and Trilby stayed with Aunt Louise, who didn't have enough room for all three of us. I would enjoy staying with the Holmes girls, he said. Carrie, the middle one, was the same age as me.

"Carrie's not my age," I said, the first words I'd spoken all day. "She's just in third grade because she flunked first grade. She's not even in my third grade; she's over in Mrs. Ballard's class."

My father missed my point once again, just as his logic escaped me when he assumed that I'd enjoy playing with the Holmes girls, who always had dirty fingernails and smelled like mold. What I enjoyed most was spending as much time as possible alone in the woods or sitting beneath the blue window on the stair landing with an encyclopedia, a library book, or the latest issue of *Dynamite*. Trilby was usually available if I needed company or a partner in crime, with the TV and record player serving to fill in the cracks. My nature had already molted to fit our family's introverted household and I had no interest in changing it.

My father gave me a red Towncraft suitcase of my mother's, along with a Navy footlocker donated by Manard Stang, the mechanic at the Whites' garage. I'd heard all about Manard serving in the Navy aboard the *U.S.S. Coral Sea* a year earlier when it tried to save a merchant ship's crew from the Khmer Rouge in international waters. It made me feel privileged to be using the footlocker, even if I didn't know who or what the Khmer Rouge were supposed to be.

My father told me to pack whatever I wanted. I took most of the records but left the record player behind since the Holmeses had one of their own. I also threw in a few of my favorite toys and books, along with the summer clothes I liked best. My father didn't suggest packing any fall or winter clothes, any pictures, or any of Grandma's things since he knew it would make me ask questions that he didn't want to answer. Herman was already at Uncle Luther's house and Elvin Witt was buying the chickens. My father said no when I asked to take one of the cats. Mrs. Holmes didn't like them.

"Who's going to feed them?" I asked as we walked outside.

"They can feed themselves," Dad said. "There's all kinds of animals they can catch and eat in the woods. They do it all the time." He tucked me into the back seat of the Holmeses' trash and toy-strewn Impala station wagon and gave me a quick kiss on the top of my head before shutting the door, reminding me over his shoulder to keep out of trouble before he walked away. I wouldn't see him again for a year.

The two younger Holmes girls were waiting in their front yard when we arrived. Ruthie, the five-year-old, ran up to get a closer look at me. She was skinny, with her father's straight dark hair and a miniature version of her mother's moon face and porcine little nose. Ruthie always enjoyed having something to tell, sometimes improvising in the absence of cold hard facts.

"Hi," said Ruthie. "Did you know your grandma's dead? That's how come you're staying with us."

"Shut up, Ruthie," Carrie said as she grabbed my hand and pulled me into the house. Her palm felt grimy and I resisted the urge to pull away. "You're going to share our room," she announced, bursting with magnanimous satisfaction.

Carrie was about my height, with the same hair and face as her sisters but while Ruthie and Tammy were string beans, Carrie was a dumpling who frequently endured taunts from the other kids at school about stealing her sisters' food. She led me to the room that I was going to share with her and Ruthie, explaining that I was originally supposed to go in with Tammy in order to have two girls in each room but Tammy had literally screamed and carried on until their father gave her the belt and their mother felt guilty and changed the plan. I barely heard Carrie—my attention was caught by the sour, unwashed smell of the house, a one-story shotgun with small windows in each room.

Carrie and Ruthie's bedroom looked like the inside of a laundry hamper. Beneath the mess I was able to make out a full-sized bed with a brass headboard and a twin with no frame, each covered with a homely pile of dingy sheets and stained blankets. Grandma East would have fainted; the rooms in our house always looked like they were waiting for nosy visitors.

Mr. Holmes came in then with Manard Stang's footlocker. He dropped it on the floor next to the brass bed and walked out again without speaking. Ruthie ran over to look at it. "Is that your stuff? Can we see it?" I agreed, having no ideas of my own at the moment. Taking the key from around my neck with a hint of ceremony, I turned the lock and undid the latches. My Cookie Monster doll was sitting on top where I'd packed him at the last minute.

Tammy's voice came up from behind us. "Oh, that's so cute, a Cookie Monster. Let me hold him." I lifted Cookie up and Tammy snatched him from me. "He's mine now," she announced before turning and running out the bedroom door, the rest of us in outraged pursuit.

Mrs. Holmes had just started supper and wasn't in the mood to settle any custody disputes. When Carrie, Ruthie, and I ran to her for help, she waved us away with the wooden spoon she was using to stir macaroni, flicking hot water on us. She had no time to worry about a stupid toy.

"You're just going to have to learn how to share, anyway," Mrs. Holmes said to me. "Your dad told me you were greedy."

My first week with the Holmeses came and went with no mention of my father returning. Since I refused to sleep in the brass bed with Carrie, it was a week spent on the floor in my Juicy Fruit Gum sleeping bag. I started asking Mrs. Holmes when he was coming back, already knowing better than to ask Mr. Holmes anything, or to even be in the same room with him if I could help it.

"How much longer is my dad going to be gone?" I asked Mrs. Holmes.

She giggled. "Is staying here so terrible?"

It was but I was trying to be polite about it. The shotgun house was a noisy place in the middle of Mount Olive. There were between forty and fifty houses inside the village—a quarter of them barely standing—the general store, my father and Uncle Luther's store, a gas station, a grain elevator, a souvenir and tackle shop hoping to cash in on the state route that ran through the middle of the village, and three churches. The view from the edge of the village on any side was a narrow paved road running through corn, wheat, and soybean fields, broken up by the occasional pasture or pond. No forests or even a decent-sized patch of woods could be seen and there weren't any creeks or rivers within walking distance. There was no place to think or even exist without outside interference and my nerves were getting raw.

"Your dad's gone away for a few days and he's not sure when he'll be back so he wants you to stay here for right now," Mrs. Holmes said when week three was drawing to a close and I was demanding a departure date once again.

"Can't I call him?"

"No, we can't afford the long distance. You'll need to wait till he calls here."

"Why is he long distance?" I asked.

"Because he's out of town. Now be quiet."

I went to the Methodist Sunday school with the Holmes girls. Carrie and I were in the class taught by Alma Schultz, an opinionated and disoriented lady of seventy-nine who kept referring to me as Charity Holmes; nothing could sway her from her notion that I'd been adopted. When I asked Alma to change my name to Sintz in her attendance book, she refused.

"You have a new family now," Alma said with a beatific smile that was all the more infuriating since her age didn't allow me the luxury of violent retaliatory fantasies.

Mrs. Holmes's wide, moon-shaped face was authentic down to the craters and framed by a short mass of crinkly dark hair that she cut herself without using a mirror. Built along the same lines as a snowman, she always managed to choose outfits that flattered her as little as possible. Mrs. Holmes could usually be seen in undersized tank shirts with Bermuda shorts in the summer or outdated pedal pushers and too-tight sweatshirts in the winter. On Sundays she wore boxy straight skirts that hit her mid-calf and button-down shirts that gapped in front, allowing everyone to know that she wore Playtex cross-your-hearts whether they wanted to or not.

Mr. Holmes was his wife's physical opposite: tall, lean, and mean with facial bones that jutted like rock formations, Abe Lincoln's beardless evil twin. He always smelled like tar. Mr. Holmes drank more beer and watched more TV than my father, who'd grown up doing chores on the farm from the age of six and preferred to be active. The only time Mr. Holmes moved quickly was when he was chasing someone with a belt in his hand.

As far as the girls went, Carrie was an awkward, exasperating sort, the only one in the family who never intentionally offended my sensibilities. She marveled at how quickly I could finish a library book, memorize a Bible verse, or make a bread-bag jump rope like they'd shown us in Brownies. Even so, I could never warm up to Carrie beyond room temperature; she reminded me too much of Herman and anyone who thought I was exceptional had to be in pretty sad shape.

Tammy was eleven, with a snide, banal sense of humor like her mother's. Outside of that, she was as ordinary as her name. But whatever Tammy lacked in brains or originality, she still had the persistency of a gnat whenever it pleased her to torment me or her sisters.

"When's my dad coming back?" I demanded from Mrs. Holmes after a full month had passed, my tone of voice getting ruder and angrier each time I asked her for information.

"I've told you for the last time, I do not know and I don't want to hear another word about it," she said.

"You're a liar," I cried, furious with my own impotence.

Tammy laughed when she saw her mother grab me by my hair and fling me into a kitchen chair with enough force to knock it backwards. It took me a minute to regain my wind and I opened my eyes to see Tammy's mocking face above me. "You know your dad's gone and moved to Florida," she said.

"No he didn't." I wanted to slap Tammy's face and make it split open like a can of biscuits.

"Uh huh, he did," she insisted cheerfully. "He took your little brother but he didn't want you so my mom and dad said they'd babysit you if he sent them money each month."

I got up and walked out of the house. Tammy knocked on the window from inside the living room and stuck her tongue out at me like one of the stupider first-grade kids. Later that night I stole a few hairs from her brush and tried making a voodoo doll. Hexing the messenger since I couldn't shoot her.

Ruthie alternated between pestering me to play with her and trying to get me in trouble. Having learned early on that her words carried slightly more weight with her parents than mine did, the thrill of having power over someone larger than herself was sometimes too much for Ruthie to resist. She would accuse me of bullying her and then bask in her father's fury when he came after me with his belt, which was probably as close as Mr. Holmes ever got to treating Ruthie like she meant more to him than his oldest pair of socks. The most annoying part was when Ruthie would creep to my side after watching her father whip me and politely ask the reason for my tears, as if the phony gesture of concern would cancel out her false-witnessing.

"I'm crying because there's no creek here," I told Ruthie once. "My house had a creek."

"Oh," Ruthie sighed sympathetically, unaware that she'd caught me in the middle of a daydream about pushing her into that same creek and drowning her. "Well, maybe we'll get lots of rain and it'll make a creek in the backyard. We'll ask Jesus for rain."

Yes we would, among other things.

Other times were more congenial and I used Ruthie as a cheap substitute for my brother, reading to her from my school books or the encyclopedias sitting under the TV table, a set even older than Grandma East's Funk & Wagnalls and so outdated that Sri Lanka was still Ceylon and Algeria was still a jewel in the much-tarnished crown of France. They were the only books in the house besides an elaborate hardcover copy of the Living Bible that was rarely opened, a wedding gift to Mr. and Mrs. Holmes. On the positive side, they had a subscription to the *Cincinnati Enquirer* since Mr. Holmes liked reading the sports page. I introduced Carrie and Ruthie to the crossword puzzle and *Dear Abby*; sometimes I could even get them interested in the news.

I looked through the Bible on occasion to reread my favorite stories and search for verses about the return of a prodigal father or the vindication of an unwanted daughter. I never found any, though it was gratifying to read about Jacob's sons taking action when some jerk from a neighboring tribe raped their sister Dinah in Genesis 34, a chapter that Alma Schultz refused to allow as a classroom topic. I was unclear on what rape entailed beyond a fuzzy idea that it started with a man forcing a woman to kiss him when she didn't want to.

Pieces of the truth about my new life were revealed to me over a period of months and I absorbed them grudgingly. The biggest piece was that my father had sold his share of Mount Olive Feed & Seed to Uncle Luther in order to buy a decrepit fixer-upper motel located less than two miles away from a newly opened highway exit off of Interstate 95 in eastern Florida near Port St. Lucie, with Trilby riding shotgun. It was probably like the plot of a western for the two of them, the men stoically venturing away from home to seek the fortunes, allegedly regretful about leaving the womenfolk behind. And at some unknown point I went from hoping for the best to acknowledging that I'd been had. It wouldn't be the last time.

Chapter Six

The first of my four years with the Holmeses was a year with no phone calls or letters from my father besides the checks he sent to Mr. and Mrs. Holmes for my keep and their trouble. On the first of his annual visits I cried and ran to hug him. He hugged me back but laughed at my presumption when I asked him where we were going to live.

"You aren't going nowhere, missy," my father said. "You're staying put."

His words were a knife in my liver but I tried not to show it. "Where's Trilby?" I asked quickly, hoping he didn't notice that my eyes were filling with tears. Showing hurt feelings would have everyone calling me a crybaby.

"He's down in Florida where you and he can't get into any trouble together." My father's voice was smug; any sinister plots I might have hoped to hatch with my brother's assistance were safely thwarted.

I took my father literally and tried to recall anything truly terrible that I'd ever done to Trilby, or caused him to do. It was true that we'd argued and even gotten into fisticuffs on more than one occasion, which record to play, which TV show to watch. And the winter before Grandma's funeral I'd tried to help him across the creek one day and he fell and got stuck in the snow; I'd been

68

spanked for letting him walk there when I should have known better. Maybe Trilby was a nicer child now that he wasn't living in the same house as me, which meant I'd been ruining him all along without knowing it. My right hand began to hurt. I ruined people.

I jumped in headfirst nonetheless as soon as there was a lull in the conversation between my father and the Holmeses, afraid it might be my only chance to speak. "Why can't I live in Florida with you and Trilby?" I demanded recklessly, knowing before the words were halfway out of my mouth that I was going to regret speaking them; they made me sound greedy and petulant. And jealous, of course.

"You really hate staying here so much?" my father asked me in a way that said he was unimpressed with my manners. He looked from me to the Holmeses, who were sitting at the kitchen table with us, arms folded.

"Oh, yeah, she really hates it here," Mrs. Holmes said, her giggle coming on like hiccups. "She thinks she's too good for us. Even said she'd commit hairy-carry if I tried to make her wear Tammy's old underwear."

"I sent you money for clothes." My father was squeamish about such things himself.

There was a small but unmistakable shift in the grubby kitchen's atmosphere. Mrs. Holmes quickly assured my father that I had plenty of clothes and that she would be taking me and the other girls to Danner's the next day to shop for swimsuits. Danner's was the single and essential discount store in Hazelwood, selling everything from paperbacks to hamsters to material by the square yard and trips there were always a bonus. I ran outside to tell the other girls and happy shrieks floated in through the kitchen window.

"It never did take much to cheer her up," I could hear my father saying.

My chance, real or imagined, was blown. It was obvious that the Holmeses were neither starving me nor beating me black and blue; therefore, I couldn't have any legitimate gripes coming. Mr. Holmes usually left welts with his belt but I didn't happen to have any at the moment and I was hardly going to reveal my backside to my father, who would probably only be mad at me for getting in trouble after being given explicit orders to stay out of it.

My father only stayed for a few hours, turning down the invitation to supper. Like everyone else in the county, he knew Mrs. Holmes was a miserable cook. We all walked my father out to his truck and I saw that that he and I weren't going to have any time alone. It was embarrassing after he left, even before Tammy stuck her head in our bedroom door and sing-songed, "Daddy doesn't want you!"

"Tammy, shut up," Carrie said as she and Ruthie helped me examine the contents of a box my father had left for me. "Look at all these presents her dad brought her."

"Yeah, shut up, Tammy," Ruthie said. "It's not Charity's fault her daddy doesn't want her."

My favorite item in the box was a straw hat with a brim that curved away from the face like Tom Sawyer's. A boy's hat belonging to a boy with a turbo-charged imagination who took matters into his own hands and made things happen. The hat was about all I had in common with Tom Sawyer.

Sometimes I dreamed that Grandma East was alive and the two of us were sitting on her front porch, drinking Pepsi from cold, sixteen-ounce glass bottles as we petted the family cats. No one else was with us and we weren't speaking, only drinking and petting the cats. I stopped having the dream after seeing Mrs. Holmes kill a cat.

As my father had warned me, Mrs. Holmes didn't like cats. What he didn't warn me about was that she hated them enough to enjoy strangling them with her bare hands. This I learned for myself when we were taking in the laundry one morning and a beautiful yellow tabby confidently approached us in the yard. When the cat began to nuzzle Mrs. Holmes on her shin, she snaked one arm out and grabbed it around the neck, squeezing and shaking until its limbs stopped thrashing and the gurgled meows were silent. I fainted for the first time in my life.

Tammy laughed at me when my cracked senses were regained. "You're a sissy. Mom always does that to cats."

"You're as stupid as a rock and nowhere near as pretty," I cried, borrowing one of Uncle Luther's platitudes to his ex-wife. "And your mother is a Medusa who will burn in hell."

Tammy's chin fell and for the first time I succeeded in shutting her up for longer than the count of five. But I was too upset to enjoy it, unable to close my eyes without seeing Mrs. Holmes smiling grimly as she strangled the golden cat and tossed its still-warm body into the trash barrel. From then on the other girls were quick to help me shoo away any stray cats that came near the yard. Even Tammy helped. The incident was rattling for all three of them, almost as if they'd seen me being slain by the spirit and speaking in tongues.

Fifth grade began with a different kind shakeup when Carrie and I walked into our classroom to find that Mrs. Huff, who'd been teaching the class since before the Second World War, had retired and in her place was Mrs. Campbell, young, thin, and ivory-skinned, with long dark hair and earnest eyes like the model in Eugene Thirion's portrait of Saint Joan that I'd seen in one of the library encyclopedias. Mrs. Campbell and her husband were newcomers from Dayton, Ohio, which would automatically put everyone's parents on guard. Newcomers from Ohio were potential troublemakers first and last until a minimum of trust could be established and even then it was only a guest pass.

Mrs. Campbell flashed a mouthful of pearl teeth and held her hands out towards us as she spoke. "Good morning boys and girls, my name is Elizabeth Campbell. I can't tell you how happy I am to be here with all of you and I want you to know that we are going to accomplish some terrific things this year."

Eyes shifted and telepathic messages were exchanged as we all speculated on the name and constellation point of Mrs. Campbell's home planet but inside of five minutes the entire class was idolizing her as if she really was Saint Joan. It was fantastical enough to see a teacher who was young, pretty, and enthusiastic; that she could also wear patchwork brown and tan jeans with an orange t-shirt, a matching headscarf, and platform sandals made her straight out of Hollywood. When Mrs. Campbell added that she'd been married for seven months, rode her own horse, played the violin, and had a black and white rabbit named Oreo, our cups were running over. No one could wait to spread the word.

But our experience wasn't unique. At recess everyone rushed to tell everyone else about their new young teachers, the end result of a mass retirement for everyone over the age of sixty-five the previous year. There was an unspoken question among us of whether or not school could even be kept without its usual phalanx of silver-haired, eagle-eyed women stepping firmly through the hallways in their thick-soled orthopedic shoes. At least Mrs. Huber was no longer around to subject the first-graders to her trials by fire.

Another change was the absence of an ancient dead sycamore with branches that kept snapping off and breaking the windows of the school building whenever there was a thunderstorm. The school board had finally arranged to have it cut down over the summer. In its place was a yard-wide, two-foot high stump that the girls immediately began calling dibs on at recess.

Lindy Albertson was new that year too. Her parents were chemists at Procter & Gamble in Cincinnati, a forty-five minute drive east into Ohio. The Albertsons were restoring a red brick Shaker house that sat twenty yards back from the road, the state route that was one of the few streets outside Hazelwood to be marginally well-paved enough for two full lanes complete with white and yellow stripes. Mr. and Mrs. Albertson were probably the usual suspects, seeing the move as a chance to afford a larger house with more land and lower taxes. And their chipmunk of a daughter could go to a safe public school in the country and revel in the fresh air. Reveling was what Lindy did best.

"How come you're sitting here by yourself?" A puckish voice spoke directly above my head as I woolgathered on the sycamore stump during recess on the first day of school. "Did you just fart or something?"

I jumped up, banging the top of my head on Lindy's chin. Both of us yelped like smacked puppies and fell backwards in the dirt. "Ow, sorry about that," Lindy said, rubbing her chin. Her eyes were browner than a beagle's and her shag-cut hair was the same color. They went well with her late summer tan.

"I was watching a cricket fight," I complained.

"Who won?" Lindy asked. She sprang to her feet and laughed like Sonny the Cocoa Puffs Cuckoo.

"Quit," I said as her laugh reached out to me like a tickling hand. Lindy pulled me to my feet and told me to stand still while she dusted me off, making downward slapping motions on my backside until I was pronounced clean. I did the same for her.

"I just got these pants yesterday and now they're already dirty," Lindy said, twisting her head over her shoulder to check them. "Oh well, I'm going to play baseball." She bounced away towards the baseball field, sporadically flapping her arms and making chicken noises like Bruce Lee. After a moment she stopped and turned back to see why I wasn't following her.

"Aren't you playing?"

"Nope," I said, settling myself back on the stump. "I like it here."

Lindy walked back to me. "This would be a neat place to do a tap dance. Do you know how to tap dance?"

"No."

"I had to take ballet when we lived in Cincinnati," she said, climbing onto the stump with me. "Look, I've got Barbie knees."

I watched as Lindy drew herself up by the ballerina's invisible straight line and turned her feet outward until her heels and knees were pressed together. She followed by moving her right foot outward, forward, inward, and then back so that her feet were nesting heel to toe. Lindy made it look simple and impossible at the same time, like an M.C. Escher drawing. What would it be like to have parents who made me take ballet lessons?

75

Mrs. Holmes cut our hair off that fall after Carrie and I were sent home from school with lice. Carrie wept for days every time she caught sight of her reflection or whenever Tammy teased her. I was thrilled; everyone said I looked like a boy and I begged Mrs. Holmes for a touch-up trim after learning that my father was coming for an unexpected visit right before Halloween.

We were in the middle of an exceptionally fine Indian summer and my hopes were high on the golden Saturday afternoon when my father's truck pulled up. I swaggered outside in Wrangler jeans and a Pepsi t-shirt, my favorite outfit, and ran to tell him how much I needed a Bowie knife so that I could practice throwing it, a hobby whose only purpose was to help secure my status as an honorary boy. But Dad only frowned and held me at arm's length when I tried to hug him.

"What do you think you're doing, running out in the middle of the road like that?" he demanded. "You got rocks in your head?"

I slipped out to the backyard as soon as it was possible to do so without anyone noticing and didn't see my father again for more than three years. From my station outside the kitchen window I heard him tell Mr. and Mrs. Holmes about business at the motel being slow, broken windows and other damage from a tropical storm, the tourist season ending before he could recoup the losses. Friends from his church had donated their sons' outgrown clothes so that Trilby would have something decent to wear to school. And then after a long, miserably hot drive from Florida to Indiana, Miss Gimme-Gimme had come running to demand a Bowie knife before he could even catch his breath.

"I had half a mind to slap her mouth right off her face," my father said. Mrs. Holmes giggled.

I went to hide in the shed and spent the rest of the afternoon crying and rubbing my right hand. Somehow I'd lost the privilege of living with my family and opportunities for winning it back never appeared. If I were to cry, beg, and make a hullaballoo, I'd be in trouble for acting foolish but if I appealed to my father in a quieter, more reasonable way, he would take my composure as an affirmation that my lot was acceptable enough and that I was only whining, always wanting what I didn't have. And it was true; I did always want things.

The Holmeses and I were used to each other by then anyway. Each morning I got up with the other girls, dressed, nibbled at overly peppered scrambled eggs, and caught the school bus for nine months of the year. Summer meant carpools, with Mrs. Holmes and other mothers hauling children of all sizes to Bible school, day camp, or the municipal pool in Hazelwood.

For privacy I started taking walks around Mount Olive, often detouring through the old cemetery behind the Presbyterian church that hadn't been used since the Spanish-American War. My favorite marker was a plain, thick slab of sandstone bearing the name "Aurelia," followed by the phrase, "Consort of John Matthias Hamilton." The only other detail was the year of death, 1792. There was no last name or date of birth for Aurelia. I looked up 'consort' in the classroom dictionary.

My walking habits didn't go unnoticed by the people who lived inside Mount Olive, which meant it was soon being whispered that I took after my great-grandfather Ansgar and should probably be given a wide berth. This might have been the reason why I was rarely sick during those years, although one memorable exception was a case of scarlet fever that came complete with a strawberry rash that itched like poison ivy, razor blades jammed in my throat, and a hurricane in my stomach. Mrs. Holmes brought me cold foods that I could swallow and made the other girls sleep in Tammy's room, forbidding anyone to come in contact with me until I was better.

The rare privacy, the orange juice and ice cream twice a day, and the complete set of *Little House on the Prairie* books sent from the school library by Mrs. Campbell made scarlet fever almost like a holiday when I wasn't throwing up or coughing and adding fuel to the fire in my throat. I worried a little about losing my eyesight, like Mary Ingalls, but not too much. A school for the blind was bound to be an improvement over chéz Holmes and I was confident that I could learn to read Braille in a snap.

Chapter Seven

Tammy offered to teach me how to smoke for my tenth
birthday if I was willing to steal a pack of cigarettes
from the general store. Smoking seemed like a useful
skill to have and I lifted a box of Marlboros while
Dorothy White's back was turned. Tammy and I went
to the basement steps in the back of the Presbyterian
church to finish sealing the deal. My launch as a weed
fiend left me nauseated and reeking but curiously
liberated. Like most children, I thought it made me look
older and less unthreatening. It also gave me something
in common with my father, even though he might
object. I almost hoped he would since there was nothing
he could do about it.

Mrs. Campbell told the girls in our class that it was
traditional for some of the Native American tribes to
hold a special party for their daughters when they
reached puberty. "It's like a celebration of the new
possibilities that life offers once you start to grow up,"
Mrs. Campbell explained. "The Navajos call it a
kinaalda."

Not long after learning how to smoke, I got my first
period. When I told Mrs. Holmes, she shoved a Modess
box into my hands and said, "Isn't that just dandy. Like
we don't have enough to spend money on as it is."

This was the extent of my kinaalda.

In the fifth grade it was now an unwritten rule that two girls or two boys were no longer allowed to sit next to each other at the movie theater in Hazelwood without an empty seat between them unless the theater was full. Resting an open hand on any part of your own body could lead to jeers and accusations of engaging in self-stimulation and I got into the habit of clenching my fists whenever my arms were at rest. It was all new, the taboos and the stupid games that always involved trying to embarrass someone.

But there was still Lindy Albertson, who became the undisputed comic among the girls from the moment of her arrival. A female Peter Pan who would have had Captain Hook in a straitjacket, Lindy could mimic a dog, a cat, any cartoon character I named, the school principal, or President Carter equally well. Sometimes Lindy jumped up from behind me on the playground and pounced like a puma kitten, yelling "Shazam!" More often than not she would snatch a hat or book from me, making me chase after her to retrieve it. It became my habit to look for her in the mornings after getting off the bus.

Kathleen Stevens was a volunteer aide at school and hers was also a face I sought in the mornings, if only for the pleasure of looking at it. Kathleen was an authentic Irish Traveler with black hair, snowy skin, and eyes the color of a twilight sky. As seventeen-year-old Kathleen Barry she'd broken ranks with her clan when they were passing through the county in 1963 on their way to

Richmond for the purpose of hustling a few home improvement scams, or so the story went. One year later Kathleen married Charlie Stevens, a childless widower twenty years her senior who owned the reputable Stevens Nursery & Landscape and was soon to be the most indecently happy man in Roosevelt County.

Kathleen's son Chuck was in my class, a cheerful rogue with a kind and irreverent word for anyone, including the homeliest girls and the grimmest teachers. Chuck enjoyed flirting with Lindy and me both; she had the sparkle but I had tits like grapefruits, as he so suavely put it. It was a childish exaggeration but my breasts had arrived literally out of nowhere near the end of the summer and were rudely taking up more and more of my space. By the middle of the fifth grade I was ready for a B-cup and Mrs. Holmes bought me a bra at Danner's, grumbling as always about the extra expense.

"Charity's probably going to be a whore in high school," I overheard Jodie Hampson telling her entourage one afternoon during recess when the rain kept us inside and Jodie was using her outdoor voice from habit. "My mom says girls who grow too fast are always like that. They have too much hormones."

The other girls nodded sagely, as if Jodie were delivering a lecture on the pitfalls of gambling or voting Libertarian. None of them noticed me sitting on the floor behind the teacher's unoccupied desk listening to them, or Chuck slipping up beside me to see what I was doing. "Hey, Cherry, you got anything besides cantaloupes in that fruit bowl?" he whispered as he slipped his hand up my Star Wars t-shirt. "How about a banana?"

"Cut that out," I whispered back, jabbing Chuck in the ribs hard enough to make him gulp. "I'm trying to hear what Jodie's saying."

"What's she talking about?" he asked.

"Me. She says I'm going to be a whore in high school."

Chuck looked impressed. "Really? Well if you are, be sure to keep me in mind," he said gallantly. "That's what my grandpa told me to say if a girl won't let you mess with her."

I laughed; Chuck was good at making people do that even when they didn't want to. He was equally popular with girls and boys, pleased with himself and everyone else. Girls found it difficult to smack Chuck's hand and pretend to be angry if they became the object of his attention on the playground and more than one of the boys probably wanted that attention for themselves.

What I wanted was to be Chuck. Or possibly Han Solo, whose costume was sharp and whose ability to ride the frayed, flapping edges of disaster without falling in suggested a generous combination of luck and brains that I could well use. It wasn't a question of wanting to be a boy anymore; the idea of having a penis—or a peter, as they said at school—was creepy. All I wanted was the freedom to be a cheerful rogue myself. I didn't see it happening anytime soon.

Lindy kissed me with no advance notice one morning to test my claim that the new lip gloss I was wearing tasted like grapes. Pulling away, I poked her in the ribs where I knew she was ticklish, making her flop into the air like a fish being reeled in. Our eyes locked for an instant of perfect empathy before I broke the spell.

"What kind of fairy are you?" I laughed.

"*I am a hairy fairy*," Lindy sang, improvising her own lyrics to "The Adjective Song" from *Schoolhouse Rock*. "*I also am a scary fairy . . .*" We danced around the playground arm in arm and did the can-can. Our first kiss.

Tanya Yeager was one of the more popular girls in our class and her parents gave permission for a twelve-guest slumber party in May. Lindy and I made the cut and got our chance to see the inside of the Yeager house, a century-old structure that once served as a bordello until a nearby brewery was demolished in a 1905 tornado, throwing most of the house's regular customers out of work. All of the local ministers except the priest at St. Helen's in Hazelwood reportedly had a field day insisting that it was a case of divine judgment all around. The bordello's employees packed up and headed west in a group to start fresh.

In accordance with its reputation, the house had several small bedrooms. Lindy and I found an empty one and unrolled our sleeping bags. Lying side by side on the floor, we talked long after everyone else was snoring. Lindy surprised me by asking if my parents had really loved each other. It was a question I'd never considered in view of my father's near-debilitating grief after losing my mother.

"I think my parents are getting a divorce," Lindy said. For once there was no laugh waiting beneath her words. She reached for my hand and I rolled sideways, draping my left arm over her. Lindy snuggled closer to me. "What kind of shampoo are you using? It smells so nice."

"It's called Body on Tap." I murmured. "It's got real beer in it. I bought it in town with my Christmas money. I have to hide it or Tammy steals it."

"I wish you could come live with me instead of at the Holmeses," Lindy yawned. "You and me could wear each other's clothes and you could have your own bedroom, unless you wanted to share."

"That'd be nice." Lindy and her clothes always looked comfortably clean and shiny, like freshly minted dimes.

"I'll ask my mom," Lindy promised. "Our house is all fixed up now too and they were finally going to start having company and let you spend the night sometimes."

Lindy had once made the mistake of describing the Holmeses to her parents and for this reason wasn't allowed to visit me at the shotgun house. That meant we never saw each other outside of school unless it was at someone else's house or a public place like the movie theater or the county fair. Rumor had it that the

Albertsons would have preferred a different playmate for Lindy, someone who didn't like walking in cemeteries and wasn't insufferable to her own family. Though it was hurtful knowledge, at the same time I was touched by their concern for Lindy and sometimes pretended that the Albertsons were my own parents, doing their best to shield me from life's malevolence.

As fifth graders Carrie and I were now eligible for 4-H. We joined Tammy as members of the Mount Olive Busy Bees and went to meetings at other homes, nicer homes where cookies were always served and cats sometimes lived. Cats always approached me, even the ones who weren't normally friendly to guests.

I took mean pleasure in watching Mrs. Holmes's face whenever she was obliged to stay and visit at such homes, where etiquette forbade her to even frown at the cat if anyone was watching. If the cat in question was cooperative, I would deliberately provoke Mrs. Holmes by cuddling and crooning to them like babies, certain that the ability to appreciate such a creature was only one more indicator of my natural superiority to my foster mother aka babysitter, as my father always insisted on calling her. He explained to me once that foster parents were for welfare kids whose real parents couldn't pay for their keep.

Being in 4-H also meant the chance to exhibit projects at the county fair and it was obviously a good excuse to go to the fair itself. I had a short apron on exhibit, sewn by hand, while Carrie had labored over her mother's ivory Kenmore to produce a green paisley peasant skirt with the material folded into just the right proportions over the elastic waist band, generously bunched and with the ruffle flaring evenly at the bottom. At home we'd all been amazed; Carrie found something she could do.

"Sweetheart, I'm afraid we'll have to give you a second place on this one since it doesn't have a zipper," said Edna Blankenship, the head of the judging panel.

"But it's got an elastic waist band," Carrie said. "That's what the pattern had."

"A zipper is always better," Edna insisted. She didn't say why. The other judges nodded and simpered, a clutch of biddies telling Carrie without words that her family was one empty beer can short of being certified white trash and it was their duty and pleasure to remind her of her place.

Carrie sat down dejectedly and we watched together as Edna turned to Nancy Fitzpatrick's project, a square yard of roughly woven pink twill material with a cross cut in the center. Nancy had also taken the trouble to shred the edges for a fringe. Nancy's mother Marian was an officer on the 4-H council for Roosevelt County and had a reputation for tormenting people out of their will to live if they failed to pay her children sufficient tribute. The sewing panel was quick to cough up.

"Well my goodness, this is lovely," Edna gurgled. "I guess you could use it for a poncho, or a skirt, or any number of things . . ." The other judges cooed their agreements like a flock of pigeons.

"She could walk in here with nothing and they'd give her a blue ribbon with a state fair recommend for the emperor's new clothes," I stage-whispered to Carrie, hoping to be overheard. Some of the women and girls sitting near us laughed loudly enough for Edna to notice but she only smiled like a sheep and continued to fondle Nancy's hank of pink twill like it was the shroud of Turin.

Since my last name was Sintz and not Holmes, I received a blue ribbon and a dollar for my apron and one more of each for the puppet theatre I'd made with a cardboard box and some white paint, my childcare project that was to become Ruthie's property after the fair was over in exchange for letting me use her dolls as puppets. I bought Carrie an elephant ear to cheer her up and we rode the Scrambler. After that we played the Lucky Duck game for a dime each, which was like buying a box from a grab bag since there was always a small prize like a bandana or a wide-toothed comb made of sturdy, bright-colored plastic. We avoided the other games; Carrie and I both hated watching the younger, more gullible children cry when they lost all their money trying to win the tacky stuffed animals on display.

"I have to pee," Carrie said after we got off the Scrambler.

"Shoot, look how long the lines are." I pointed to the outdoor bathroom, a small concrete and timber structure sitting halfway between the food tent and the entrance to the race track. Women, girls, and smaller boys were lined up nearly all the way back to the food tent. "Let's just climb over that fence in back of the buildings and do it in the field there. Nobody'll see us."

The fence was only four feet high and taut enough for us to reach the top and jump down without wobbling if we were fast. I was fast; Carrie wasn't. She wobbled, scraping her hand as she tried to grab the top of the fence before falling to the ground like a rag doll.

"Ow, darn it," Carrie said, holding her hand to her mouth and sucking hard on the spot where she'd been caught by a wire spoke. We dusted off and took care of business.

On our return climb over the fence we nearly fell on top of a man in a plaid flannel shirt and baseball hat who was crouched against the fence, nearly hidden by the weeds and frantically yanking on his stupid peter. Carrie screamed. Our voyeur bolted upright with his hands still grasping his brain, which he waved at us before quickly yanking his jeans up and running back to the exhibit area, where men in jeans, baseball hats, and plaid flannel shirts outnumbered the mosquitos.

"Could you tell who that was?" Carrie asked in a trembling squeak.

"No," I said. "He must of seen us walking this way and just followed us."

"What a creep," she said, her voice returning to normal. I agreed, unable to think why a man would get excited—or whatever it was men got—from watching two unremarkable girls taking a pee in a field or anywhere else.

Against my advice, Carrie shared the incident on the ride home that night, making Tammy and Ruthie giggle just like their mother.

"Sounds like you two have delusions of grandeur," Mrs. Holmes said.

"Oh brother, now they're going to start thinking they're sexy or something," Tammy added.

"What's delusions of grander?" Ruthie asked.

Mr. Holmes drove and said his usual nothing. More than likely he hadn't been listening anyway. No one suggested that Carrie might need a tetanus shot for her hand, or even a Band-Aid.

Chapter Eight

The Tree of Ténéré was a single acacia growing in the Nigerian Sahara, the only survivor from a grove that filled the area before it became a desert. In 1939 it was determined that the tree was approximately three hundred years old and no one could understand how it continued to live without being desiccated by the sun or gobbled up by camels from a passing caravan. The Tree of Ténéré was even featured on a one-to-four million scale map of the area until 1973, when it was run over by a drunk driver who managed to strike the only object in a 400-kilometer radius.

One of the first things we learned in Mr. MacDonald's sixth grade class was that burning books was a sin against humanity because it sought to repress knowledge that was part and parcel of human civilization and should be accessible to anyone choosing to seek it out. Mr. MacDonald's particular beef at that moment was with someone named Ayatollah Khomeini, who was burning books in a country called Iran, which I knew as Persia from Sunday school. Mr. MacDonald added that President Carter was an imbecile with a loony wife and that the economy was in the toilet.

"And who's going to be running against Mr. Peanut in the primaries?" he asked rhetorically. "Ted Chappaquiddick Kennedy, God save us all. Our government has become a circus act, boys and girls." He went on to give equally dismal reviews of the Republican party's favored candidates. Mr. MacDonald was outspoken for a Roosevelt County man.

Mr. MacDonald's claims about the economy were verified for me and Carrie that same afternoon when we got home from school and found Mr. Holmes sitting at the kitchen table with a bottle of Wiedemann in hand, his face more red and hatchet-like than usual. The atmosphere had a hissing edge that led me, Carrie, and Ruthie to silently concur that grabbing a snack and quickly disappearing would be our best option even though we'd been hoping to watch the afternoon cartoons. Then Tammy walked in from the back door and opened the refrigerator to get herself a Pepsi, oblivious to the undercurrents as usual and too arrogant to heed the warning signals Carrie and I tried to send her.

"What are you doing home, Dad?" Tammy asked, sunny and smart-alecky. "They can you or something?"

Mr. Holmes was too frugal to throw a beer bottle that was still half full. He threw the bottle opener instead, catching Tammy in her upper arm. She yelled and clutched her bicep as he got up and lumbered toward her.

"Don't you touch me," Tammy cried. "You can go to jail if you do, they said so on TV."

Carrie, Ruthie, and I stood in a frozen lump like a Greek chorus waiting to sing a dirge for Tammy. Mr. Holmes stared at her, slowly raising his eyebrows. Then he jerked his head forward, the display of sarcastic, theatrical surprise made by someone drunk as a drain.

"I can go to jail, huh?" he said, shaking his index finger in a semi-circle to include all of us in his address before turning back to Tammy. "Well, point the way, girl, just point the goddamn way. Then I won't have to kill myself every day trying to keep food on the table for a houseful of she-brats who couldn't care less if I lived or died."

We were afraid but fascinated; even at his coldest, angriest self, Mr. Holmes never became talkative or emotional. This was a new side to him, potentially dangerous but interesting. Obviously something significant had happened and we were seeing the beginning of a sea change that might mean good or evil.

Mrs. Holmes told us over TV dinners that Mr. Holmes and the other first-shift employees had arrived at work that morning to find the factory shuttered. Not enough building was going on to keep up the demand for shingles, which meant no need for shingle-makers. The next day Mr. and Mrs. Holmes drove into Hazelwood to apply for welfare, food stamps, and Medicaid, while we girls were told to pick up the free lunch applications from the principal's office. Too many kids were getting them for it to be embarrassing anymore.

Luxuries disappeared. Mrs. Holmes no longer bought cookies, chips, Pepsi, or a subscription to the *Cincinnati Enquirer*. Mr. Holmes switched from cigarettes to pipe tobacco. No spending money was available for me or the other girls, even though I knew I was supposed to be getting an allowance from the money my father was sending them. I also knew that asking about it was liable to get me a crack across the face, or at the very least a diatribe on greed that would leave my stomach aching for hours. Fear could prompt discretion more easily than valor.

My father sent me a card with ten dollars at the beginning of November for my eleventh birthday. I assumed he couldn't remember the actual date and so sent the card on the first of the month each year, like a license plate renewal. The card was sitting on top of a stack of overdue bill notices when Mrs. Holmes took them out of the mailbox as she spoke with Ethel Gabbard, who lived nearby and was out having a walk.

"Is that a card from my father?" I asked loudly, pointing to the mail in Mrs. Holmes's hands. "Can I see it?" Asking to see sounded less greedy than asking to have. Ethel gave her usual empty smile and Mrs. Holmes had no choice but to scowl and hand me the card instead of pocketing the cash and telling my father the whole thing had been lost in the mail in the unlikely event that he asked about it. Ethel could see the card with her own eyes and she loved having a story to twist as much as ever.

"You don't see your daddy too often," Ethel said to me, her voice gleeful. "It's too bad he took Trilby with him and left you, isn't it?" When I ignored the question, she turned to Mrs. Holmes. "She was always so jealous of her little brother. The first day they brought him home from the hospital she went and tried to make him eat Vaseline and almost poisoned him."

There was a quiet but definite commotion at school the next day—the same Khomeini who had so riled Mr. MacDonald with his book-burning was now into hostage-taking, or at least into endorsing it. But this time Mr. MacDonald wasn't alone in his outrage; all of the teachers seemed surprised or livid. Strange things were always happening in remote places but this was somehow different and an air of disbelief permeated the school. Could there be a war with Iran like the old one in Vietnam? Maybe Chuck Stevens and the other boys in my class would all get drafted and be killed in a few years. Maybe they would start drafting girls and I'd be killed too since I was hopeless at thinking on my feet.

Pictures of blindfolded hostages and veiled women appeared in the newspapers and magazines that everyone was asked to start bringing to class. Gas and fuel prices shot up and thermostats went down at school. Mr. Holmes brought a kerosene heater in from the shed and shut off the heat. The smell of kerosene got into everything, including our hair and our clothes. I came to associate it with a sense of shame and defeat, which didn't keep me from hunching closer to its source as the weather turned colder.

Mrs. Holmes spent Christmas morning staring bitterly at the artificial white tree on display in the living room. It was a tacky-looking tree with the same uniform blue and silver ornaments that was hauled out each year the day after Thanksgiving. There were at least half a dozen people in the township who would have let us cut down a real tree from their woods but Mr. Holmes didn't want to admit to anyone that he didn't even own a saw. I was always embarrassed by the Holmeses' rush to put up the tree even before the first of December, which would have been seen by my own family as a vulgar display of obsession with the material side of the holiday.

Not that there was much to obsess over. Mr. Holmes chased down the few rumors of work that came his way without much luck; a few weeks of harvest labor from some of the local farmers was all he could find and it didn't help that everyone knew he hated animals. There were three small packages with candy, socks, and underwear sitting beneath the tree with tags addressed to Tammy, Carrie, and Ruthie—and nothing else. Mrs. Holmes wanted to send me a message and she wanted to send it with the force of a sledgehammer. With my usual lack of tolerance for uncertainty, I cut to the center of the cake.

"Is anything wrong?" I asked Mrs. Holmes, like an actor being forced to deliver canned lines in a badly written play.

She responded on cue. "Nothing's wrong for you, that's for damn sure." A bit of paper was held out and waved in my face. "This is what your dad sent for you, fifty dollars. And since he doesn't seem to trust me anymore, he's written a check and made it out to you."

I'd never had so much money in one sitting and my surprise made me tactless. "That's a check for fifty dollars? For me?" I asked, not stopping to consider that Mrs. Holmes must have been planning on using money from my father to buy Christmas gifts for everyone.

"Yes." Mrs. Holmes flung the check towards me. "So you can buy yourself all sorts of junk while my girls didn't get anything for Christmas. Isn't that nice?" She left the room in noisy tears.

I'd never seen Mrs. Holmes expend that much sentiment on behalf of her daughters before and it was more disturbing than touching, a crack in an already brittle shell. The other girls and I looked from their mother's retreating brown terrycloth robe to each other and then to Mr. Holmes, who was already tomato-faced and finishing up his third Wiedemann of the morning.

"You girls clean up this paper and stuff," he said, standing up to head to the kitchen for another beer. "I come back here and find anything on the floor, you're all getting the belt."

We hustled to do as ordered. I tried to cheer up Carrie and Ruthie by promising to use half the check for something everyone would enjoy, likes games or records. Tammy ignored the three of us and yanked up a few bits of paper, flinging them in the general direction of the garbage can in the kitchen.

"There's no money for Christmas but there's always money for beer," Tammy said loudly as she stood outside her parents' bedroom. Her words had the expected effect, if not the desired one. Mr. Holmes charged out of the bedroom, pulling off his belt as he walked toward Tammy. She taunted, cried, and threatened as he swung at her. As usual, Carrie and Ruthie stood and watched with wide eyes, looking like idiots. I kept my own eyes down for the most part, furious with Tammy for destroying any hope of a peaceful day. She knew we all caught it when her father was this angry.

"You girls get to your rooms this minute. I hear a sound out of any of you, you're going to wish you were never born."

And to all a good night.

The sea change we'd all been hoping for came in March, almost literally. Mrs. Holmes had a cousin in Port Isabel, Texas who ran a fishing business with her husband and a grudging invitation was issued, probably under pressure from other relatives. An empty houseboat could be used by the family, a job in the business scraped up for Mr. Holmes. Port Isabel was a small coastal town in southeast Texas with a climate like Florida's. It sounded slightly dangerous and mostly wonderful to all of us. We were to leave in June, three weeks after school let out.

"I'm going to the beach and swim every day," Ruthie boasted.

"You'll probably get eaten by a shark," Tammy said.

"I've heard if you know how to swim the right way, the sharks won't notice you," I said.

"What's the right way?" Carrie asked.

"In a pool," her mother replied. "Now shut up and get to bed."

Topping off the luxury of reflections on beaches and pan-fried trout was the news that my father was paying for me to spend three weeks at Willow Lake, the Girl Scout camp in Coldwater, a two-hour drive to the north from Mount Olive. Though I'd never gone beyond Brownies, Mrs. Holmes explained over our scrambled eggs and fried potato supper that inactive scouts could stay for an extra fifteen dollars. I was impressed by the sum and naïve enough to assume that my father was trying to make up for his long absence.

"How come we don't get to go?" Carrie asked.

"Cause her dad is paying for it," Mrs. Holmes said.

"Her dad always buys stuff for her and not for us," Ruthie complained. "That's not fair." She'd been nursing a sense of injustice since Christmas, even after I used part of the fifty dollars to buy a tabletop pinball machine and an LP of *The Gambler* that everyone in the family had been wanting.

"Life ain't fair," Mr. Holmes said. "You better shut up and get used to it if you don't want your neck broke."

"You're hating me again," Ruthie cried as she jumped out of her chair and ran weeping from the table.

Over the next few weeks I packed two sets of belongings: camp and Port Isabel. There were forms to be filled out from Willow Lake that included a list of things a camper needed, along with a list of items that might be useful. Mrs. Holmes saw to it that I had everything on the needs list and even a few items from the usefuls. The solicitude should have made me suspicious but I was too caught up in the pleasure of acquisition and the thrill of being allowed to choose my first bikini from the junior rack at K-mart, periwinkle blue with a halter-tie top, a junior size five.

"You might as well learn how to flaunt it," Mrs. Holmes said sarcastically when I tried the suit on for her. She reached out as she spoke and unexpectedly gave my left breast a contemptuous pinch, digging her blunt fingernails into my skin for a quick, painful moment that ended before I had a chance to react. It was the same way she touched her daughters, taking care to hurt someone for at least a millisecond with a quick pinch, hair tug, or face flick.

Saying good-bye to Lindy on the last day of school made my hand ache. Her parents had filed for divorce right after Tanya Yeager's slumber party and Lindy was getting used to the idea that the life she'd lived was over. The remodeled brick Shaker house was being sold at a loss and Lindy's mother was taking her to live in Indianapolis, where it would be easier to find a job. Her father was already back in Cincinnati. Lindy had repeatedly begged her mother to let me live with the two of them and even tried waking her up in the middle of the night to trick her into saying yes while she was still half-asleep. I knew that such a yes wouldn't hold up in any kind of court but Lindy's efforts were touching.

"My mom always keeps her promises to me," Lindy said. "I wish I'd made her promise that she and my dad would never get divorced. But I never thought they would."

Lindy and I hid behind the Rumpke bin on the edge of the playground during our last recess together instead of sitting on the oak stump. After three false starts when it sounded like someone might be coming near, it was finally time to begin the project we'd been planning for weeks. We started by kissing each other's foreheads, followed by the noses, eyes, chins, and finally lips. Our hands remained pressed to our sides.

"Should we try it with our tongues?" I asked.

"Definitely." We rolled our tongues in each other's mouths, cautiously at first, then more easily. Then we tongue-wrestled and I let Lindy win so that I could trap her tongue in my mouth. She reached up and touched my nipples.

I was only just working up the nerve to put my hands in the back pockets of Lindy's jeans when we both heard a soft sound a few feet away. Over her shoulder I saw Jerry Corbett crouching next to the Rumpke, chin halfway to his knees and just as much of a mama's boy pissant as he'd been back in kindergarten when he accused me of crashing into him on purpose after he'd gone and jumped in front of my swing like a bozo. As if he fully expected me to jump out of the swing, fall in the dirt, ruin my dress, and tear up my hands and knees to avoid hitting him.

"Lezzies!" Jerry hooted as he ran off to broadcast his discovery to a group of kids standing nearby at the edge of the drainage ditch.

Lindy and I gave chase. Just as Jerry was about to open his mouth and condemn us before the crowd like Robespierre Maximilien or Joseph McCarthy, I caught up and delivered a lucky kick to his gabardine-covered ass. Jerry flew into the ditch and landed face-down in the algae and green mud, which meant his dignity was now in crumbs and any accusations he made against me or Lindy would be seen by everyone as feeble comeback attempts.

From my spot at the edge of the ditch, I regarded Jerry's foolish, dying-calf face with satisfaction and said, "I did that on purpose." No one could hold a grudge quite like me.

Chapter Nine

It was Mrs. Holmes who took me to camp. She didn't like making long drives but the aging, rheumatic Impala's engine now coughed and heaved whenever it was shut off and getting it back on again always made everyone tense to see if it would turn over by the third try. Any more than that and Mr. Holmes was liable to become dangerous for the rest of the day, ignoring all speed limits and stop signs. Carrie and Ruthie came with us.

Halfway through the ride, Mrs. Holmes unexpectedly pulled into a McDonalds, making Ruthie squeal at the sight of the golden arches. I inhaled the signature French fry aroma and my stomach growled; breakfast had been buttered toast and Tang for everyone. Mrs. Holmes warned us that it was to be hamburgers and Cokes only but she relented once it was her turn in the drive-through and added a medium order of fries for us to share. Ruthie shook the fries onto a napkin and divided them by four. We lapped up the high-fat mini-meals and sugary drinks almost before Mrs. Holmes was able to get the car from the cashier's window to the street.

The welcome center and administration offices at Camp Willow Lake were inside a green, two-story craftsman house with a shaded front porch that looked big enough for a dance class. The house was concealed from the road by a driveway that wound around a grove of black walnuts in a squared curve. Before we got to the parking area I noticed a log cabin on the right side of the driveway and a row of archery targets neatly set up on easels. Would I learn to use a bow and arrow?

"Why'd we come so early?" Carrie asked. "There's nobody here."

"We have to get back before the garage closes," Mrs. Holmes said. "Manard's got some used parts he said he might be able to put in our engine but he's leaving for Kentucky tomorrow and he won't be back for a week."

A tall, lean woman with short black hair and deeply tanned skin came out of the green house and approached us with a wave as she explained that the camp director had just gone into town. "We usually don't get any kids this early in the day. I'm the camp nurse. You can call me Lakota, we all use nicknames here."

"Lakota?" Mrs. Holmes giggled. "You're not an Injun, are you?"

I wanted to die where I stood and never be reincarnated, assuming there was an option for it.

"For a car or a boat?" Lakota asked, her voice ten degrees cooler. Mrs. Holmes looked blank, the barb having sailed safely over her head. Carrie and Ruthie didn't get it either. Lakota suggested that we go inside the green house where her office and records were; each girl's papers had to be checked for medical needs before she could join her assigned unit and unpack. "Are both of you here for camp?" Lakota was looking at me and Carrie.

"Just that one." Mrs. Holmes pointed her thumb at me. Lakota asked my name.

"It's Charity Sintz," said Ruthie, who was going through a pun-making phase and was likely to be smothered in her sleep by one or more of us if she didn't grow out of it soon. "We take *charity since* we don't have any money."

"Ruthie, shut up." Mrs. Holmes turned to her, hand raised for a slap.

Lakota made a quick, involuntary move towards Mrs. Holmes with her own hand raised. "Let's go inside," she said, an order barely disguised as a polite suggestion. She ignored the contriving smirk that Mrs. Holmes tried to offer her.

We were led into the room that doubled as Lakota's office and the infirmary. It was filled with white fixtures, white paint, and white furniture, underscoring the colors of the woven rugs and pictures hanging on the wall. I took a closer look at one of the pictures, a framed print of a bird that I'd never seen in life, large and shiny with cobalt-blue feathers and a narrow, pointed beak like a lance. The caption gave the artist's name—John J. Audubon, who always appeared in volume one of every encyclopedia set I'd ever read—and the bird's species: Blue Crane or Heron. Crane or heron? Didn't they have to know which one it was before they went around selling pictures of it?

Before I could raise the question with Lakota, she took my file from a stack on her desk and opened it. "I remember getting your enrollment form. We don't see too many Charities." Then she added in a lilting voice, "And now abideth faith, hope, charity, these three; but the greatest of these is charity." I was surprised; not many people quoted the King James version of that verse.

A framed picture on Lakota's desk showed two girls and a boy close to my age. All three were black, with the kind of smiles that suggested they were used to having their pictures taken and didn't much mind. My picture was rarely taken unless the school photographer was making rounds for the yearbooks and I would have been happy to skip that as well; the pictures never looked like me anyway.

"Those are my children," said Lakota, noticing my interest in the picture.

"Oh, for the love of Mike," Mrs. Holmes muttered audibly.

Lakota turned to her with one eyebrow raised, like Spock. A moment of dead silence was broken when Ruthie exploded with a window-rattling belch, the Coke from McDonalds coming back to haunt her. Lakota gave Ruthie a quick onceover and then did the same to Carrie, whose seam-strained t-shirt had visible sweat stains and ketchup spilled on the front. I quickly checked my own shirt, noticing how threadbare and grungy the three of us looked.

Then Carrie laughed. "Injun, engine, I get it!"

After my papers were gone through and the footlocker unloaded from the car, Mrs. Holmes walked to the driver's side door and waved at her daughters to get in. Carrie and Ruthie tried to hug me and Mrs. Holmes told them to stop being silly. "Well, Charity, you be good now." Mrs. Holmes was giggling so hard by this time she almost couldn't speak. "Don't let people say I haven't taught you how to act."

I didn't tell Mrs. Holmes that I hoped people would say exactly this, a politeness I would later regret. Then they were pulling out of the driveway, the car having started on the fourth try. My newest life was beginning and I didn't even know it.

Lakota led me, my footlocker, and my Juicy Fruit sleeping bag across a broad lawn behind the administration building, down a slope, and into a circular glen that was ringed with woods. The air was damp with the smell of pine and sassafras and scattered with small bursts of sound: birdsong, insect chatter, the rustling of leaves as the mammal and reptile enclaves went about their business. And the trees themselves, breathing quietly in the humidity. It was all too green and glorious for words.

The seven tents inside the glen were arranged in a horseshoe, with the counselors' tent resting at the bottom of the curve. The khaki canvas roofs had side flaps that could be rolled up and tied or unrolled to create walls. The tents were held up by wooden beams under the roof and posts at each corner, sitting on platforms a meter off the ground that were reached by steps in the front. Each tent held four cots.

Lakota's daughter Joy was already setting up shop in the tent of her choice nearest to the latrine, though not so near that the smell would bother her. Joy was small for her age, a slender sprite with short black curls and skin like chocolate butter cream. Her eyes were even browner than Lindy's and I felt disloyal for noticing.

"Hi Charity, how come you came so early?" Joy asked when Lakota introduced us. "That's cool though, you and me can have the place to ourselves for a while. Everybody else usually gets here around four or five o'clock. Come on and I'll show you the lake."

"No, there's no lifeguard right now," Lakota said.

"But Mommy, I'm a blue cap this year," Joy protested.

"N-O spells what?"

Joy showed me the latrine instead. It was a single server made of knothole-filled boards and about the size of a large closet. The reek of Pine Sol nearly sent me under. Joy warned me to bring my flashlight or I might not be able to find the toilet paper in the dark. She added that some girls never used toilet paper and that it was important to keep anyone like that from sharing our tent. Joy had been coming to camp every year since the age of five and she swore by her ability to determine if someone was unhygienic or liable to wet the bed.

"A lot of those girls don't like black people anyway," Joy added. "Not at first, I mean. My mom says some kids are just raised bad so they're afraid of anyone who looks different than what they're used to."

"I think black people are prettier than white people," I said to my own surprise. "White people look kind of dead or something."

Joy considered this. "Well, maybe some of them do. You're really pale but you've got some freckles so that helps. Do you ever wear make-up?"

"No way, I'm only eleven. Is there any place I can smoke?"

Joy led me to a spot in the woods that seemed safely out of view from the glen or the latrine, though it was still on a dirt path. She warned me to stay away from the evergreens and to always use a can of water to catch the ashes. A girl scout for all seasons.

At four o'clock Joy insisted that we return to the glen and sit in the front of our tent where we could be in plain sight and have a good view of everyone as they came down the slope with their luggage and parents. Her vigilance bore fruit as one runny-nosed specimen after another glanced our way and then veered in the opposite direction with their suitcases. Not that it mattered; Joy would have nearly everyone in our unit wrapped around her pinkie toe within forty-eight hours.

"Oh, we want that one," Joy whispered as if we were horse traders. Too polite to point, she gave a conspicuous nod in the direction of a chubby, soft-skinned girl in a pink gingham shirt and blue shorts who was armed with an extra pillow and a Holly Hobby sleeping bag. "There's room in here," Joy called out to the girl and her mother as they stood in the center of the glen, speculatively eyeing the ring of tents.

The mother beamed at Joy, who looked as wholesome and reassuring as a child in a Crest commercial. "What's your name, hon?" she asked.

"Joy. My mom's the camp nurse."

"Well, that's handy. I'm Mrs. Hoffman and this is my daughter Rochelle."

Mother and daughter had the same softly curling brown hair, blue eyes, and unusually high color in their apple-shaped cheeks. Their shirts were the same pink gingham material, although Mrs. Hoffman wore a blue denim skirt instead of shorts. I was willing to bet Mrs. Hoffman had made all of those clothes herself from the way they fit, like carefully arranged flowers. I'd worn such clothes before. Mrs. Hoffman noticed my scrutiny and didn't seem to like it, probably because of the analytical frown that was usually on my face whenever I met someone's parents. She asked me my name without calling me hon.

"Charity." My voice sounded like overused sandpaper.

"Well, Charity, you look kind of gloomy. You shouldn't be that way, your parents brought you here to have a good time."

"Are there any bears in the woods?" Rochelle finally spoke. I laughed without meaning to and immediately ducked my head.

"Honey, we've been over this already. The only animals you're going to see in those woods could fit in a shoe box, am I right?" Mrs. Hoffman looked to Joy for confirmation, which was readily forthcoming. Then she turned to me, arch with maternal pique. "And as for you, your parents might want to teach you a few more manners."

"I don't have any parents," I said, emboldened by the surplus oxygen. "I was raised by weasels." With this I jumped out the back of the tent like a burglar making an escape and went to sit in the latrine, feeling like I'd blown another chance somehow. After a few minutes I made my way back, hoping my eyes weren't red. Rochelle was kissing her mother good-bye and I walked past the two of them without saying a word even though I was bursting to tell Mrs. Hoffman that only a moron would try to stick a raccoon in a shoebox.

"What's wrong, you look like you been crying," Joy said, sitting next to me on my bunk. "How come you said you didn't have any parents? Wasn't that your mother that brought you here? I saw you guys getting out of that big old car."

The idea of having been spat out by Mrs. Holmes courtesy of Mr. Holmes was enough to activate my gag reflex. I explained my situation to Joy as Rochelle reentered the tent, watching me as carefully as her mother had most likely just told her to. Resolving to be civil, I flashed Rochelle a peace sign, which she returned with a puzzled look.

"So how come your dad left you with those people?" Joy asked.

"He said I needed to live in a house with a woman, or something." This was not what my father said; it was what people who liked me said. My father had never given me any reason other than the occasional joke about what a she-devil I was or how I was better off not having to change schools and move to Florida where it was always hot. Non-answers tailored to be non-rebuttable.

"That's amazing," Joy said. "My mom died when I was a baby. That's how come I'm adopted. I can't remember her but I like the parents I've got just fine so it's okay."

"I couldn't stand it if I lost my mom," Rochelle said, a tender expression on her heart-shaped face. "You two must be really brave."

Gretchen was the last to arrive. Twiggy-thin with cropped hair the color of a tiger lily, Gretchen had so many freckles that it was hard to say where they ended and she began. The colors were fitting; Gretchen knew how to light a fire under anything.

"Hey guys, I'm Gretchen. My dad calls me Vetchin' Gretchen. I've got striped undies on and don't you dare laugh at them or I'll put a snake in your shoe while you're asleep. Just kidding. Do any of you pee in bed? I don't but I snore sometimes, I can't help it. If you've got a kidney problem just say so and I won't be mean about it."

After setting up her bunk, Gretchen took out a deck of cards and shared everything her father had taught her about poker, winning hand after hand of Blackjack and

Five Card Draw as she told us stories about her school back home in Greenwood and some of the kids there who were foolish enough to have gotten on her ugly side. Gretchen enjoyed going at it with the bullies, bigots, and narcissists and she took no prisoners. Her crackling energy was infectious and by suppertime the four of us were halfway convinced that by working together we could take over the world, or at least the camp, plus form a rock group in our spare time. Rochelle produced a pack of Bubble Yum from a goody box her mother had packed for her to share with the new friends she was bound to make and Gretchen showed us how gum could be used to imitate the sounds of firecrackers and heavy artillery. I never questioned Joy's judgment again.

Chapter Ten

Willow Lake's dining hall was a lodge-style building with exposed log beams and hardwood floors covered with long, heavy wooden tables and benches. Everyone stood in line for food that came on trays, like the school cafeteria. The corned beef, cabbage, boiled red potatoes, and sliced apples served at the first evening's meal were delectable to some of us, revolting to others, and acceptable to most. A short grace was said and everyone was urged to clean their plates.

There were four units of girls in the camp, with each unit holding fifteen to twenty campers between the ages of eleven and seventeen, a Humbert Humbert's paradise. I saw rows of white faces seated at the tables with a sprinkling of black ones but no other varieties that I could make out besides Lakota. Four counselors were assigned to each unit, along with others who were in charge of activities like waterfront or arts and crafts. There were also women like Lakota and Hootie the camp director who lived and mostly worked in the administration building.

No men were in sight, which Joy explained as the general policy while camp was in session. Too many girls running around in shorts and swimsuits and too many Baptist or Pentecostal parents who wouldn't let their daughters go to camp without such a provision in place. Joy's father and older brother were the only occasional exceptions unless there was an emergency.

"A girl scout loves to make music," Hootie announced after supper was over on the first evening. A barrel-shaped woman in her late fifties, Hootie was what people would call hearty, I knew. Hearty Hootie. To me the word implied someone whose enthusiasm was in fifth gear while their wits could barely make it into first. Songbooks were distributed and Hootie led us into the first of the sing-alongs that were held after each meal. The songs were traditional camp fare like "Land of the Silver Birch," "Little Tom England," and "The Ash Grove."

"From out of the shadows their loving looks greet me,
And wistfully searching the leafy green dome,
I find other faces fond bending to greet me,
The ash grove, the ash grove alone is my home."

Our unit was known as the Ponies. We were the youngest girls at Willow Lake and always left the dining hall first, followed by the Pintos, the Mustangs, and the Appaloosas. On the first night of camp we gathered in a circle back in the glen to listen while Marigold, the senior counselor, gave a talk about camp rules and customs. Marigold was a tall brunette whose nickname was ill-chosen, in my opinion. Anyone so glorious should have been called Helen, Venus, or Bathsheba, at the very least.

Marigold began by introducing the other three counselors to us. First was Chipper, a hefty young woman with Buster Brown bangs who enjoyed making lame jokes. Chipper was followed by Bambi, a lean, pony-tailed blond with a snowy Colgate smile who played the piccolo. Last and socially least was Lämm, a young Austrian woman with sober gray eyes who expressed her hope that we would all become friends in a hesitant, heavily accented English that reminded me of my old friend Veronica from second grade before she stopped stuttering.

"Oh brother, she talks stupid," said a blonde girl named Dede who was sitting next to Rochelle. "I hope vee vill all become very gut friends."

"Nah, she talks fine," Gretchen said blithely. "You just hear stupid."

"That's a really mean thing to say," Dede huffed.

"No meaner than what you just said," Joy countered. Rochelle seconded her. I watched the exchange silently, proud of my new friends.

A tall, awkward girl named Vicky rested her fingertips on the brim of my Tom Sawyer hat. "Your hat is so cute. Can I have it?"

I was too surprised to speak but Gretchen wasn't. "Damn, what's wrong with you?" she asked. "You can't just go around asking people for their hat and stuff."

"You cussed. I'm telling Marigold," Dede said.

"Go ahead," Gretchen said, leaning towards Dede as she spoke. "I'll just tell them what you said about Lämm." Most of the other girls muttered and nodded; it was easy to see that Gretchen had the stronger position, not to mention the red hair.

Dede saw which way the wind was blowing and decided to change the subject. "Well if Charity was nice, she'd give Vicky her hat."

I was saved from having to be nice by the small goat's bell that Marigold rang to let us know it was fifteen minutes till lights out. Everyone went to bed and Bambi played "Taps" on her piccolo. I liked the sound; it reminded me of the music I sometimes heard on the PBS channel like "Appalachian Spring," or "Rondeau" from *Masterpiece Theatre*.

"Taps" was followed by several minutes of catcalling from everyone and loud singing at odd intervals by me and my three comrades; Gretchen said the idea was to be quiet long enough for everyone to relax and then take it from the top.

"*Anticipaaation is making me late, is keeping me waaaiting . . .*" the four of us harmonized at full throttle. A background chorus of complaints rang from the other tents.

"Joy, Charity, all you girls need to get to sleep," Marigold called from the counselors' tent. "You're going to be plenty tired tomorrow if you don't."

"*These aaare the good old days . . .*"

I finally slept after saying my prayers, giving thanks to Jesus for my new friends and for protecting my hat. The sound of Marigold calling my name across the glen was frosting on the cake with ice cream on the side. I dreamed of palm trees and Gulf Coast beaches layered in warm-sugar sand.

The woods surrounding our campsite were mostly snake-free but one day a garter had the bad luck to run into Dede, whose reaction could probably be heard by people sitting down to their afternoon tea in Papua New Guinea. I spent as much time in the woods as possible, not only for privacy and smoke breaks but also to wreak havoc on the wild raspberries and blackberries that were growing everywhere I turned. There were paw paw trees too but their fruit wouldn't be ripe for months. Raccoons always got to them first anyway.

One day Lämm persuaded me to surrender my blackberries to her and then borrowed the dining hall kitchen to make an upside-down cake, substituting the blackberries for pineapple. The cake boosted her standing and Lämm's inability to grasp w's and th's was partially forgiven by some of the girls. Others remained diehards, refusing to speak to Lämm or sit next to her in the rowboats or around the campfires.

"You know, if Lämm does anything wrong, she could get kicked out of the country," Dede said during the first week when the Ponies were walking to the dining hall for lunch. "We should watch her and see if she does anything so we can tell the police."

Dede didn't notice Gretchen slipping up behind her, armed with a mouthful of Bubble Yum that she blew into a beach ball-sized orb before popping it directly into Dede's hair. Everyone laughed at Dede, who was troubled to find herself under attack instead of leading a charge. I could see that she was the type who was used to running the schoolyard, always being the one to decide which girls were allowed to occupy the privileged circle and which ones were banished to the lower tiers. Camp politics were better than a movie; the good guys could win without getting steamrollered in the first half.

Marigold told us on our first rowboat outing that Willow Lake's manmade beach was roped off from a small lake that eventually merged with a larger one. For anyone who could row the distance, it led to another manmade beach at the edge of Hazelwood. It hardly seemed possible that lakes, rivers, and oceans could operate like highways and lead to any port in the world, depending on the boat and the currents. What was there to stop me from getting on a boat and simply taking off down the Whitewater River until it met the Ohio? Then it would be down the Mississippi to the Gulf of Mexico just like Johnny Horton's bloody British and after that, the world. I wouldn't even need a driver's license.

Gretchen was changing out of the swimsuit she'd been wearing all morning when she suddenly grabbed a hand mirror from her suitcase and peered at the underside of her tight beginner breasts with obvious dissatisfaction. "God, I wish I had some boobs."

"Well, I wish I could give you some of mine," I said, impulsively pulling off my t-shirt to show off for the first time in my life.

"Geez Louise." Joy was truffle-eyed.

"Guys!" Rochelle made sure the Legion of Decency was represented.

"Big whoop, everybody's got a body, Roach," Gretchen said. She put her arm around my waist and rolled her hips as she imitated a strip joint saxophone. I picked up the rhythm and danced a slow grind with Gretchen in the middle of the tent while Joy and Rochelle fell on their bunks and howled like hyenas. We stretched the hijinks with a game of strip poker; I was the only one with downstairs hair, which the others tried not to stare at, while I noticed that Rochelle smiled whenever Gretchen called her Roach.

Chipper came to our tent one afternoon during the last week of camp to announce that I was wanted in Lakota's office. "Hup to, on the double," Chipper said as she followed me to the administration building, imagining she was being witty while I imagined swinging a pickaxe or at least a sharp marshmallow stick right between her empty eyes. Chipper's manner suggested that I was in trouble and she was enjoying it. Someone probably ratted on me for smoking.

"Charity, there are some favors it's not a good idea to ask your friends for," Lakota said, her horn-rimmed eyes holding mine from across her desk as she waited for me to respond.

"Like what?" I asked, confused by her approach.

"Like asking their parents to adopt you?"

Dear little Joy had secretly gone and asked her parents to give me a place at their table and Lakota was assuming that the idea had been mine. Her eyes were kind but cool as she waited for me to explain myself but after seeing my stricken face, Lakota misunderstood and tried to explain why adopting me wasn't a practical option for her. "My husband and I already have three children," she began.

"So?" My shrug was as haughty as I could manage without dislocating a shoulder. "I never asked you to adopt me," I said. "It was Joy's stupid idea."

The conciliatory way that Lakota held her mouth suggested that an apology was expected and she was waiting to graciously accept it but I was nowhere near being gracious enough to give it. Instead I walked out of her office and went to the archery yard to shoot arrows until my shoulder gave out, ignoring the rule about not being in the yard without a counselor. Even if I only apologized as an act of diplomacy it would feel compromising. In my experience, adults usually took such courtesies as admissions of defeat and behaved like bad winners.

It was Joy who apologized while we were getting into our pajamas that night. "I'll tell Mom it wasn't your idea," she promised, seeing how humiliated I was. "It's just that I heard her telling my dad that your foster mother was a redneck who probably couldn't find her own mouth with her fork if she closed her eyes and it was too bad because you seemed really smart and nice-acting. Besides, she's got three black kids and I thought it might be nice if she had a white one too."

In all honesty, so did I.

The parents were supposed to pick up their daughters by noon on the last day at Willow Lake. The older girls had to pack and carry their gear to the administration building but the Ponies were allowed to wait at their campsite since it was near the parking area. Rochelle gave each of us a tearful hug when her mother appeared to collect her.

"Good-bye, Charity," Rochelle said. "Send me a postcard from Port Isabel, or wherever you go."

I noticed that Rochelle and her mother didn't look as much alike as they had three weeks earlier but couldn't put my finger on the reason for it. They both still had the same eyes and baby doll brown hair but something was different. I decided that it must be Rochelle's skin, which was now tanned and lightly freckled. And she was slimmer; the scale in Lakota's office confirmed the loss of twelve pounds. As they walked away together, I could see Mrs. Hoffman frequently turning to look at Rochelle and take in the changes.

"So long, Rocking Chair." Gretchen reached out to hug me. I was fool enough to hug back and immediately got poked in the ribs.

Joy and I sat and watched the rest of the girls disappear one by one, singing "Another One Bites the Dust" each time someone drove away with their parents. When lunchtime came and went with no sign of Mrs. Holmes, my regret over leaving camp turned to mild anxiety. At three o'clock Joy and I went to the administration building to see if anyone had called for me. There was always a chance that the Impala had finally collapsed like an overloaded donkey.

The conversation that Lakota and Hootie were having on the front porch of the administration building was mildly animated and I noticed that they were facing each other, which suggested a matter of some relative importance. Lakota's arm gestures were abrupt and above the waist, implying accusation, while Hootie held her hands out slightly from her hips in a stance that was flaccid and appeasing. They froze at the sight of me and Joy walking towards them.

"Joy, I need you to go help Daisy," Lakota said as she came down the porch steps towards us. "She just got a new delivery of supplies for the craft house and it all has to be organized." Over Lakota's shoulder I could see Hootie slipping back inside the green house.

"Okay, we'll both go," Joy said, reaching for my hand. "You can come get us when that woman gets here. Did she call or anything?"

Lakota shook her head. "I need to talk with Charity for a minute."

"What about?" Joy asked.

"It's private business, honey." Lakota sounded uncharacteristically tense. "Now go help Daisy."

"All right, I'm going." Joy frowned over her shoulder as she walked away, making me want to hug her. She definitely belonged in commercials.

Lakota told me to wait in her office. Sitting in the rocking chair, knees tucked under my chin, I inventoried the details of the infirmary once again, noting the cot, the white cabinets and drawers full of medical supplies, the woven rug on the floor, the fluid beauty of the blue crane or heron on the wall. It was cool inside but the moist weight of the air outside still reached through the window. The sky was gray, hinting at a summer shower. The rain would be welcome but the mosquitoes would be a nightmare. I always forgot to use insect repellent and my legs looked like I had the measles. Was it possible to get malaria in this part of the country?

Lakota returned a moment later. She pulled up a metal stool and sat to face me, taking my hands in hers. The gesture was unexpected and I thought it might mean she'd had a change of heart about adopting me.

"Charity, there's something I need to tell you."

That didn't sound like the opening statement for an offer of parenthood.

"Did something happen?" I asked. "Did Mrs. Holmes call?" And did grownups always have to dole out information as if it were candy they secretly wanted to keep for themselves?

"No, not exactly." Lakota's near-baritone voice wavered. "The thing is, she's not coming. They're in Texas now."

"No they're not," I said. "They'll be leaving for Texas tomorrow. We'll be leaving tomorrow."

"I'm afraid not, Charity. I've just found out from Hootie that the Holmeses actually left for Port Isabel the day after they brought you here."

"No they didn't." I shook my head and started to go on but Lakota cut me off.

"Do you understand me, Charity? The Holmeses have already left. They're in Texas now and they're not coming back."

Lakota emphasized her last sentence to leave me no escape from another one of those pieces of the truth that hit like asteroid chunks. It seemed that after deciding in favor of the move to Port Isabel, Mr. and Mrs. Holmes had made other plans for me. A social worker would be driving me to a school just outside Darketown up north where some other kids lived. It was supposed to be nice. The whole thing had been arranged weeks earlier between the Holmeses, the Indiana Guardian Angels' Home, and my father, who thought it was best for me to remain in Indiana in case he decided to move back there.

So this was what other plans meant. I never got to make plans, other or otherwise. Lakota's voice sounded like it was coming over an antiquated telephone line, with words fading in and out as she explained to me that the Home was not an orphanage, but more like a boarding school for kids whose families were having problems. How could I have family problems when I didn't have a family? Not even a cheap fake one. I was indistinctly aware of Lakota putting her hands on my shoulders.

"I'm really sorry, Charity, I honestly didn't know anything about this until today," she said. "Hootie told me just before you and Joy showed up, that's what we were talking about. She said she forgot."

Hearty Hootie, who'd known everything before my arrival since Mrs. Holmes needed to explain why I was going to be picked up by a social worker instead of a parent. Hootie and Mrs. Holmes had agreed that keeping me in the dark until camp ended was the right thing to do. Hootie must have known better than to tell Lakota, who would certainly have told me. Right in front of Mrs. Holmes, if possible.

As if on cue, Hootie popped her head in the door just then, a tight, farcical smile on her face like the Joker. "How's it going in here?" she asked, dense enough to suppose that I couldn't get mad if she smiled at me, which made me even madder. I gave Hootie the look of death and not just any death either, something slow and excruciating. For three weeks I'd been played for a fool and my dignity cried out to be saved.

"I think you're a big fat fart, that's how," I spat out.

Hootie's smile fell down and her hand rose. "You watch your mouth, young lady. It's no wonder that family didn't want to keep you."

Lakota steered Hootie outside the infirmary. "You wanted me to handle this so why don't you just let me do that?"

I could hear them arguing on the other side of the door, Hootie urging Lakota not to be a sap. I'd undoubtedly given the Holmeses good cause to leave me behind, never minding the fact that my own father found me unmanageable. And look at me, not even twelve years old and I could probably buy myself a beer with no questions asked.

"You know she's going to turn out bad." Hootie sounded like she was enjoying the idea.

"I don't know any such thing," Lakota replied. "And neither do you."

"Well, it's not like she's being thrown out in the cold."

I gave the rocking chair a furious kick, hard enough to hurt my foot and make myself even angrier, which in turn made me want to demolish the infirmary and see what everyone had to say about that. Tearing the mattress off the cot didn't make much of a dent but kicking the trashcan across the room was enough to get the big people's attention. Lakota and Hootie came back in the room just in time to watch me toss the coat rack against the wall, barely missing the window. The blue crane or heron rattled and fell off the wall.

Hootie stormed over and grabbed me by my elbows, a poster woman for righteous outrage who shook me hard enough to rattle my teeth. "Do you want to pay for that window, missy?"

"Charity, try to stay calm and think for a minute," Lakota said as she moved in between us. "This school could turn out to be a good place. Joy told me about the way your foster parents treated you so it might be for the better."

"Couldn't I stay with you?" I asked, clutching for the straws as I yanked an elbow free of Hootie's grasp.

"You've got some gall," Hootie said as she walked out of the infirmary.

Lakota set the rocking chair upright and tried to make me sit. I refused. She put her arms around me. I tried to pull away but she held on.

"It's a rotten thing to have happen, I know," Lakota said softly. She stroked my hair, which hadn't been combed for a couple of days. "When I was your age, my father died."

"What from?" I croaked inelegantly through my tears, feeling obliged to keep up my end of the conversation with Lakota, who gave me her undivided attention even as she told me about her father dying when she was twelve after getting beat up by three men who then ran him over with his own car. Three white men who were drunk and mean and had nothing better to do. They'd knocked over a stop sign and a mailbox during a post-murder joyride in her father's car and the county tried to bill Lakota's mother for the damage since the car's brakes were worn out. The three men had gotten probation by using their intoxication as a sort of temporary insanity defense.

"The only fair in this world is the kind that gives the prizes for cakes and cows," Lakota finished. "Our circumstances can change without any warning, like an earthquake, and we adapt because we must. You'll be able to adapt too, so try not to worry any more than you need to."

The purple haze in my head was clearing up and the corners were sharpening again. At the peripheral edge of my brain was the question of whether or not I really could get away with buying a beer. The drinking age was eighteen in most states, though it would be back up to twenty-one in a few years. How old were the men who killed Lakota's father? At least I understood now why she didn't want a white child in her house. And so I shuffled along like a lobotomy patient as Lakota gently steered me to the door, her story having put me in such a fugue that I forgot to say good-bye to Joy.

Chapter Eleven

The Tree of Heaven, also known as the Chinese palm, is a tree often seen in poor urban neighborhoods because of its ability to thrive in heavily polluted air. The tree resembles an overgrown weed and no one welcomes the sight of them since it usually means the neighborhood is going downhill. Novelist Betty Smith wrote in A Tree Grows in Brooklyn *that if there were only one such tree in the whole world, everyone would think it was beautiful. The problem with such a theory is that it can never be tested.*

My social worker's name was Mrs. Doyle and the first thing anyone noticed about her was the stiffness of her implausibly black hair, which was ratted up into an unfashionable bubble cut. Her long-sleeved yellow polyester blouse and rust-colored pants looked too warm for the day and her layers of dark pancake, clumpy mascara, penciled black eyebrows, and frosted pale pink lipstick were equally implausible. I could see that her bra was the old-fashioned cone style, probably with straps that didn't stretch or allow her any bounce. It was a neo-Victorian look for the kind of woman who wanted her appearance to be ladylike and overtly sexual at the same time, like a cartoon.

"Hello, Charlene, I'm Mrs. Doyle. I'll be looking after you from now on." She checked inside the file she was carrying. "I see you have no police record yet. Good, let's keep it that way for now." A hint of scorn in her voice for my lack of sophistication.

"My name's Charity," I said.

"Was your family Mennonite?" Mrs. Doyle asked as she pulled the driver's seat back to make room for my footlocker. "Maybe you should change it to a regular name."

I got in the car, wondering if Mrs. Doyle's hair was fireproof as well as bullet-proof, or if it might be possible to find enough strands of it on the seat for a voodoo doll. Her Volkswagen Rabbit smelled like Lysol and Charlie perfume and the engine sounded like a muted lawnmower. I closed my eyes to avoid getting carsick, the Lysol plus Charlie smell working its way into my head like slow poison. When I asked Mrs. Doyle to stop somewhere and let me use the bathroom, she refused.

"There's nothing along the way except truck stops and the men in those places are always so fresh," Mrs. Doyle said, as if me throwing up on myself or peeing my pants was the lesser of two evils against being in the vicinity of fresh truck drivers for five to ten minutes. She finally agreed to stop by the side of the road and let me squat in a ditch, staring at me the entire time to make sure I didn't run off.

"Don't smile, your face will crack," Mrs. Doyle said when we were back in the car. My pressed lips and rolling eyes had no effect; as a social worker, she was probably used to driving with silent, hostile kids in the seat next to her, no doubt preferring them to the loud, angry ones. The business with refusing to stop until I was almost begging and the staring turned out to be part of a routine she employed to put kids in their place, even the boys.

After driving another hour north, we arrived at the Guardian Angels Home for Boys and Girls. The Home was originally opened as a boarding school and vocational training center for the male descendants of Civil War veterans but by the turn of the century it was opened to girls as well. The Home was whites-only until 1962.

I wouldn't learn any of these things until later. Mrs. Doyle had her own ideas about what sort of information I might find interesting. No smoking was permitted at the Home, half the children there were inveterate thieves, and I would do well to keep my valuable items under wraps. Church service was mandatory, in the summer everyone worked or went to summer school, and all of my clothes were to be dropped off at the resident laundry for fumigation and labeling, including my underwear.

It was just after five when we drove through the wrought iron and brick front gate of the Home and I was handed over to Miss Arlen, one of the two girls' officers supervising the house parents who lived in the dorms and looked after the kids. Miss Arlen was a small woman, no taller than me, and her only distinctive feature was a set of oversized front teeth that she enjoyed flashing in a disdainful smile. She opened my footlocker for a contraband search and I was thankful to have kept my cigarettes tucked inside the waistband of my shorts. Miss Arlen looked me over, reaching out to touch my hair. I drew back.

"Long hair is a privilege that has to be earned," she said. "By demonstrating consistent good hygiene."

With these words I was handed over to a barber who made quick work of the hair I'd been re-growing for almost two years after cutting it failed to impress my father. I sat stone-faced in the chair and made no protest. The barber left the entire length just above my chin—a look that wouldn't be in style for another ten years—and washed it with something that smelled like vinegar. I wondered if they were going to make me strip and take a shower too.

They weren't. Instead I was taken to a dormitory on the far side of a lake that sat between the girls' dorms and the laundry. The boys' dorms were on the opposite end of the campus, as far from the girls as possible. Miss Arlen pointed out the dining hall, bakery, school, sewing shop, and vocational center. The Home was self-contained to keep the children politely out of the public eye, although runaways were a frequent sight in Darketown.

My dorm was one of four in a newly finished brick building. Girls were assigned according to age, with mine holding the seventh, eighth, and ninth graders. Each dorm had five bedrooms, with four of them designed to hold four girls and the fifth one meant for two. Mrs. Kelly, the dorm mother, was a white woman of later middle age whose brown and slightly silver hair was short and neat in a Toni Wave. She eyed me with a quick, jaded purse of her lips.

"Hello young lady and welcome to my dorm," Mrs. Kelly said as I was handed over to her by Miss Arlen. "You and me will get along like spaghetti and meatballs so long as you don't play games."

Mrs. Kelly always kept her word.

I was put in the dorm's fifth bedroom to be roommates with a girl named Annabelle who was twelve years old and had blond hair almost the same color as mine but hers hung to her shoulders in smooth waves; presumably Annabelle's hygiene was consistent even if her vocabulary could embarrass Cyd Vicious. Annabelle swore not early and often but endlessly. It was a habit at odds with her unassuming personality but was actually a byproduct of it. Annabelle had had no upbringing, as my Grandma East would have said, and she wasn't exceptional enough to raise herself.

"Hi, I'm Annabelle, what's your name? Charity? Son of a bitch, that's kind of a weird name. I mean, don't get me wrong but shit, I never knew anyone named Charity before. How the hell did you get a name like that?"

"My grandmother picked it out."

"Shit, why'd she name you that?"

"No idea," I said. "Anyway, she had a cat named Annabelle once."

"That's weird. Who the hell names a cat Annabelle?"

"Why not?"

This Annabelle could not answer so she turned her attention to the contents of my footlocker that I was in the middle of unpacking once again. After showing me which side of the closet and which dresser was for me, Annabelle expressed her disappointment over my sparse wardrobe; it meant lean pickings for borrowing and trading. It struck me then that all I had to my name was my footlocker and everything inside it. My winter clothes and most of my books, records, and other sundries were either in the trash or shared out among Carrie, Tammy, and Ruthie Holmes. They would benefit from my disappearance just as I had when Adam Irwin was shot down over Haiphong and his worldly goods were given to me and my brother.

"Don't you have any nice clothes? Hell, this isn't any better than the shit they give us here from the sewing shop." Annabelle flipped through my collection of t-shirts, jeans, and shorts. "Holy shit, you've got a bra. Make sure you hang on to that."

"Why?"

"Cause they won't give you a fucking bra here till you're thirteen, that's the rule."

"You're not allowed to wear a bra here till you're thirteen?"

"Well, yeah, you're allowed to wear it but the sewing shop won't give you anything but an undershirt till you're thirteen. They're so goddamned stupid. But I've got two bras anyway, I traded some cigarettes for them. They're nice ones too. The ones from the sewing shop are those dumbass ones that make your boobs look all pointy and the straps don't have any elastic in them. They're so fucking retarded."

I wasn't sure if Annabelle was referring to the bras or the bureaucracy of the sewing shop so I gave a noncommittal nod and continued to unpack. Without being asked, Annabelle filled me in on some of the Home's rules, both written and unwritten. Smoking inside a building was worth three weeks' restriction if you were caught but only one week if you were outdoors. Cigarettes were twenty-five cents a piece on the black market, a steep price when they were selling for sixty cents a pack in the stores. Some kids were able to build small fortunes from the cigarette trade and there were twin sisters in one of the downstairs dorms who regularly sent money to their heroin-addicted mother in Kokomo. Each child over the age of six was given a dollar a month for spending money that usually went for candy, pop, or the jukebox at the recreation center. Anyone twelve and older could earn bigger money by working in the cafeteria or one of the other sites on campus, like the bakery or the janitorial service.

"Do you like to dance?" Annabelle asked hopefully.

"No."

"Shit, that's too bad. I love to dance. Everyone says I'm pretty good, too." Annabelle turned on her transistor radio and fiddled with the dial until it came to a top forty station. She bounced and snapped her fingers with undeniable skill. "*Nowadays you can't be too sentimental, your best bet's a true baby blue Continental,*" Annabelle sang. "Billy Joel is a fucking hunk."

"You sure cuss a lot," I said.

"Not really," Annabelle said. "You should have heard Tina Bartlett downstairs. She used to call the house parents motherfuckers all the time. She was messed up on account of how her mom and her grandma used to beat the shit out of her and make her peddle ass from the time she was five to keep them in smack. She wasn't right anymore, you know what I mean?" Annabelle tapped the right side of her head. "She tried to cut her stomach open and they sent her to Edison. That's the loony bin over in Kingston. They say it's real nasty there and they've got these son of a bitches who walk around wearing cattle prods to make the patients be quiet."

The cattle prods sounded farfetched to me, making the rest of Annabelle's claims suspect. Still, anything could happen and it obviously did. How else could I be standing there listening to such things in the first place?

At six-thirty it was time to report to the dining hall for supper and everyone in the dorm gathered at the entrance in front of the stairwell to say grace. *"Heavenly Father, we thank thee, for thy bounty spread before us: bless it to our use, help us to do right, and keep us through the night, amen."*

I walked between Annabelle and Mrs. Kelly while the other girls shared whispered judgments about my looks, potential character, and possible reasons for my presence among them. "Maybe her stepfather was screwing her and her mother got jealous," said a black-haired, cherry-cheeked girl who looked like an illustration from an Edwardian candy box.

"No, they said her mother was dead, remember?" said another girl with tortoise shell glasses. "Maybe it was a stepmother who didn't want her."

"Ignore them," Mrs. Kelly said. "They're always nosy whenever a new girl shows up."

Like Willow Lake, the dining hall at the Home was run cafeteria-style, with three hundred children plus staff lining up with trays to receive their meals. Dinner was square slices of meatloaf that looked like cheap carpet samples, potatoes au gratin, canned peas, and lime-flavored Jell-O set with gooseberries. Seconds were allowed on the potatoes, peas, and Jell-O. I sipped milk from a cardboard container and ignored the food.

When Annabelle asked if I was going to eat my meatloaf, I abruptly flipped it onto her tray with my butter knife.

Once the meal was halfway finished, everyone replayed their day's events, shared gossip, or engaged in half-hearted arguments. The black-haired girl gave me a hard, careful look. "You sure got huge tits," she said.

"Cindy, do you think you could try pretending to have more manners than God gave a jackrabbit?" Mrs. Kelly asked.

"Well shit, they are," the Edwardian-looking girl now known as Cindy protested.

"Just like those tonsils you're always showing us."

The walk back to the dorm after dinner was more casual, with girls making deviations to chat with friends from other dorms or walk near the lake. A few boys stole up to their girlfriends for a quick kiss or hand squeeze before anyone could stop them. Since it was summer, there would be at least a few outdoor rendezvouses taking place after lights-out at ten. The younger children were sent to bed earlier.

I took a shower in the communal bathroom, using the Dial soap and Prell shampoo that was issued to everyone in the dorm. The shower stalls were lined with cream-colored ceramic tiles and had no curtains. The tiles were new-looking with no mold or mildew, which made me feel slightly better about everything until Cindy walked by the stall I was using and snatched the towel Mrs. Kelly had given me.

"You better keep your hands off my fucking towel if you don't want your ass kicked," Cindy warned me.

"Just ignore her, she always does shit like that." Annabelle advised from where she was brushing her teeth by the sinks. She gave me her own towel, damp but better than nothing.

The beds in our room were bunks, with no ladder for getting to the top. Annabelle offered me my choice and I took the bottom. She listened to Pink Floyd becoming comfortably numb on her transistor radio while I watched the bed slats above me, my eyes adjusting to the darkness well enough to make out their shapes. It didn't take long.

Chapter Twelve

My first days at the Guardian Angels Home were spent trying to reach Mrs. Doyle. Having an imprecise idea that she was my link to the Outside, as everyone called it, I kept trying to catch her at her desk, hoping she would see fit to put me in touch with my father. The first time I went to her office she called Miss Arlen, who flashed her oversized teeth at me in a triumphant smile and put me on a week's restriction for being in the administration building without a pass.

"All you had to do was ask me for a pass," Mrs. Kelly said.

"I didn't know." Needing written permission to enter a building and beg for information about my family was the latest of many new experiences.

I tried a second and third time. Mrs. Doyle was rarely in her office, especially in the afternoons. After three weeks I was finally able to catch her talking with someone on the phone about a church picnic gone awry after it was discovered that the minister's fourteen-year-old daughter had dumped a fistful of chocolate-flavored laxatives into the brownies that everyone found so delicious. I noted the deed for possible future use and continued to wait.

"I have a thundercloud sitting across my desk," Mrs. Doyle said to her phone after five minutes went by. "It wants me to know that I've been on the phone entirely too long for its liking."

My stomach tightened to an impotent fist as I realized Mrs. Doyle had no intention of giving me the time of that particular day. I walked back to the dorm as quickly as possible to prevent anyone from seeing my furious tears and found Annabelle dancing to "Video Killed the Radio Star" in the living room. I immediately switched course, tiptoeing out the backdoor exit for a walk by the lake.

Two days later I tried again. This time Mrs. Doyle was off the phone and sifting through the contents of a blue folder, which meant a boy's file. Yellow was for girls. What part was Mrs. Doyle playing in this unknown boy's life and what unhappy circumstances were to blame for him being in her hands?

Mrs. Doyle looked up after five minutes and forty-two seconds had passed and gave me a smile that used her lips but didn't extend to her eyes, just the opposite of Mona Lisa. "Well, Chelsea, are you ready to be civil?"

I tried to start from scratch. "I know you have a lot to do . . ."

"You're darned right I do."

"But I really need to find my father."

"And you expect me to find your father? I'm not a detective." Mrs. Doyle tapped her pencil against a paperweight that had a ceramic pig inside it. She leaned forward and looked hard into my face without blinking, telling me with her Maybelline-crusted eyes that I had sadly underestimated her significance in my new universe and could count on paying for my disrespect. "You have to accept the fact that some parents don't want to be in the picture and you've got plenty of company in your misery. The Holmeses were just trying to help out when they took you in after your mother died. You couldn't expect them to keep you forever."

"They didn't take me in when my mother died." I seized on the technicality. "My dad sent me to live with them four years after that, when my grandmother died."

"And anyway, do you know how many kids here have missing parents?" Mrs. Doyle asked as if I hadn't spoken. "It's the rule, not the exception. So if you want to live in a fantasy world, that's your problem, kiddo."

I did want to live in a fantasy world, so much that I left myself for a bit, as Grandma East used to call it when someone had an out-of-body experience. Hovering, or whatever it was called, up and to the right side of my body as it walked out of Mrs. Doyle's office and left the administration building. I could see myself hunched over, my hands in their usual loose fists pressed against my legs. My face was sour, the ugliness cooking inside me like an ulcer and sweating its way to the surface. I looked every millimeter a Wednesday's child.

I scrambled up a maple tree on the girls' side of the lake with a formless idea of settling there permanently, like one of those people in California who supposedly climbed trees and refused to come down until the police or someone came along and shook them out. I could see a group of high school girls roughhousing near the water, at one point five or six of them converging on another one and tearing her shirt off, tossing it up a tree. Somehow they were all able to laugh, wrestle, and make lewd jokes, having accepted the idea that they mattered to no one except possibly themselves. And eventually I'd be able to do the same if what Lakota had said was true about being able to adapt when we had no choice.

There were seventeen girls in our dorm between the ages of twelve and fifteen, many of them with portfolios of more foster parents and group homes than they could remember. There were also some like Annabelle who came to the Home at the age of four, the youngest allowed by regulations. Born out of wedlock to a Pepsi bottler in Muncie, Annabelle was forfeited when her mother landed a husband whose family persuaded her to eighty-six the bastard and try for some certifiable issue. Annabelle received an occasional card and some cash from her mother but visits only occurred when her mother and stepfather happened to be passing through the area, which was rare. Annabelle had no idea where her father might be and no interest in finding out.

"Why the fuck would my father want me?" Annabelle asked when I suggested she try tracking him down. She was confused, not bitter, as if I were suggesting that she write to the White House and ask the beleaguered Carters to adopt her and let her share little Amy's room. I saw her point; most men would probably choose to skip the father/daughter experience.

Cindy was another girl who'd lived in the Home since preschool. Her father's whereabouts were unknown and her mother was serving five years at the women's prison in Indianapolis for drug-dealing and check forgery, either to earn enough money to get Cindy out of hock or to support a drug habit and a parasitical boyfriend; rumor had it both ways. Cindy and I would never reach the confidence-sharing stage so there was no way to be sure. Either way it was an ordinary story at the Home.

Worse than Cindy were girls like Holly, an eighth-grader who always had a smile on her face, especially when she bragged about having tormented Tina Bartlett into her suicide attempt.

"Holly's mother brought her here two years ago," Mrs. Kelly told me privately. "Her father is serving a life sentence in Michigan City for killing his second wife. Idiot went and bought a $50,000 life insurance policy on her and didn't even wait a month before he shot and killed her while she was in the shower and tried to say it was a suicide."

Holly chose to follow in papa's footsteps. At the age of thirteen she was arrested and expelled from school after beating a fourth-grade boy with a dog chain when he refused to surrender his lunch money. Holly's mother was waiting with crossed fingers for her to turn eighteen; after that it was only a matter of time before she'd probably be sharing a cage with Cindy's mother in Indianapolis and everyone would sleep easier.

Mrs. Kelly wasn't in the habit of sharing personal information about one girl with another but Holly was an exception. Her ability to win someone's confidence without difficulty and betray it without pause if it benefited or amused her to do so had left more than one girl shell-shocked. I was more resentful than thankful for Mrs. Kelly's warnings, having hoped no one would notice that I was too gullible to be a decent judge of character.

To get even with girls like Cindy and Holly for the times they bullied us or stole our cigarettes, Annabelle and I invented a passive-aggressive game called What the Hell that involved sneaking into someone's room and placing a small but obvious object on their pillow, like a crucifix made of twigs or a layer of sycamore leaves. In lieu of a mystery gift, a cryptic message like "Free Pumpkins" or "Sarsaparilla 26 to 1" could be written on the mirror with lipstick. Nothing threatening or ugly was permitted; this would spoil the art of the game. Points were awarded if the gift's recipient could be overheard saying the game's name, with bonus points if they said what the fuck instead.

A factory whistle pierced us awake every morning at six on weekdays and eight on weekends. Once everyone was dressed and assembled at the doorway, the morning prayer was recited and then we could leave for breakfast. "*For care through the night, for another day's light, we thank Thee. We thank Thee for the food, for the life, health, and good, amen.*" There was no porridge or gruel. Instead it was toast made with the bread from our bakery, usually with cold or hot cereal, orange juice, and apples or bananas.

Brunch was served on Sundays, which meant extras like oranges, sausage, fritters, and scrambled eggs, with unlimited seconds on most of the non-meat items while supplies lasted. We were also allowed to go to the dining hall on our own instead of having to stay with our dorms. The exception was the last Sunday of every month, when a formal afternoon dinner was served for the purpose of teaching and reinforcing mealtime p's and q's. On those days everyone had to stay in their church clothes and sit at an assigned table. Everyone hated formal Sunday, including the house parents.

There were two months before the school year began and not much to do except wander the grounds and talk to the trees, whose conversation was usually better than Annabelle's. Summer jobs were available but when Mrs. Kelly gave me a pass for the administration building to see Mr. Drew, the supervisor of the job program, I found him chatting with Bobbie Ann Johnson, the previous year's homecoming queen, and not welcoming interruptions from plainer, less articulate girls. Mr.

Drew was like most of the tweed-suited men who worked in the administration building: red, oversized, and porous, in his late fifties but looking ten years older.

"What do you need, gal?" he demanded without ceremony when I walked into his office.

The right words refused to spit themselves out. Mr. Drew's abruptness coupled with the beautiful Bobbie Ann's polite smile was giving me aphasia. "Um, Mrs. Kelly said . . ."

"Speak up, gal, I can't hear a word you're saying." His voice was adenoidal and bellowing, a congested elephant.

"Nothing." I turned and walked out, hurrying back to the dorm. Mr. Drew put out the equivalent of an APB with the house parents in our building, claiming that I'd been sassy to him and was messing around the administration building for no reason. Another enemy made without even trying. Besides the tobacco shortage and lack of reading material, the worst thing about the Home was the never-ending supply of tripwires and landmines.

At suppertime Mrs. Kelly told me to try again the next day and not to worry about Mr. Drew. "I told him you're just shy," she said. "He's always been a horse's ass."

Everyone laughed and I soaked up the vindication. Mrs. Kelly's position on such conflicts was usually in our favor. Some of the house parents were exceptional, like her, while others were tolerable, heavy-handed, or fit for poison. Just like real parents.

The Home library was closed during the last two weeks of August for maintenance. There were comic books in the rec center, *Little Lulu*, *Casper the Friendly Ghost*, and *Richie Rich*, which I read out of desperation until the sight of their Fisher Price colors made me queasy and hostile. I was saved from what felt like an impending nervous breakdown aggravated by nicotine withdrawal when a spot opened in the cafeteria on the breakfast shift. Mr. Drew called the dorm himself to tell Mrs. Kelly after she'd had a few sharp words with him about not treating girls looking for jobs as if they were panhandlers in off the street. Mr. Drew's behavior became downright solicitous and he addressed me by my name instead of calling me gal.

There was no Sunday school at the Home's nondenominational Protestant church for anyone past sixth grade, only a one-hour sermon by the Reverend Whitcomb, a small, dark man who used the Children's Living Bible and always wore gray or black as he delivered middle of the road homilies that were easy enough to follow if I was careful not to let my mind wander, which I usually wasn't. The high school choir performed one Sunday a month and on special occasions. Communion was only served on Easter Sunday. I liked Reverend Whitcomb better than Reverend McCleod at the Methodist church in Mount Olive, who wore polyester suits in different colors and used hair oil.

Miss Lott was a tall ogress who shared duties with Miss Arlen and didn't hesitate to deliver a clop around the chops to any girl who failed to use caution. Like Sheila Martz, who punched a hole in her bedroom wall after a promised visit from her older brother was canceled at the last minute. Or Justine Bolser, a wilting flower of sixteen who held the Home's current record for lake dates with Tony Chase, her boyfriend since seventh grade. Not that this made any difference to Miss Lott when she saw Tony sneaking out of Justine's dorm at three in the morning. She immediately ran inside and slapped Justine upside the head with her hand and the riot act.

It was rumored that Miss Lott had an overactive libido and Claudia, the girl with the tortoise shell glasses, advised me not to take a shower during the weeks that she was on duty. "She won't want you if you smell bad," Claudia said. It was her habit to serve as the voice of logic and reason in our dorm, as if wearing glasses obliged her to play the sage.

"Mrs. Kelly won't like that," I said to Claudia as I tried to imagine what being seduced by Miss Lott would involve.

"Fuck Mrs. Kelly. She has a lock on her bedroom door."

I liked the way Claudia could say such things and still sound so rational and unruffled. At the same time, I knew that skipping the shower wouldn't sit well with Mrs. Kelly, who didn't mince words when it came to good hygiene. Too many of the girls came from backgrounds where no one had seen fit to inform them that people who bathed daily, flushed the toilet, and refrained from masturbating in public were likely to be more popular at parties than those who didn't. Our housemother had no qualms about filling in the gaps.

"Miss Lott is not a rapist." Mrs. Kelly said after she caught me sneaking to my room one night instead of scrubbing myself as ordered. "Have I ever steered you wrong?"

It was a fair question. But steering someone right wasn't enough to prevent sneak attacks from the rear. Lakota could have told her that.

My Tom Sawyer hat disappeared during my first week at the Home, never to be seen again. Theft was as endemic as Mrs. Doyle had promised; in addition to the hat, I also lost a necklace of my mother's and the bra that Annabelle had warned me to guard with my life. I went without both until Mrs. Kelly noticed and sent me to the sewing room under orders not to return without foundation garments. The sewing shop gave me two cone bras of my own that I altered with a needle and thread borrowed from Mrs. Kelly, who admired my ingenuity. By sewing a two-inch seam tuck across the center of the cups and snipping away the bit of excess material on the inside, I turned the cones into bowls.

Annabelle had misunderstood the clothing policy, which was that only girls over the age of thirteen were automatically given bras; anyone younger had to demonstrate obvious need, which she hadn't. The ability to consider variables was never Annabelle's strong point. And while I was always quick to try and gauge the mood of any group of girls I came upon to avoid any volatile or unwelcome situations, Annabelle had no more instinct for avoiding trouble than a Dodo. More than once she was yelled at or punched by someone for saying the wrong thing at the wrong time, taking someone else's seat on the bench outside the dorm, walking around with blood stains on the back of her shorts.

"What are you doing, sitting in the grass?" Cindy demanded when she saw me and Annabelle sunning ourselves on the lawn in front of the dorm. "Sit on the fucking bench, you stupid bitches."

I pretended to ignore Cindy, the best way I'd found of dealing with her, and tried to do a handstand. Being ignored might lead Cindy to come closer, poke at me, call me an ugly name or two to see if she could provoke me into a fight, and then wander off out of boredom. But for reasons known only to God and Freud, Annabelle cheerfully invited Cindy to force her from the sidewalk if she was able. Since Cindy wasn't able, she kicked Annabelle in the back, hard enough to make her cry. I had to help her to her feet and upstairs to get an infirmary pass from Mrs. Kelly.

"Why do you do things like that?" I asked Annabelle as we limped up the steps. "You've known her longer than me and you still act like a dumbass." Annabelle conceded my point but was unable to explain her impulses. Hoof in mouth disease, Mrs. Kelly always said.

"I fell and hit my back on the bench," Annabelle said to Mrs. Kelly, with me backing her up. Mrs. Kelly sighed and wrote out the pass, as irritated by the no-snitching code as she was by the persistently filthy toaster oven in the kitchenette. The two problems could be minimized but never eliminated. She soldiered on against both anyway.

I hated fights and dreaded getting into one. There was always the possibility of being set on by a group of girls, broken teeth or a disfigured face that the Home probably wouldn't pay to have fixed decently as long as I could still eat and talk. Or of getting trapped into a back and forth vendetta with someone, which would mean keeping one eye over my shoulder every second like the protagonist in a John LeCarré novel, a habit that could never come naturally to me.

I also dreaded the possibility of losing my own temper, becoming so angry that I did ugly and irreversible deeds, like jumping on Cindy after one of her taunts and using the element of surprise to maul her like a coyote tearing into a chicken, or offering Holly an arsenic-laced candy bar. My dark side at work, I assumed. Everybody was supposed to have one.

Chapter Thirteen

The library at the Home was run by Miss Haas, a credulous maiden lady in her late sixties whose gray pageboy wig lay draped over a moth-eaten scalp. Sometimes one of the boys would hide behind the encyclopedia stacks and yank the wig off with a coat-hanger fishing pole. Miss Haas would invariably screech, slap her hands over her head, and run to Mr. Morton the principal to weep about what cruel monsters we were, with the guilty party receiving five whacks. Miss Haas never made any connection between the scalping incidents and her habit of treating us like something she'd scraped off her shoe. It wasn't unusual for Miss Haas to banish all of the kids from the library in a sudden fit of pique and refuse any checkouts for the remainder of the day.

"You welfare kids don't have the manners of a goat," Miss Haas cried once as she ordered everyone out of the library after someone farted loudly and refused to self-identify.

"*Behhh*," I said. Miss Haas couldn't see who was doing it since she was looking at our backs. Some of the boys started making goat noises too and then everyone was doing it. Miss Haas became downright hysterical, screaming for Mr. Morton as if we were children of the corn.

"That old biddy, who does she think she is?" Mrs. Kelly said to Mrs. Sorensen, the flute-voiced Norwegian widow who took care of the dorm below us. "Calling them welfare kids. I'm going to have a few thousand words with Mr. Stewart about that."

"You know she's a little bit off," Mrs. Sorensen said. "And she never had children of her own so she's not so patient."

"Then she's picked a damned strange place to supplement her SSI." Mrs. Kelly wouldn't budge.

"This time she said it was because we were making faces at her," I complained to Annabelle after yet another shutdown. "She's always closing the library for some dumbass reason so she can sit on her own fat ass and read *The National Enquirer* all day long."

"Why don't you just pick the lock?" Annabelle asked as she passed me the cigarette we were sharing behind the vocational school building.

"Shit, I don't know how to pick a lock."

"It should be easy, that door's old and it's got one of those giant-ass keyholes that you can just about stick your hand in."

"So why haven't you ever done it?" I asked.

"Who cares about going to the fucking library?"

Passes weren't required for the school building. Armed with a bobby pin, a protractor, and an alibi about looking for a lost necklace if anyone saw me, I found the library door as easy to open as Annabelle had guessed. Once inside, I ran straight to the high school fiction section and grabbed a copy of *Gone with the Wind*. Since it was big enough to be three books, I decided it would suffice for the moment and peeked out the door to see if the coast was clear. From the corner of my eye I noticed a box of paperbacks; a recent donation from a sorority at Butler University. I grabbed as many of them as I could hide under my clothes and hurried back to the dorm.

"So this is the book were the guy says 'frankly my dear I don't give a damn'?" Annabelle asked as she flipped through *Gone with the Wind* that night just before bedtime.

"Yep."

"Cool, read that part to me."

"That doesn't come until the end," I said. "I'm starting at the beginning."

I read aloud from page one, giving Annabelle an occasional translation of the text in a more modern vernacular. Scarlett O'Hara was not beautiful but men seldom realized it once she decided to add their scalps to her collection. The Wilkes/Hamilton family only married their cousins and it was starting to make them weird. The good slaves of Tara had no concerns beyond their work and no desires beyond a bit of fun and games at Christmas because they weren't allowed to know that there was anything better going on.

Mrs. Kelly had grown up in a country town that was too small for a movie theater, bowling alley, skating rink, or any other form of diversion for young people that was both legal and socially acceptable in the post-war 1940s. Mrs. Kelly and her friends would sometimes spend their Saturday evenings passing the hat for a bottle of White Lightning mixed with 7-up and then head to their favorite drinking spot, the upper branches of an old mulberry tree that grew outside the back entrance of a local fundamentalist church. A second-story window offered them a perfect view of the church's Saturday evening services.

"You have never laughed until you've seen a 300-pound dame with a beehive hairdo dancing in holy rapture after she's been slain by the spirit," Mrs. Kelly promised.

One of the regulars at those Saturday evening services was a boy from Mrs. Kelly's class named Jimmy who suffered from a messianic complex and allegedly killed small animals to see if he could bring them back from the dead. Sometimes Jimmy walked around town in a bedsheet pretending to be a prophet, always stopping at the saloon to warn his alcoholic father and any others present of the eternal damnation waiting for anyone who consumed the devil's water. Little Jimmy grew up to become a minister with a flock that slaughtered itself and a number of others on his command.

Like the rest of the girls in the dorm, I had no trouble remembering Jim Jones and the Jonestown massacre that had taken place a few days after my tenth birthday. Scores of children dead in the Guyana jungle after being tricked or forced into drinking the cyanide-laced Kool-Ade that was served to them and their parents was hardly a forgettable event. Some of the people who tried to escape were shot and killed, including a U.S. congressman named Leo Ryan who was investigating a series of complaints about Jim Jones using and abusing his followers. November was a bad-luck month.

"I kept looking through the papers and magazines to see if anyone I knew was dead," Mrs. Kelly said. "There were a lot of foster kids in that group they found. Kids that weren't even supposed to leave the state, let alone the country. They did evil things to those kids."

The articles Mrs. Kelly found in *Time, Newsweek,* and the *Indianapolis Star* told how the once energetic and forceful young minister had corroded himself with pill-popping and bed-hopping as his inner megalomaniac came out and laid claim to everything his followers had, right down to their bodies, their children's bodies, and finally their collective essence. Mrs. Kelly warned us in her sternest no-shit voice that such individuals were to be treated like tornadoes; under no circumstances did we want to be caught up by one or the other.

"You girls need to remember this," Mrs. Kelly said of Jim Jones. "Those kind don't want to change the world, they just want to be worshipped. And they always have an eye out for young people without families."

Mrs. Kelly never did say if she knew anyone at Jonestown.

Miss Lott never chose to favor me with her attention, even though I received no visitors or letters, obvious indicators that no one on the Outside was taking a personal interest in my well-being. But her physical contact with me never went beyond the occasional jerk, slap, or hair-yank; she preferred the mouthier, bravado-ridden girls. Someday I wanted to be bravado-ridden but this didn't seem like a good time for it. Taking Claudia's advice might have helped as well.

"Don't you ever shower?" Miss Lott complained as she stood behind me in the cafeteria line at suppertime. "You stink to heaven and back."

"I want to conserve water," I said. "For ecology."

"What about air pollution?" she retorted.

I could at least take comfort that I wasn't in the same shoes as Sonya Wheatley, a sixteen-year-old from the neighboring upstairs dorm who was caught by nature after dallying with Tom Applegate, the chief of custodians. Tom made the usual sapsucker's plea that the father could have been anyone but it didn't keep him from being bumped down to everyday janitor after Sonya described his unusual circumcision scar and the contents of his on-campus apartment. Nor did it keep Sonya from being sent to the Florence Crittenton Home in Indianapolis.

"Maybe Tom would do it with me," Annabelle said as we were lying on our beds after a formal Sunday and listening to the rainstorm that was keeping everyone inside.

"Tom Applegate is a bastard," I said. "I heard he never even gave Sonya any presents, just that pie in her oven."

"If he'd do it with Sonya he'd do it with me. And I bet I could get some presents from him."

"So go ask Tommy the slut if he'll roll with you," I said, hoping she'd hush up soon.

Annabelle corrected me. "Only girls can be sluts. Just like with bitch."

"Fine. You be a slut and I'll be a bitch." We both laughed.

My thirteenth birthday was notable for one reason only; a peep heard from my father in the form of a Western Union money order for fifty dollars that Mrs. Doyle grudgingly handed over to me.

"Did he send a letter or a return address?" I asked.

"Nope." Her pink crayon lips smiled.

No letter or anything personal telling me anything about himself, my brother, or if I would ever be deemed worthy of entering their presence again. But now I was thirteen and supposedly too old to get soggy about such things. At thirteen you wrote off missing parents as defaulters and turned up the radio.

Chapter Fourteen

Annabelle came down with a stomach virus during the last month of the school year and spent a week in the infirmary. I brought her some of my own books to read since the library was closed again after Miss Haas complained that someone was making piggy noises intended for her ears alone, which must have been why no one else could hear them. As I complained about the library, Annabelle suggested that I try writing my own stories.

"You can write about doing it with someone for the first time," she said. "People always want to read stories like that. Have you fucked anyone yet? Maybe we should do it together."

I wasn't sure if Annabelle meant choosing a pair of boys and copulating as a quartet or if the two of us should improvise and do it on our own. Nor did I ask since one scenario held as little appeal as the other. I returned to the dorm without giving her an answer and found everyone watching TV. Cindy rose and did a halfhearted belly dance during the commercial.

"You like my ass?" she sneered at me. "I know you're a lez."

"Don't you be rolling your eyes at her," Holly said to me with her usual easy smile. "I'll wait till you're asleep and cut you up like a frog." A deaf person would have supposed by Holly's expression that she was saying nighty-night and not to let the bed bugs bite.

I went to my room to daydream about Marie Brown, a senior girl I was crushed on who lived downstairs in Mrs. Sorensen's dorm. Marie led the honor roll at school each semester and held herself with a radiant confidence that protected her from the slings and rocks of girls like Cindy and Holly. Without understanding how, I knew that Marie was the kind of girl who could uplift those she chose to favor with her friendship, like Helen Burns in *Jane Eyre*. Annabelle, on the other hand, was dead weight. No doubt Marie would see me in the same light if I were to come within arm's reach of her, which I was careful not to do in case she noticed.

I was always being careful. An old habit, like worshiping in a church that threatened to excommunicate me every time I turned around. Why not let it and go the way of all apostates?

And it was a perfect spring evening with soft air and sweet smells. I jumped up and put on my Wrangler jacket, a Christmas gift from a secret Santa at the Lutheran church in Darketown. Five minutes later I slipped out the front gate just past the house of Mr. Stewart, the Home's superintendent. It was shortly before lights-out, normally a bad time to be going AWOL but with Annabelle in the infirmary, there was no one to loudly notice me missing from my bed. I had a dollar and thirty-seven cents in my pocket and not an idea in what passed for my mind besides putting as much distance as possible between myself and the Home in the shortest amount of time. If Huckleberry Finn could do it, why the hell couldn't I?

Once past the front gate, I had my choice of two directions. Going east would lead to Darketown four miles away, the most popular destination for runners. The alternative was Kingston, seven miles away but less obvious. Believing that a delay of gratification would be in my best interests, I chose Kingston and put my thumb out. Within a few minutes I had a ride with a middle-aged man in a Buick who was dressed too plainly to be a pimp—at least according to pulp fiction standards—and who reluctantly dropped me off on a main drag once we were inside Kingston without asking for so much as a handshake in return. I was off to a good start and untroubled by the fact that step two was nowhere in sight.

It was a Tuesday night, which meant most of the few businesses in Kingston were shuttered for the evening. One exception was a sad-looking tavern whose lights were still on. The smoke and cheap beer smell that greeted me when I opened the door prompted a memory of the times my father would go to the White Light Tavern for a binge, maneuver his truck home, and leaf through an old photo album that Trilby and I were never allowed to touch as he cried over his wedding pictures.

The barmaid inside this tavern was a large woman in her fifties with frosted hair and a kind face, just like the ones on TV. This had to mean I was on the right track. A handful of men sat at the bar; the youngest one looking to be in his late twenties. His tanned and reddish face suggested that he either worked in the elements or was too fond of what was in the glass in front of him. Or both. A red baseball hat and zipped up navy sweatshirt. He reminded me of Robby Gallagher, one of the regular customers at my father's store.

"Buy you a beer, sweetheart?" he offered. That was also what they said on TV.

"Not unless she's got an ID," the barmaid said.

"I'd rather have a Pepsi," I said; diplomacy seemed best. A red plastic glass with a straw was put in front of me.

"What's your name, hon?" the younger man asked.

"Aurelia," I decided. Burying myself in the part, I added, "It was my great-aunt's name and she died from scarlet fever when she was nine."

"That's one I ain't never heard before," the man said. "The name, I mean."

I took this as an unintended compliment on my creative skills. The barmaid's name was Lynette, which was spelled out in script on the silver necklace she was wearing. I thought it suited her. Lynette asked me why I was up so late instead of being home in bed for school the next morning.

"I graduated last year," I told her. "And I'm heading down south to be with my father." It was a near-snap decision; the South was in vogue and everyone else seemed to be going there. Why should only I be left to contend with snow, ice, and Holly, while my father,

Trilby, and the Holmeses were strolling under palm trees and collecting sand dollars?

"Where's your daddy live?" Lynette asked.

"Dallas." It hit me suddenly as a great idea. Head to Dallas and get a job as a maid for a family like the Ewings, who might take a liking to me and send me to a real boarding school, an all-girl one with nice-looking uniforms, a generous allowance, and trips into the city once a week. I might not have had much of a brain but I did possess an imagination chock full of clichés.

Lynette gave me the careful look of someone with her own misspent youth in mind. "How you planning to get to Dallas? Greyhound?"

"I don't have enough money for a ticket." I hesitated. "I'll just have to hitch."

"That can be dangerous." Her tone of voice suggested she knew I wasn't going to listen to her.

"I can give you a ride to Muncie in the morning when I go to the Army recruiter's," said the man in the red baseball hat. The others called him Ira, which sounded like a girl's name to me. "And you can spend the night with me and my granny."

A house shared with a grandmother sounded like a safe enough haven. Lynette said goodnight to Ira and wished me luck as I followed him out the door like a stray cat who'd just been fed. We drove outside of town in his formula rattletrap Ford pickup, a palsied hulk with gaps in the floorboards.

Ira's house was even less inspiring than his truck. The front porch was a layer of ancient wooden boards that were warped and partially covered with scabby green paint. Once we were inside, Ira turned on a lamp with a ruffled cloth shade, yellowed with age and nicotine, and I could see that the wallpaper and furnishings were probably concurrent with the truck. There were no overhead light fixtures, even in the kitchen. The small living room was dominated by a couch and a pot-bellied stove that didn't seem to be earning its keep. Spring or not, the house was freezing. How could someone with the freedom to live on his own not choose to do it in a better-kept home?

"Come on, let's get to bed and get warm," Ira said.

"Bed?" I bleated like a sheep. "Where's your grandmother?"

"She stays in that trailer across the yard. She mostly just comes over here to cook and stuff for me."

I considered the situation. On the one hand, if a grown man thought I was pretty enough to have sex with, perhaps I wasn't a lesbian after all. On the other hand, I wanted to run screaming into the night. I couldn't decide if it was Ira or his nasty little house that was putting me off more. While I was trying to decide what good manners called for in the situation, Ira proceeded to strip. Then he turned on the portable heater that was sitting on the bedroom floor. The smell of kerosene filled the room, making me nauseous and depressed.

Once his boxers were off, Ira began tugging at the shoulders of my jacket. "How old are you, for real?"

"Thirteen," I blurted. The truth might set me free. I tried not to look down at his arced penis.

"Holy shit, I bet you taste like peppermint."

"I've got the curse," I said quickly.

"You're lying. I bet you're a virgin."

I took the Fifth Amendment.

"Hey, don't worry about it." Ira's voice softened as he stroked my messy hair and sat down on the edge of his lumpy, unmade bed. "There's more than one way to skin a rabbit." Pulling me towards him, he held my elbows and pushed me to my knees. Then he took my head in his hands and guided it to his crotch. "Go ahead, get started. I bet you'll love it."

It didn't take long but Ira gripped the sides of my head the entire time to keep me from stopping until he was ready. I didn't try to leave myself, which would have meant having to watch the whole thing. He was reasonably clean though I had nothing to compare him to but it was impossible to forget that the object of my unenthusiastic attention was utilized for other purposes and my gag reflex went into overdrive. Ira was a good sport about this, slowing down when I appeared to be choking to death and not taking offense when I ran to the bathroom to throw up afterwards.

I was awake most of the night, unable to determine exactly what had happened or what it meant. I knew that I was still a virgin but not what people would call a nice girl anymore. What I didn't know was whether to worry about it or not, unsure if I'd just been ruined or initiated.

The next morning I got up and found a lean, gray-bunned woman in an oversized sweater and polyester pants making scrambled eggs in Ira's kitchen. "How do, young lady," she said, her eyes never leaving the stove.

"How do," I replied, wondering what sort of explanation she might be imagining for my presence. I felt chilly and achy.

"Is Ira up yet?"

"No." Was the sight of an unknown and possibly underage girl in her grandson's house too ordinary to stir a reaction in the woman? Grandma Ira was a much cooler customer than either of my own grandmothers would have been under the same circumstances.

"Well, he better shake a leg if he wants to get down to them army people today."

I couldn't think of anything intelligent to say, or even anything stupid. Grandma Ira told me to sit down and asked if I wanted coffee, which I didn't. Her accent was pure Appalachia; she could have been both a Hatfield and a McCoy. It was the sound of lonely places.

Ira came out of the bedroom a few minutes later. "Hey, Mamaw, what do you know?" he asked.

"Not a whole lot, honey. How about you?"

"Not a damn thing."

Grandma Ira motioned for him to sit as she set the eggs and a plate with slices of toast on the table. Ira sat down and talked with his grandmother about a TV she'd seen the night before about a man with a multiple personality disorder. Or as Grandma Ira put it, a man with more than one mind to him. What would it be like to return to consciousness after being in a blackout for days or even years while someone else occupied my head and lived my life for me? A setup like that could have its benefits.

We left for Muncie after breakfast, for which I forgot to thank Ira's grandmother. Ira himself seemed preoccupied and hardly noticed me next to him on the seat. We pulled into a truck stop just outside of town. "You ought to be able to get a ride with someone here," he said. "I'd keep you with me if I could but I've already enlisted so I have to show up or they'll get the MPs on me. Take this in case you need something to eat."

"Thanks," I said, speaking to him for the first and last time that morning as I accepted the two twenties he was holding out to me. It might have been his way of making things more principled and less sickening, this show of giving me money out of generosity instead of handing it to me the night before as soon as I was able to lift my head from the toilet bowl, a miserly payment for a service grudgingly rendered.

I climbed out of the truck and walked away without looking back at Ira, who drove off the edge of the earth and into a pile of compost for all I would ever know or care. From my conversation with Annabelle in the infirmary to Cindy's ass-shaking, Holly's lighthearted threats of dismemberment, and fellating a grown man of less than two hours' acquaintance, it was less than a day and more than a millennium. I decided to blame

Miss Haas for closing the library and setting the chain of events in motion.

The truck stop was one of the newer franchise ones with a large dining room and counter area on one side and a shop on the other. Not being hungry, I explored the shop and bought a cheap brown suede hat with a narrow, curling brim like John Denver's and a man's red t-shirt to replace the vomit-stained one I was already wearing. The dining room was full of breakfasting men and an occasional woman who were mostly dressed like me and the air jangled with Southern and Midwestern voices. I sat at the counter and ordered a Pepsi, listening in on the crowd to see if any ideas about what to do next could be culled from their chatter.

"Hey, amigo, they say you're badger-bound.

"Yeah, I got a load for Beer City and then boundaround to Chi Town with a honey wagon."

"Hear you got bit in the ass at a bear trap."

"Damned right. That's going to wipe out my trading stamps."

A tall, thin man in a blue baseball hat with a white letter 'T' on the front walked in and sat two stools away from me at the counter. He took his hat off, which meant at least a hint of some upbringing. His dishwater blond hair was wiry and he looked so much like Jerry Reed that I half expected him to start singing "East Bound and Down." The waitress brought my check and he reached for it.

"You don't need to do that," I said.

"Why don't you have something to eat?" he suggested.

"I'm not hungry," I said. "I'm just trying to find a ride to Texas with somebody."

"Texas? Well, if you're going anywhere near Dallas I could give you a lift. That's where I live."

It was like winning a contest. His name was Phil and he had a load of steel pipes to deliver in Pittsburgh, with a second one to pick up in Illinois and bring back to Dallas. I was welcome to join him if I could pay for my own meals and keep out of sight at the weigh stations. In return he would keep his hands to himself. When I agreed, Phil asked my name.

"Ellie," I said. Whatever my name was, all I cared about now was being someone else and getting to Dallas. Phil told me to be ready in an hour.

The sign behind the cash register said: "Showers, 25 cents." For a quarter and a one-dollar deposit, a room could be used for taking a shower or a nap. After two hours the dollar was forfeit and after three hours someone would come looking for me. I handed over five quarters and received a key and a yellow towel. Equipped with a new toothbrush, a tube of Crest and a bottle of Breck, I stepped into the shower of the threadbare but clean bathroom and scrubbed with the complimentary bar of Ivory, which I tried holding in my mouth. It wasn't too bad.

Chapter Fifteen

The horn in Phil's truck didn't work right. Instead of a loud, satisfied honk, all it could manage was a medium-sized beep. Sometimes a child in a passing car would jerk their elbow at us and Phil would oblige, pulling the cord three times to make up for the missing volume. I was a little disappointed myself but tried not to show it since I was pretending to be eighteen.

"Do you ever go to Florida?" I asked Phil as we headed east. "What's it like there?"

"Some parts of it are nice." He offered me a Kool and I shook my head; menthols made me sick. "Like Fort Lauderdale, that's a real nice town. But those swamps down there, not for me. I'm not a crocodile and I sure as hell ain't no orchid."

"Me neither," I said, to be polite.

We ate dinner at another truck stop in Ohio just outside Cincinnati. It looked exactly like the one in Indiana where we'd joined up. The same miniature jukeboxes were at the tables and I played "Eastbound and Down" until Phil nicely asked me to give it a rest.

"We're not supposed to pick up riders," he warned me. "So if anybody asks, tell them you're my daughter."

"Sure." I liked the idea of being Jerry Reed's daughter.

We reached the Pennsylvania state line late in the evening. I was exhausted but determined not to miss the event. As soon as the "Welcome to Pennsylvania" sign appeared on the side of the road I climbed back into the sleeper and was out within minutes, not waking up until Phil nudged me to let me know we'd arrived at the Travelodge where he had a room for the night. It had only the basics, a single queen-sized bed, dresser, nightstand, and a clean bathroom. I'd never stayed at a motel before. Maybe my father's place looked like this.

"Do you mind sharing the bed?" Phil asked. "You can sleep in the truck bed if you want. The sheets are clean."

Since he was offering an option without acting as if it mattered to him one way or another, I agreed to share. If he wanted the same thing that Ira did, maybe I could do it without getting sick this time. At least this way I knew there was no chance of getting pregnant.

Phil used the shower and came out of the bathroom wearing a t-shirt and pajama bottoms. "Tomorrow morning I'll be going to drop off those pipes at a construction site and then I'll come back and get you," he said as he rubbed his hair with a towel. "I don't want to take a chance on someone reporting me for having a rider."

We talked for a while before going to sleep; it seemed expedient to get acquainted since we were going to be sharing the bed, if nothing else. Phil made no move in my direction as he talked about his marriage and four-year-old divorce; his wife said he was on the road too much, that she was lonesome. Lonesome enough to have three different men to carry on with and a fourth for spare parts, as Phil put it. She started calling some of them by the wrong names.

"Did you and your wife have any kids?" I asked.

"Nope. Neither of us really wanted any."

"Oh."

After leaving Pennsylvania the next day we went back the way we came, only on I-70 West instead of East. This, I learned from Phil, was what boundaround meant. We stopped at a Texaco outside Columbus and I splurged on a cheap, sturdy silver pendant shaped like the state of Ohio that had 'Eleanor' engraved on the front.

Twice I collected the nerve to say yes after being approached by one of the drivers at a rest area parking lot. It was beginning to seem easy enough, especially after I discovered how to leave myself by reaching inward instead of out. While my hands or mouth were doing one thing, my mind could visit a galaxy deep within myself and the men were finished or near to it by the time I exhausted its possibilities.

The first of the two men was a friendly and uncritical grandfather type who only asked me to use my hands. The second man was equally atypical— young, good-looking, and generous enough to share his pot with me afterwards. "My name's Kenny," he said, handing me the joint he'd just lit. "What's yours, little bit?"

"Alice." I thought it suited the occasion.

"Cute. Well, Alice, haven't you ever smoked pot before?"

"No," I admitted. "Just cigarettes."

Kenny told me to inhale only a little and hold it in for as long as I could. I had no special expectations but once the THC kicked in, my mind slid to neutral and trying to steer myself was hopeless. Sensory input processing was operating on reserve. I watched Kenny next to me, trying to remember who he was. Was it important for me to remember? I couldn't decide. My eyes slid over the small contours of the truck's sleeper, trying to remember why I was there. Then it occurred to me that I should leave, that this truck wasn't my place in the world. Did I have a place in the world? I couldn't remember if that was important either.

After climbing down from Kenny's truck, I felt the miasma of the novice pot user filling up my air. It was pleasant but bewildering and I sat down on the blacktop in the parking lot with my knees drawn under my chin, unable to decide where I was going or if I even needed to be going anywhere at all. It was in this state that Phil found me and hustled me back to his truck, pulling away as quickly as he could before the wrong person might notice me. I always thought that was decent of him; Phil would have lost nothing by ditching me except the possibility of being charged under the Mann Act.

At four the next morning we pulled into a truck stop near a town called Mattoon. Phil immediately went to sleep but I decided to go inside for an early breakfast. The waitress at the counter had eyes like dishwater ready to be let out. I ignored the menu and asked her for scrambled eggs and toast.

"Shouldn't you be at home getting ready for school, honey?" she asked me.

"I graduated last year," I said, wondering why strangers seemed suspicious about my age while the people who knew me all agreed that I could easily pass for eighteen or nineteen. It was probably my habit of standing cautiously at the threshold of any establishment I entered, a quick scan of the room to check for cops and then edging my way in, always stopping to study the candy displays and carefully browsing through the souvenirs and postcards. It was the body language of a thirteen-year-old space cadet, no matter how developed the body might be.

The counter was crescent-shaped, curving around a half-kitchen with a three-burner coffee warmer, a sink, and a cooler filled with slices of pie and cake. The only other person sitting there was a silver-haired man in a tan trench coat who stirred his coffee and munched on a Danish as he read his copy of the *Mt. Vernon Register-News*. He didn't look like a trucker and I guessed him for a traveling salesman. The waitress came over to refill his cup periodically and the two of them shared a few words of conversation that I couldn't hear.

The man looked over and winked at me after the waitress left the counter area to serve two men sitting at a table. I didn't like it when people winked; it seemed like a silly thing to do and I never knew what it was supposed to mean. I twisted my mouth to the side in response and turned away from him, which he took for coy friendliness.

"How about a cup of coffee?" he asked me.

"Nope," I said.

"You can't start the day without coffee."

"Yes I can." I gulped down the last of my orange juice and reached for a cigarette. It was a chance to show off my new lighter with its silver and turquoise cover, a freebie that came with the matching fishing knife I'd bought the day before in Kankakee to keep tucked in my waistband, in advance of need. I thought it was beautiful.

"A pretty girl like you shouldn't smoke," the man said.

"Why not?" I asked, knowing that some bullshit rhetoric was on its way.

"It'll make your fingers and teeth turn yellow and you won't have a pretty smile."

"Fuck off." I stood up and grabbed my check.

His ears were pinned back. "You've got a nasty mouth for such a pretty girl."

"I didn't ask you to talk to me so you can just piss up a pole." I slapped fifty cents on the counter and went to pay my bill. The etiquette of tipping wasn't entirely clear to me but I wanted to seem worldly.

I used the bathroom and went outside, where the sun was rising to make an opal sky. Having the freedom to tell off a jerk and walk away from him was a rare and tasty dish. I didn't notice the car at first, pulling up next to me with a hum that didn't register in the middle of the snoring-lion sound of idling Mack engines.

"Excuse me, miss?"

"Yeah?" I turned to see a man with mirrored sunglasses and a black felt campaign hat. Lights on top of his car.

"You mind telling me what you're doing around here?"

"I was just inside eating breakfast." My throat was tight, making my voice even raspier than usual.

He turned off his engine and got out of the car. The black and yellow patch on his jacket identified him as a state trooper. A policewoman appeared from the passenger side in a blue raincoat. They approached me from either side, his face blank and hers slightly worried. She was a maternal-looking woman, black with light skin and plastic-framed eyeglasses in the new, upside-down style.

"Honey, we got a complaint that you were soliciting a gentleman inside the restaurant," she said to me.

"What?" My deal blown to hell because a pissant in a trench coat had to get even with me for wanting to be left alone? Naturally. The only fair in the world was the kind that gave prizes for cakes and cows. And then came the inevitable; I was asked for my age and an ID I didn't have to verify that I was none other than eighteen-year-old Eleanor O'Bryan on her way to Texas to join her father.

"Which of these trucks are you with?" The policewoman gestured to the parking lot.

"None of your business. I'm not bothering anybody."

"I think you better put your hands on the car, honey."

Being told by a cop to put your hands on a car was another one of those things that was only supposed to happen on TV.

"She said put your hands on the car," the state trooper said, grabbing my elbow and pushing me down over the hood. One of them quickly ran their hands over my legs, crotch, and hips. I couldn't see if it was him or her.

"Stand up and turn around," the woman said. "Hold your arms up."

There went my new knife and the pack of Marlboros I'd stashed in my bra. She opened the pack and dumped the contents into her hand. After satisfying herself that my cigarettes were made of tobacco and could only cause lung cancer, she gave them back to me.

There was no chance for a good-bye to Phil. We'd ridden together less than two weeks but it felt much longer; the truck had become my home. Phil probably wouldn't miss me since he didn't want kids. And it was the truck I would miss more than him anyway. Riding in it was like escaping on the back of an elephant.

I was photographed and fingerprinted at the local police station. The inkpad looked dirty and I held back until someone took my hand and firmly pressed it down, once on the pad and again on a form. I kept my hands closed to avoid getting ink on my jeans.

"So how about telling us your name, young lady," the policewoman with the upside-down glasses said to me as she held up the form with my fingerprints on it.

"What if I don't have a name?" I asked. The situation was obviously heading straight back to Indiana and I saw no reason to help speed things along.

The state trooper saw it differently and told me to identify myself and my lawful place in the world or be taken to the local juvenile hall. Given the option, I sang like a sullen canary and was placed in a glass-walled holding cell for minors. Three boys close to my age were already inside and it wasn't even seven in the morning. The world was a much busier place than I'd realized.

The boys watched me passively. "What are you here for, chick?" one of them finally asked.

"Running away," I said, thinking too slowly to invent something more interesting.

"Well, nobody's going to fuck with you in here," he said.

Another boy with a pale, pinched face and a headful of curly red hair kicked his foot against the cell door to get the attention of the desk officer posted outside our cage. "Of course nobody's going to fuck with her in here, it's those cocksuckers out there you have to worry about. They're all pimps, every last fucking one of them!"

"Shut your hole, woodpecker," the desk officer said in a sleepy voice.

"I could get out of here in five minutes just by sucking off the right person," the red-haired boy continued as he paced along the wall. The deep, bruise-colored circles around his eyes were harsh against his translucent skin. "Hey, who wants a blow job? A blow job for anybody that looks the other way when I walk out the door. Get me on a Greyhound to Chicago and I'll take it up the ass."

"I said shut your rabbit trap unless you want to be upstairs." The desk officer was standing up now; he'd had his fill of the little mad prophet with the strawberry curls. "I hear one more word out of you, that's where your freckled ass is going."

"What's upstairs?" I asked the boy standing nearest to me.

"Adult holding. Those fuckers would eat him alive before anybody knew it."

The red-haired boy made a rude face and threw himself on the concrete floor with an angry cry, like someone who was ready to give up.

I never learned what happened to the red-haired boy, just like I never learned what would have happened to me if I'd kept my mouth shut in a time when there were no national registries of missing children or the computers to access them, especially after a state line was crossed. I would have been sent to the local juvenile hall, perhaps, and then what? Could I have convinced people that I was at least sixteen and knocked three years off the road to emancipation, started a new life as Eleanor O'Bryan? And would my father have tried to find me or would he have placidly taken my departure as proof positive that I didn't need him?

Chapter Sixteen

Joshua was a different breed of social worker than Mrs. Doyle. Young and nice-looking with thick, sandy hair and silver-rimmed aviator glasses, his plaid flannel shirt, ski vest, and Levis were ninety degrees from Mrs. Doyle's early sixties fright-face and helmet hair. And while Mrs. Doyle's hostility was always quietly slithering beneath the surface, Joshua's was overt and upfront, unfurling itself like a Jolly Roger as soon as we were in his car.

"You must have a serious lude problem if you think I've got nothing better to do than drive some stupid little cunt all the way across the state of Indiana," Joshua said to me in place of a hello. "And don't even think about running off from me because I was on my high school track team. I'll catch you and you'll regret the day your mother ever shit you."

With his how-dos out of the way, Joshua slammed his car door shut, reached over me to lock the passenger door, and ordered me to put on my seat belt. When we stopped at a rest area to use the bathroom, Joshua frog-marched me over to the door of the women's room after doing a quick scan for windows that might provide an escape. I toyed with the idea of passing myself off as a kidnapping victim and asking for help but there was no one inside.

Maybe Joshua wasn't even a real social worker. For all the talk about lude problems, he was acting like someone who'd been interrupted in the middle of a much-needed coke fix when tapped to take charge of me, behavior I thought someone might reasonably expect from a hired goon whose day off was revoked at the last minute in order to see about me. I could almost feel sorry for him.

"Hurry up, I haven't got the whole goddamned day."

But not quite.

We pulled up in front of the administration building late in the afternoon. Instead of going directly to the dorm, I was to first meet with Mrs. Doyle, Miss Arlen, and Mrs. Kelly. Although I walked willingly enough, Joshua still found it necessary to grip my elbow and drag me. His antagonism hadn't let up over the long drive and I almost envied his energy.

"Now where would this woman's office be?" Joshua glanced around the hallway of the first floor. I pointed to Mrs. Doyle's office at the end of the hallway where a light was on and he slapped my gesturing hand with vicious pleasure. "Were you raised in a barn?"

The worm finally turned. "If you don't want to know where something is then don't ask because I don't want to be here either but you don't see me shitting on other people about it," I nearly screamed even though I was trying to sound chilly and dangerous.

Joshua looked hurt and surprised, an obvious shift in tactics now that we were out of his car and soon to be among witnesses. "Well, there's no need to get so wound up. You're too sensitive."

"Fuck you and the jackass you rode in on," I hissed, nearly overpowered by a desperate, aching wish to hurt Joshua more, smash his glasses, throw used motor oil and pig shit on his clean, friendly clothes that were such a lie. I wanted to make Joshua look as nasty as he was and as dirty as he'd made me feel.

The sounds of our voices brought Mrs. Kelly out to the hallway. "Charity Sintz, I couldn't sleep worth a damn these past two weeks. I could throttle you." She belied the statement with a quick, rough embrace that I returned awkwardly.

"Well, you'd have thought I was driving her to Alcatraz the way she acted on the way over here." Joshua smiled at Mrs. Doyle and Miss Arlen, who joined us in the hallway. Everyone laughed except for me and Mrs. Kelly, whose character judgments were usually on the nose. Mrs. Doyle took Joshua to the cafeteria for coffee and I was left to hear Miss Arlen pronounce sentence on me, which was the standard thirty days' restriction for going AWOL.

"You know, kiddo, you really took everyone by surprise," Mrs. Kelly said as we walked back to the dorm. "You've always been so quiet." She took a sharp look at me. "All the way to out to Illinois, no less."

Mrs. Kelly filled me in on the dorm. Everyone was well except Holly, who'd been turned over to the local police after dousing one of the fifth-grade girls with gasoline and trying to set her on fire. Holly was being charged with theft and vandalism along with assault since the gasoline had been swiped from Mr. Stewart's car, sometime immediately before or after she slit the tires and keyed the passenger side door. Holly was probably on her way to Green's, the reform school up north in Wabash that was held over our heads like a fishnet. She wouldn't be back; the Home had a strict no-arsonists policy.

Then Mrs. Kelly stopped and turned to face me. "There are some people in this world who always want to do good things, have you noticed that? People like that Mother Theresa in India, or Eleanor Roosevelt." She began walking again. "And then you have people like Ted Bundy or Charlie Manson who are just the opposite, they love to do evil things. Why do you suppose they're like that?"

"They're ate up," I replied dutifully, seeing that Mrs. Kelly was about to toss one of her pearls to the ungrateful little swine that was me.

"You mean crazy?" Mrs. Kelly asked. When I nodded, she continued. "But some people think it's crazy to have visions from God and then go working someplace for free without worrying about yourself. Would you work your butt off taking care of lepers for free, like Mother Theresa?"

I considered it. "Probably not."

"There you go," Mrs. Kelly pointed with her cigarette. "It's just something they feel compelled to do without having what you could call a logical reason for it. Some people are like that in a bad way and I'm afraid Holly is one of them."

"I guess."

"And you are lucky, you are so goddamned lucky that someone like that didn't get ahold of you while you were out God knows where," Mrs. Kelly finished with her piéce de resistance and hurried me on to the dorm. Though I didn't argue her point, I thought I was at least equally lucky to have been on the road while Holly was dabbling in pyromania. Not to mention that there was something seriously dirty pool about kids like Holly being sent to the Home in the first place because people were afraid of her on the Outside but somehow it was all right for us to live with her.

"Shit, I'm so glad to see you." Annabelle threw her arms around me. "I've been so fucking lonesome." Annabelle didn't ask the reason for my flyer; someone was always running away for any number of reasons. It was considered a natural act, like wanting to dance or go swimming.

Within twenty minutes every girl in the dorm was in our bedroom wanting details, as if I'd just returned from a choice vacation spot that few could afford. No one could believe that I'd managed to cross three state lines until I held up an empty Marlboro box with the Pennsylvania stamp on the bottom. Even Cindy spoke to me with a hesitant respect, as if we were meeting for the first time.

Chapter Seventeen

Annabelle received a surprise visit from her mother and stepfather at the end of July the summer after I ran away. Her parents' church had a new young minister with modern ideas, one of them being that wrong side of the blanket or not, Annabelle belonged with her family, not hidden away in an institution because of circumstances that weren't her fault. Arrangements were now grudgingly being made to take Annabelle out of the Home. These details she learned from her mother, who shared them to remind Annabelle that it was all the minister's doing and not her own preference. Annabelle's radiance was undimmed by the knowledge.

"I'm going to live on the Outside, can you fucking believe it?" Annabelle gave a loud, ecstatic sigh. "My mother wants me."

"Her mother doesn't want her," I complained to Mrs. Kelly. "She's just being bullied into taking her."

"Just like she was bullied into leaving her here in the first place," Mrs. Kelly agreed. "If you never take a stand, all you'll ever have is what other people are in the mood to give you and that's never going to be much."

Mr. Waltz, Annabelle's stepfather, was red-faced and ridiculous in his starched white dress shirt and high-rider pants that made him look old enough to be her grandfather. Mrs. Waltz wasn't much more promising as a taller and more careworn version of Annabelle with peroxided hair and a turquoise polyester summer dress that belonged on someone twenty years older and twenty years earlier. Mr. Waltz enjoyed waving his index finger in the air and addressing Annabelle as 'young lady' whenever she swore, as if he even had the right to say please, thank you, or kiss my ass to her.

"Good-bye, Chair, I'll write to you every week," Annabelle said as she climbed into her parents' tank-sized Oldsmobile station wagon, the kind with the fake wood paneling on the sides. While she and her mother arranged the suitcases, Mr. Waltz motioned me to one side to keep Mrs. Kelly and the other girls from hearing him.

"I don't want you to waste your time and stamps writing letters to Annabelle because me and her mother will throw them in the trash," Mr. Waltz said solemnly, as if being so direct pained him to the quick. "She needs to start a new life."

"At least I know how to write," I said, secure in the knowledge that Mrs. Kelly would come running armed for bear if she saw Mr. Waltz trying to hit me. "Annabelle sure as shit never got any letters from you two."

"I can see you're going to end up on the street," Mr. Waltz said in a satisfied way, as if this counted as getting the last word.

My new roommate Diana was the first to speak after Annabelle and her parents rolled out of the front gate. "I sure feel sorry for Annabelle's mama if she has to make it with that farty old honky. I bet his thing looks just like a little pink slug."

Such a profound observation sent everyone into a whooping dog pile. "Stop being so damned ridiculous, all of you," Mrs. Kelly said from the sidelines as we rolled and laughed. "Charity, you sound just like a drunken goose."

Annabelle's parents dealt with the possibility of undesirable friendships by moving a month later without leaving a forwarding address. Though I didn't miss her drivel or having to keep an eye out for her, I still wondered how Annabelle was going to fare in a world occupied by people like the Waltzes. I could see her being introduced to the congregation at her parents' church, all of whom would listen to Mrs. Waltz's tearful testimony about her sinful past. Annabelle would be introduced to a crowd that was probably expecting her to wear a white dress and make a speech about how living at the Home all those years had taught her to love Jesus more or something along those lines.

And then Annabelle would open her mouth and tell everyone how her ideal sweet sixteen birthday party would include a naked Tom Selleck jumping out of a cake. Maybe the Waltzes would find another church and send her back. I was glad to have Diana safely in place as my roommate.

The Home was a quieter and less demanding place in the summer; at least two thirds of the kids were staying with relatives or foster parents while those of us who remained worked, went to summer school, saw free movies twice a week at the rec center, and had use of the pool from three in the afternoon until eight in the evening. As an added bonus, no one was hassling me since my return from AWOL, Holly was gone, and I was stockpiling money from my job in the cafeteria for a Greyhound to New York, my latest notion taken after watching *Breakfast at Tiffany's* on TV. In the meantime I thought about signing up for the auto mechanics class at the vocational school in the fall to help overcome my fear of machinery.

It should have occurred to me that things were going too smoothly. One month after Annabelle left, I came back to the dorm after working the lunch shift to find an explosion of clothes and books on the bedroom floor. Everything of mine and Diana's yanked from the closets and dressers and flung into a single pile. Claudia told me Miss Lott had done it.

"Was she looking for smokes?" I asked. Mine were well hidden but Miss Lott wasn't above trying to slap the desired information out of someone if she got angry enough.

"No, she said we need to use less bedrooms right now since so many people are gone for the summer and it's been so hot that we have to keep the air on all the time." Claudia said. "You and Diana are moving in with me. And Mrs. Kelly wants to see you in private. She said to tell you the minute you came in."

I went to Mrs. Kelly's office, which doubled as her sitting room. She told me to close the door and sit down. I obeyed, wondering what was up and unable to think of anything I'd done that might have gotten me in Dutch, or at least anything I was careless enough to get caught at.

"Charity, how long has it been since you've seen your father?" Mrs. Kelly asked me as soon as the door to her office was closed.

"My father?" She might as well have been asking about my horoscope. "I guess about three years now. Why?"

"He got in touch with Mrs. Doyle a week ago," Mrs. Kelly explained. "She forgot to tell me till today, naturally. Your father told her that he's moved back to Indiana and he's coming to visit on Sunday."

I asked Mrs. Kelly for a cigarette. Normally she was strict about not giving them to us for fear that we'd be begging for them constantly but now she extended the pack to me, saying "Just this once." I knew she meant it but that didn't bother me. There was some comfort in consistency.

Mrs. Kelly wrote me a pass for the administration building when Miss Arlen called the dorm on Sunday to let her know my father had arrived. I walked over to meet him with all the girls from the dorm circling me like an honor guard. They hung back when we reached the administration building since the pass was only good for me. I found myself hanging back as well. We stood in a cluster and peeked through the windows on the door of the main entrance.

He was standing in the hallway, shifting from foot to foot instead of sitting on the bench, like someone with no patience for standing idle. Did he still like to drink PBR and watch *Hee Haw* on Saturday nights? My father still looked like me apart from his tan, which made his hair seem lighter. I was thankful that he didn't wear it buzzed or greased like Annabelle's stepfather. He was lean but not very muscular, smaller than I remembered. My brother was nowhere in sight.

My father saw us. Walking to the door, he turned his head sideways and tried to pick me out from the group. As a joke I grabbed Diana by her shoulders and pushed her in front of me. "Now when he comes out, yell 'Daddy!' real loud and throw your arms around him," I said.

"Shit, girl, you got squirrels in your head."

When he realized we were coming no further, my father came forward, favoring us with a tired smile. Diana played her part poorly, saying "Daddy!" like a music box tune that was warbling to a close. Instead of hugging him, she chucked him on the elbow. Everyone laughed anyway.

My father saw through the joke. "My daughter always looked like the Grim Reaper," he said to Diana. "She'd never have a pretty smile like yours."

The girls hooted their approval of his comeback and whispered to each other about our resemblance. No one made any moves to leave until my father suggested that the two of us go into Darketown for lunch. Everyone followed us to the parking lot and stood watch as we drove away in his latest Ford F-250.

"What's wrong with those girls?" my father asked as he checked his rearview mirror. "You'd think they never saw a man before."

"They just wanted to see what you looked like," I said, trying to make myself heard over the sound of the truck engine and the radio. "A lot of them don't know their fathers."

He laughed. "I'm afraid I can't help them out on that one."

"No one asked you to," I said, annoyed by his flippancy.

"Well, what's your problem?" he asked. "You sure don't seem very happy to see me."

I tried to recall any novels read or films seen that contained happy father-daughter reunions. The only thing that came to mind was a Cliff Robertson movie we'd watched in the dorm one Sunday afternoon called *Obsession*, the plot of which involved a man being reunited with a grown daughter he'd believed to be dead for twenty years or so. I pictured myself weeping, embracing my father, and crying "Daddy, you came for me," with a fake Italian accent. That would probably be enough to make him regret not taking Diana in my place when he had the chance.

"So where's Trilby?" I asked. My brother seemed like a safe topic.

"Why, he's home. He had a baseball game today." My father said this casually, letting me know it was a given that Trilby lived in a house with his family and went out in the world to do things like play baseball.

"How come you never let me have your address and phone number when you were in Florida?" I tried to sound confused instead of angry, which might give him an excuse to take offense and disappear again.

"You were always so ornery, we thought you might try to run away and come down there if you knew where we were." There was no regret in my father's voice, only the old amusement with my potential for havoc-wreaking. On the other hand, he was right.

I gobbled fried chicken like a tapeworm victim at the smorgasbord in Darketown that Mrs. Kelly always recommended for visitors while my father filled in parts of the three-year gap between us. The motel in Port St. Lucie had done well but he'd missed Indiana and wanted Trilby to grow up in his proper home. The motel had been sold for a decent profit, part of which he'd used to buy a house. Now he was working as the manager of a motel and coffee shop outside Hazelwood, just off Route 74 near the Indiana/Ohio state line that he was hoping to purchase when things settled down a bit. There was also some farmland connected to his new house that he was thinking of renting or buying, putting in some crops or an orchard of his own. He was married now, to a woman from Kentucky named Annette. My father didn't ask me what I'd been up to for the last three years.

"There was a time when I couldn't ever imagine getting married again," my father said. "Your mother was like a four-leaf clover." He paused and studied me as I gnawed on a chicken wing with the quiet determination of a rat. "You never did look like her."

He'd met Annette the previous winter while she was staying at the motel with her aunt and uncle. She had a master's degree in elementary education, which meant nothing to me. She got on wonderfully with Trilby, which meant more. She was nice-looking, with brown hair and brown eyes, she liked to wear makeup and pretty clothes, and she was a good cook. All of this meant even more since I was still naive enough to believe that anything with a trace of glitter had to mean gold.

I paid a visit to the dessert table and wiped out the cookie tray, wrapping the loot up in napkins that I tucked into my purse. "Whenever one of us comes here for lunch we always take something back for the others," I explained, seeing the disapproval on my father's face.

"Put them back," he ordered. "You don't need to be doing anything like that."

"Yes I do," I insisted. "Everyone does it. If I don't bring something back then I won't get anything when someone else brings something back." And who was he to be telling me what I needed or didn't need to be doing when he didn't know Jack or Jill shit about me and didn't even want to and why couldn't I say so out loud?

My father promised to stop at a Rexall's we'd seen on the edge of town for a box of candy that I could share with everyone. I removed all of the cookies except the ones hidden in the pockets of the skirt I was wearing in honor of the trip to Darketown. When we got to Rexall's I ran to the cosmetics department and ogled the displays of mascaras, liners, and shadows.

"Was there anything else you wanted?" My father sounded almost shy as he stood behind me with a box of Esther Price chocolates the size of a briefcase tucked under his arm. Seeing how large it was made me daring and I asked for a carton of Marlboros.

"When did you start smoking?" he asked, showing only mild surprise.

"Almost four years ago."

My father bought me the candy, the cigarettes, and paperback copies of *The Godfather* and *The Cat Ate My Gym Suit* that I added to the pile. "Anything else?"

"No," I lied, not wanting to go overboard.

Back inside the truck, I tore open the cigarette carton and hid the individual packs in strategic places as we drove back to the Home. By the time we pulled into the parking lot by the administration building I had two packs hidden in my bra, six tucked in the waist of my pantyhose, and one pack in each shoe. My father looked dubious but impressed.

"You'd probably make a good bootlegger."

He walked as near to the dorm with me as visitors were allowed, telling me to be good and clean up my speech. I responded with what Mrs. Kelly called a grod, a gesture I sometimes made that she described as half grunt, half nod. As in, "I want more than a damned grod for an answer, Charity Sintz."

"And make sure you have everything ready when I come tomorrow," my father said. "We got a long drive ahead and I want to leave here by noon."

Leave? "Am I going to visit with you?" I asked.

"You're coming home to live with us." He seemed put out by my ignorance. "That Boyle woman, I talked to her on the phone just before we moved back. I signed all those papers she sent me and mailed them back. She called me a week ago and said everything was all set. You ought to be all packed by now."

My father tossed away his half-smoked cigarette and one of the fourth-grade boys swooped in like a seagull grabbing a fish. It was a rule that cigarettes couldn't be touched once they went out or else you risked being called an ass-smoker. I tried to explain this but my father only frowned.

"Well, I don't know about all that but one thing I do know is that no one in our family ever had a social worker before. So when we get home, I think you shouldn't talk too much about this place to anyone. People might think it's a reform school, or that it's for welfare kids or something. Just say it's a Christian boarding school. That's what Hattie Holmes said it was." He sounded a little cross, as if it was partly my fault that Mrs. Holmes was a lying sack of shit.

"But how come I'm going to live with you now?"

"Because that's where you belong, with your family." My father was looking less impressed with me by the minute.

"But I've always lived somewhere else."

"Well, not anymore." He made the statement without flourishes, explanations, or promises of better times to come. We said our goodbyes at the edge of the lake near the girls' dorms.

I was too dazed to walk carefully and everyone noticed that I was carrying contraband. I put the box of candy on the floor in the living room and went to change my clothes without speaking a word to anyone. With any luck, the world was bound to come to an end before lunchtime the next day and I couldn't decide if it would be a bad thing or a good thing.

Mrs. Kelly was sent for when I refused to climb down from my favorite tree at dinnertime. "Charity, get your butt down here right now, it's time to eat."

I looked down at her and the other girls. In less than twenty-four hours we would disappear from each other's lives. "My father said he's taking me away," I said.

"Taking you away?" Mrs. Kelly asked.

"Tomorrow."

Mrs. Kelly was cynical at first; it was a common fantasy at the Home whenever a parent reappeared after a long absence but fantasies normally included packing a suitcase and I hadn't touched mine, which concerned her enough to grab my ankle and order me down. We went back to her office and she called Mrs. Doyle at home. The phone conversation was fast and furious, ending with Mrs. Kelly's suggestion that Mrs. Doyle could damn well start doing her job during office hours if she didn't want phone calls outside of them.

"I've got more than twelve girls to look after hands on and you don't spend more than five minutes a week with any of them," Mrs. Kelly said, rubbing the back of her head. She hung up the phone and turned to me. "I interrupted her and her husband during their sacred Sunday evening ritual of popcorn and *Ripley's Believe it or Not*, God save us all."

"I'm leaving tomorrow," I told Diana as she scooped green beans onto trays in the cafeteria, where I'd come under orders from Mrs. Kelly to eat dinner.

"Shit, for real?" Diana asked, the smile my father had noticed broadening her face. "Girl, you're in for a good time now."

By the time I sat down to eat, my news was making its way through the cafeteria and everyone knew that I'd been favored. Within minutes I was surrounded by well-wishers and for the rest of the evening and the following morning after breakfast everyone in the dorm pitched in to help me pack; it was easy to con someone out of their best clothes when they were moving on to a better situation. Since I had no best friend, Diana's position as my roommate entitled her to first refusal and she picked through my wardrobe with a moue of distaste on her beautiful lips.

"Shit, I never saw so many wishy-washy clothes," Diana said as she held up my pale blue summer nightgown. She received a clothing allowance from her older sister and was always one of the Home's best-dressed girls, pulling no punches when it came to fashion. "Ain't you got anything red, or at least bright-colored? This looks like something the Easter Bunny's grandma would wear."

My clothes might not have had many takers but everyone wanted my bundle of *Co-Ed* magazines that I'd hoarded over the last two years, a secondhand subscription from one of the younger women who worked in the sewing shop. I debated briefly before handing it over to the collective. My books weren't up for grabs but nobody wanted them anyway.

Chapter Eighteen

My father was an hour late on the day he came to take me away from the Home, leading to speculation among the other girls that he'd gotten cold feet; it happened sometimes. He arrived after everyone else got bored and went to have lunch. My father might have planned it that way, a bit of humiliation to keep me from getting any big ideas. Or maybe he only thought it wouldn't matter too much if he was late. Either way I was humbled.

"Ready to go?" he asked, as if picking me up from the grocery store. What would it be like to walk through a grocery store again?

Mrs. Kelly was on hand to hug me and say good-bye. "You behave yourself, or else," she warned. "And try to stay away from the boys till you're older. They'll cause you more trouble than you'll know what to do with."

I climbed into the truck next to my father and rode out the front gate of the Home for the last time. A mile further and we were passing the sign that advertised Darketown as a good place to visit and a better place to live. It didn't say why. An hour into the drive I was beginning to wish I were back in the dorm, where I knew what to expect. My father drove in a comfortable silence, comfortable for him at least. He still hadn't asked me any questions about myself.

When we took an exit leading to the southwest corner of Roosevelt County, I remembered that we weren't going home to the white clapboard house or to Grandma East. "Can we live in our house again?" I asked my father.

"What house?" he asked.

"Our house outside Mount Olive. Grandma's house." Being back in the house might help me feel clean again.

"Oh, that house burned down a year ago," my father said. "They say the chimney was clogged up. It was a pretty old house anyway. We should of just got rid of it and had your grandma move in with us instead."

I tried to remember the house my parents built. New and shiny with one story and a basement but further details were sketchy. Lots of trees; that was the only other thing I remembered. What would Trilby expect from me? If being reunited with a father was a confusing business, I was even foggier on the subject of brothers. Maybe Trilby wouldn't like having a sister again. And if he didn't, I was sure to be sent back to the Home unless I could run away first.

We arrived at a house a few miles outside of Hazelwood on the west side of town instead of the east where Mount Olive stood. It was wood clapboard like Grandma's house but smaller and painted a grungy yellow instead of white. A pale blue Nova sedan was parked in the driveway and a dirt bike leaned against the detached garage that was painted to match the house. We got out of the truck and I followed my father, dragging my footlocker behind me.

"Is that all you've got?" he asked me over his shoulder. "What happened to that nice red suitcase you had? You know that was your mother's."

"Tammy Holmes took it."

"You need to take better care of things," my father said as he led me to the side of the house where a screen door opened into the kitchen. A woman dressed in polyester pants and a flowered t-shirt stood at the stove frying chicken. Annette, my new stepmother, whose light brown hair was cut in a dated china bob that looked almost as stupid as Mrs. Doyle's bubble cut. I was immediately let down that she wasn't more fashionable.

"Hi there, honey." Annette said as she maneuvered chicken parts with a pair of tongs. Her voice had a soft, girlish Bluegrass accent. Then she turned away from the stove to get a look at me and her smile slipped. "Vic, I thought you said she was twelve."

"No, I said thirteen," Dad said.

"I'll be fourteen in November," I said. Neither of them took any notice. Annette looked put out. My father shrugged and told me to take my footlocker up to my bedroom.

"It's up the stairs, at the end of the hallway on the left." He gestured towards the staircase, which was divided from the kitchen by a wooden door. I went up the stairs.

After setting my footlocker at the top of the stairs, I tiptoed back down to the bottom and listened without shame; uncensored information was always useful. On the other side of the door I could hear Annette's voice like a pair of razor-sharp embroidery scissors as she accused Dad of selling her a false bill of goods; here I was going on fourteen and looking like twenty. I probably wouldn't listen to a word she said. I'd probably picked up bad ways from living at that school. I would probably end up embarrassing the two of them and Trilby. A bad moon was on the rise.

And it can't be denied that every word Annette said either was true or became true.

"She's only thirteen." My father's voice was tired and fading.

"She's got bigger breasts than I do."

"Don't say that."

"Breasts!" Annette cried. "Breasts, breasts, breasts!"

I laughed.

"Hi." A voice at the top of the stairs drew my attention from the argument. I looked up and saw a sturdy young boy with my eyes in his head and my impossible hair on top of it, the smile on his face as innocent as an unhatched egg. "I guess you're Charity."

"Well I'm sure as shit not Princess Diana," I said, thinking anyone so blatantly cheerful was waving a red flag at fate and daring it to yank the chair from under their ass.

"You shouldn't swear. Want me to help you unpack?" Trilby's southern accent was different from

Annette's, scratched by the nasal twang of our father's voice. "Don't worry about Dad and Annette. They fight sometimes but they'll stop by suppertime."

I followed Trilby, dragging the footlocker behind me. He switched on the light inside the room that was to be mine. There was a full-sized bed with no frame, a pair of small, unpainted chests of drawers, and a strange lamp with a long, cylindrical shade sitting in a black plastic frame wrapped with what looked like guitar strings. Trilby walked over and turned it on by rolling a switch on the lamp's cord. It didn't give much light.

"We got this new for you yesterday," he said proudly. "This and the chests. Annette bought them at the naked furniture store. She said maybe you and her can paint them in a color you like."

No one had ever bought a piece of furniture with me in mind and I wasn't sure what to make of it. Trilby waited for my reaction but I had none to offer. The room was relatively bare, like the rooms at the Home, minus the tidy white plaster walls and fluorescent light fixtures in the newer dorms like mine. I sat down on the bed, which was comfortable and bouncy at least, unlike the dense, no-spring mattresses in the dorm. The sheets were plain blue instead of pink and there were two pillows instead of one. Trilby walked over and sat next to me.

"I wasn't able to remember you at first," he said. "But now I'm starting to. We used to watch TV together and make fun of the commercials, didn't we?"

I thought a moment. "Yeah, like that one for Canada Dry ginger ale. *It's not too sweet, its flavor can't be beat . . .*" I sang.

"Yeah, and there was a fat lady singing that while she was dancing on a sidewalk and we'd yell, 'Fall in the gutter, fall in the gutter!'"

"What else do you remember?" I asked. "I bet you don't remember our mother."

"Don't mention her in front of Annette," Trilby said quickly. He explained that one too many of the local old-timers had been unkind enough to openly compare our stepmother unfavorably to her predecessor and Annette had finally pitched a fit, forbidding any references to Eleanor O'Bryan Sintz within her hearing, intentional or not. Trilby's patient voice explained the situation as a small quirk of Annette's that needed humoring if our lives were to not resemble hell on earth and I understood perfectly. Every deal had its fine print. At least my brother seemed to like me a little.

Annette hailed from the not so mean streets of Louisville, Kentucky, the daughter of retired tobacco farmers who bred horses for fun and a bit of profit, according to Trilby. As for Annette herself, she tried at first to be a friend or something equally unnerving to me before gradually relaxing into her role of wicked stepmother. My father's absent-minded idealism in attempting to turn the four of us into the photo-perfect family with a pair of each gender to grace an Olan Mills portrait that was never taken barely lasted a week. Like the Titanic, it was all so well-intended. The only thing he forgot to plan for was the human factor and that would show its ugly side in record time.

"You know you shouldn't ride a bike when you've got your period, honey," Annette told me one day right in front of Trilby. "Your hymen's more likely to tear then and your husband will think you're not a virgin when you get married."

"I don't have the curse," I lied, too furious for logic. Especially with my artless brother making no effort to look away and act like he wasn't listening.

Annette pretended to be confused by my denial and my obvious embarrassment. "Yes you do, I saw the stains on your panties when I was going through your hamper."

"I told you I can do my own damn laundry!"

"You just watch that mouth of yours or your dad's going to have something to say to you."

Annette's feigned confusion was part of her method to a madness that I'd seen before but never understood how to fight. It made her look innocent whenever she chose to cut me down to size by embarrassing me and provoking me into a state of homely, immature hostility without looking bad herself. And Annette's voice was softly high-pitched and pleasing to the ear even when she was angry, which made arguments easier for her to win. My voice was leaden and flat, a smaller version of my father's. It was just like the operas on PBS; the heroine was always a soprano.

"Can't you try being nicer to Annette?" Trilby asked as we rode our bikes along the state route, his voice more sad than critical. "She really wants to be a good mother."

"She's not our mother, idiot," I said, reveling in my meanness almost as much as in the freedom to ride a bike anywhere I pleased. "And I can remember our mother and she was nothing like Annette."

"I can't remember her," Trilby said.

"Well, you got Dad for five years while I got clan of the catfish and the fucking Home so don't expect me to cry my eyes out."

Trilby was quiet suddenly; the idea that he alone might have been enjoying privileges that should have been shared with me was a new one for him.

I found it hard to swallow that Annette had a master's degree in anything more complicated than shoe-tying. Outside of her element, she was just another village idiot. It didn't occur to me that she might be bored witless and miserable from living in such a remote location with no friends, family, or career prospects.

Any chance of a rapport developing between me and Annette was curtailed by Bibi, her beloved miniature schnauzer. Bibi looked like a troll crossed with a kid goat. She also stank, leaked, and picked up fleas almost every time she was allowed to run loose in the yard.

"Would you like Bibi to sleep with you?" Annette asked me on my first night in the house, no doubt seeing it as a comforting, maternal sort of gesture to make.

"No," I said plainly; back at the Home I would have said hell no. My shudder of disgust hurt Annette's feelings; first the breasts and now this. Strike two for me.

My father was still a man of few words but it was obvious that he was feeling shortchanged. In this we were equals, each of us glumly let down by the other and neither of us willing to yield the high ground. His occasional cautious overtures towards me were usually met with tepid indifference.

"You want to play cards?" my father asked one evening after supper.

"I don't like cards," I said. He shrugged and set up a deck for solitaire as I wandered off, sidestepping Annette's hints for help with the dishes.

Trilby tried the hardest, optimistic soul that he was. "How come you never smile or laugh or talk to anyone?" he asked me. "Are you mad because you miss your school? Dad said they had a fishing lake and a swimming pool there for all the kids. Is that true?"

"Yeah."

"You were lucky," Trilby said. "In Florida you can't go outside to swim in the summer, it's always too hot."

Annette took Trilby and me to the doctor in Hazelwood for check-ups the week before school began. Instead of seeing us separately, the nurse put us in an examining room together as if we were five-year-olds.

"Now be good or the doctor will have to give you a shot in your tushy," she joked as she walked out the door.

"Fuck you," I muttered at her retreating back, nearly giving Trilby the vapors. The nurse's hearing was sharper than the rest of her and my father came straight home from work at seven that evening instead of stopping at the White Light, something he was doing more often now than when Grandma East was still alive.

"You ought to be whipped for saying something like that," Dad said to me. "You better straighten up and fly right." This was one of his favorite axioms and hearing it made me feel like a circus animal that wasn't jumping through the hoops properly.

"You can't be behaving like you did at that school," Annette added. "You have to think of the rest of us. If you go around acting like you've been living on the streets, it's going to shame your father. Now what's done is done and maybe you've had some bad luck but I don't think you've got any room to be so high-horsed. You need to get that chip off your shoulder and start acting like a member of this family."

"Amen," my father added.

"Who the hell said I wanted to be a member of this family?"

"Go to your room."

I was treading on ice whose depth could only be guessed at. In spite of my bluster, I really didn't want to go back to the Home. I received a weekly five-dollar allowance, shopping trips to K-mart for nice clothes, takeout from Patty's Pizza once again, and I could smoke whenever I wanted. No one stole my things and I could listen to my favorite music. It didn't make sense that all of this wasn't enough to make me more than what I was. But all I wanted was to be left alone, preferably with a stack of paperbacks on my left, a carton of Cowboy Killers on my right, and the sad, gossamer voices of Simon and Garfunkel singing lullabies for adults on my new cassette player. Solitude to better enjoy my change in fortune.

Uncle Luther was still running Mount Olive Feed & Seed and sometimes drove freight for his regular customers. He stopped by the house on a Saturday morning to pick up Dad and Trilby, who were riding with him to the Kahns plant in Cincinnati to deliver a truckload of hogs. The possibility of a trip to Cincinnati was enough to make me look up from Annette's discarded copy of *Mademoiselle*.

"You think you're going?" my father asked, making me want to kick myself in the ass for being so transparent.

"I never said that," I snapped. One of *Mademoiselle*'s cover articles promised to teach what it called good manners for bad moments. I hadn't read it yet.

"Yeah, she thinks she's going," Uncle Luther said in a satisfied way and I saw that they were waiting for me to pitch a moderate-sized fit or at least a decent sulk that they could laugh about on the road. It was lowering in the extreme to know that my hurt feelings were serving as joke fodder but I forced myself to smile when Trilby, Dad, and Uncle Luther walked out the door.

"Maybe you'll get to go next time," Trilby whispered kindly as he walked past me, not in the least perturbed that I was being excluded.

"Maybe if you don't shut your yap, I'll stick my knife in your football," I whispered back, still smiling.

Annette decided that a weekend alone together would be a good opportunity for the two of us to get a head start on some fall cleaning. I didn't agree and exercised my dissent by vanishing from the house as soon as Uncle Luther's truck pulled out of the driveway, walking for hours with a half-formed idea of heading towards Mount Olive to see if anyone or anything might still be around that I could recognize and that could possibly help me become whatever it was I'd been before Grandma East died, or at least before the Holmeses left. I didn't know the words for what I needed, which was to turn back the clock. Not that knowing the words would have helped, unless understanding the need also meant understanding the futility of having it.

Everyone's corn was tall by then, more than a foot past my head. Knee-high by the Fourth of July and all would be well, the saying went. My father had promised that I'd be able work as a detasseler the next summer. Most of the fields I saw were planted; everything else was meadow or woods.

I walked past the few houses I saw without stopping since I was under orders not to bother any of the neighbors, who all had farms and were too busy for unnecessary visitors. Nothing I saw looked as if it had anything to do with me. Maybe Annette would tell Dad to send me back to the Home. I thought about it, trying to get used to the idea in advance of need. Since I loathed nasty surprises, it seemed better to anticipate them. That way it was only the nastiness without the surprise element serving to underscore my gullibility.

By evening my conscience weighed in and I decided to apologize and try making amends with Annette, who let me know when I walked into the house that it was too precious little too damned late by flinging a saucepan that hit my left shoulder. Staying ahead of the surprises was hopeless; the games began.

"You think the whole world is just tap-dancing along to keep you on balance, don't you?" Annette cried, all veils dropped.

"If it is, then it's doing a shitty job," I told her. "And you're nowhere near as pretty. as my mother was," I added for lagniappe, a favorite word learned from Mark Twain that was pronounced 'lannyap' and meant a small extra gift.

Annette sailed over and punched me in the chin before trying to wrap her fingers around my neck. I kicked her in the kneecap, which sent her howling one-footed across the room. She recovered enough to shove me into Dad's favorite chair and slam herself on top of me. I twisted my head sideways and bit into her upper arm. Annette's cries of pain were like a sharp needle into my sense of decency and I released my chops, which allowed her to twist herself around and hammer her fist into my left eye.

Twenty-four hours later I was standing in the living room of Grandma and Grandpa O'Bryan for the first time in five years. They looked almost exactly the same as I remembered even though Grandma O'Bryan was wearing pants instead of a skirt. Even their expressions were in the same unreadable set. They listened silently as my father apologized for dumping me in their laps.

"I don't know what all she got up to at that school but she's been a monster since I brought her home."

"Bullshit," I said immediately, a direct shot to my own foot.

"See what I'm talking about?"

"If you're going to leave her with strangers all that time you have to expect she'll come into strange ways," Grandma O'Bryan said quietly. "I told you this would happen if you left her with those people. You could tell just by looking at them that they were no-account."

"That doesn't mean she has to act no-account," my father said. "She comes from a decent family. I would have asked you to keep her but I figured she'd be too much for you."

"When a child has a perfectly good father she doesn't belong with someone else," Grandma said. "If she'd been with you, then she would have had someone to discipline her when she needed it. Which is not to say it's all right to be hitting someone so hard that you leave marks."

"I knew I couldn't handle her by myself," my father sighed.

"Maybe we should enlist her," Grandpa said. "She talks like a sailor."

"How old do you have to be?" I asked. Being miles away on a boat somewhere was an appealing idea.

"Older than you are," Grandma said. "And I can guarantee you wouldn't last too long with that attitude of yours. You'd be doing push-ups from sun-up to sundown."

"Or in the brig," Grandpa added. "When I was in the air corps . . ."

I went outside to smoke and the O'Bryans' house cat approached me with restrained curiosity. Her name was Katie John, a tortoise-shell tabby whose gold, brown, and black stripes were set off by white gloves and slippers. I kept still as she inched closer, carefully sniffing to determine if I was friend or foe. Then Katie John stood up and wrapped her front paws around my leg, humming quietly. I scooped her into my lap, rubbing her belly to warm my hands.

Chapter Nineteen

My grandparents' house was five miles outside the college town of Baumburg, named in honor of the county's lavish Jonagold and Empire orchards. The smell of apples mingled with the manure from Becker's, a Jersey dairy farm on the other side of town. Anti-German sentiment had provoked a temporary name change from Baumburg to the literal English translation of Tree Castle during the First World War but it never stuck.

The air smelled different in Piqua County. In town it was a smell that could change in an instant, depending on the wind. A stray breeze would carry some brief variant, the exhaust from a passing truck, French fries from the Arby's restaurant, a rattled skunk in someone's backyard, honeysuckle, a septic tank in need of attention, a dead animal, or a fireplace, all of it chased with the smell of apples. The fireplaces were the best.

"This is God's Country," Grandma O'Bryan said facetiously when I made the mistake of sharing my observations with her as we unloaded groceries from the car after a trip to Kroger's. "There's lots of things to smell out here." And I was obviously a simpleton for making such an observation aloud.

The university's student body was a seasonal population boost of five thousand plus staff that kept civic ideas reasonably fresh, the public library well-stocked, and the local farmers frequently up in arms over the latest tax levy that the college crowd was liable to be endorsing. Most of the students were gone during the summer, giving the townies a rest. A large number of Baumburg's leading citizens were descended from a group of Polish immigrants who arrived in America during and after the first and second world wars, most of them with good educations and high standards that could be taken anywhere, as Grandma O'Bryan put it.

"There are things in this world worth plenty more than shiny beads," she said to me once. "Have you ever thought about that?"

I'd thought about it plenty and resented Grandma's implication that I hadn't, knowing my father must have warned her about my materialistic streak. While some people might try to put words in someone else's mouth, the O'Bryans went a step further and tried to put thoughts in my head. If I betrayed my irritation at being told what I was thinking, it was called sulking or having the dreaded bad attitude, being too stubborn to acknowledge my faults. I also learned during a routine eavesdrop that I felt sorry for myself for having been left behind during the five years that Dad and Trilby were in Florida.

"Now she thinks the world owes her a song and dance," Grandma said.

"She's in for a mighty unpleasant surprise," Grandpa replied.

Una gave a snort of consensus and it appeared that I'd been sentenced.

Grandma O'Bryan was never overtly happy or unhappy but her words always carried weight in their measured delivery. Her speech had the same rhythm whether she was delivering a punch line, reciting scripture, or telling me about her oldest child, my mother and Una's older brother Ian who'd been killed during the Tet Offensive in Vietnam several months before I was born. No one had ever told me about my Uncle Ian, as if the information was too privileged.

"Some folks thought you might have stolen Ian's soul," Grandma told me as I ate breakfast on my first morning in their home. "I guess you would have been started right around that time."

"Is that what you thought?" I asked, studying the nicely prepared toast and the scrambled eggs from Grandma's own hen resting on my plate, their tidy perfection serving as a reproach: the meal was too good for me.

"It was just some of the older folks saying that," Grandma said. "They're always more superstitious. But sometimes they hit the bull's eye." She sounded like a teenaged girl slyly tormenting a younger sister.

I could still remember the censorious group of elders at my mother's funeral. This might explain why they'd been so spooked; they thought I might be a changeling or maybe even a reaper. Insulting or not, I tucked away the story of Uncle Ian and my alleged soul-thieving like a keepsake that might serve as a conversation piece one day.

Garfield State was supposed to have been named after President James Garfield, a Buckeye himself, but locals were in the habit of referring to the faculty and students as the fat cats. The school was Una's alma mater for her bachelor's degree; now she taught German there and was expecting to receive tenure, as Grandpa told me while we were driving into town to register me at my new school. I'd never heard of tenure.

"It pretty much means she'll have to kill somebody before they can fire her," Grandpa said, clearly taking pleasure in the idea that his daughter could afford to be useless if she chose, which he knew she never would. The O'Bryans didn't do useless.

Inside the high school building we were directed to the office of Mr. Cyrus, my assigned guidance counselor.

"Welcome to Shawnee, Charity," said Mr. Cyrus, extending his hand. "It's always great to have some new faces."

Grey-haired and blue-suited, Mr. Cyrus seemed friendly without being too hearty or patronizing and I decided to give him a chance. He helped me fill out a fall schedule and tried not to stare at the half-healed marks on my face, neck, and arms. Grandpa sat quietly and ignored Mr. Cyrus's raised eyebrows.

"So, Charity, what do you think of this heat?" Mr. Cyrus tried.

"I don't think it matters what I think of it," I said. Rhetorical questions were always potential traps. The O'Bryans would ask them for no other reason than to play devil's advocate with my answers, a game I loathed.

"Were you in an accident?" Mr. Cyrus finally asked point-blank. "Pardon my asking but you look like you took a tumble."

"She was kicked out of charm school," Grandpa said.

"My stepmother did it," I said. "But I'm not living with her now," I added quickly when Mr. Cyrus looked grave.

"It's always the wicked stepmother," Grandpa said. Later that night he would tell Grandma and Una how stagy I'd been in my role as abused child. A prouder and more dignified teenager would have lied and made up a story about falling down the stairs instead of airing dirty linen.

"Don't you want to take German?" Mr. Cyrus asked when I opted for a spot in first-year French. "You'd have your own tutor right there in your own home. How's your aunt Una doing these days? You know, she was always in the top five on the honor roll."

"I want French." My voice was unmistakably short. Grandpa said nothing but I see he was having a laugh on the inside, knowing that Una would have been as appalled as I was by Mr. Cyrus's suggestion.

Once my classes were settled, I was handed over to Anita, a pretty, dark-haired senior girl who worked in the office and offered to show me around. "Charity, I want to wish you the best of luck and I hope you'll be very happy here at Shawnee," Mr. Cyrus said as Grandpa and I walked out to the hallway.

"She isn't going to be happy," Grandpa said. "That girl has a frown tattooed on her face. We should make her stand on her head." He pressed his hands on my upper arms as if to turn me upside down and my shame was complete. I jerked away and quickly fought back the urge to punch my grandfather in the stomach.

Shawnee only had one floor but it was spread out over a large, hollowed square surrounding a center courtyard that was partially filled by a greenhouse. "Some of the science classes are held out there," Anita told me. "They also use it for growing the homecoming chrysanthemums and a lot of other plants."

Each classroom I saw had one entire side used for windows that took up the top half of the wall, allowing sunlight to flood the hallways. The gymnasium doors were open and I saw several girls performing cheers inside while a group of women sat together at a table and watched them as they scribbled notes on yellow legal pads. Cheerleading tryouts. Anita asked me if I wanted to try out; there was still time.

"This is the first time they've held them in the summer," she said. "They used to have them on a school day but so many of the girls who didn't get picked were calling home and saying they had stomachaches and all that. You'd see them lined up at the pay phones, crying."

I was unmoved; there were plenty of things to cry about and a pair of pom-poms would never make my list.

Two pictures of my mother were on display in the O'Bryans' living room. One of them was her high school graduation portrait and the other was of her and my father at church for their wedding, her white satin dress almost Amish in its simplicity in spite of the heart-shaped neckline. The veil's headpiece was a small tiara strung with tiny pearl beads that rested carefully on her Jackie Kennedy bouffant. My father's tuxedo was black with pinstripes and his hair was buzzed like a marine's. The candles in the church were lit, which meant a nighttime wedding. My mother's dress would have glowed like the moon as she walked up the stairs of the Presbyterian church in Mount Olive.

"Were you in the wedding?" I asked Una.

"No, I was too young," she answered from her spot on the couch, where she was unwinding from school by watching reruns of the fifties sitcoms that were always on late in the afternoons.

"Couldn't you have been a flower girl?"

"Eleanor didn't want one," Una said. "She liked to keep things simple."

"So what was the wedding like?" I asked. "Was the cake good?"

Una frowned. "I'd really rather not talk about it, if you don't mind."

"Why not?" I persisted.

"Like I said, I really don't want to talk about it." Una got up and walked to the kitchen, where I could hear her complaining to Grandma about my nosiness. As a result, I was fully prepared that night when I went to my room to study after supper.

"Charity has no idea what it was like for Una to lose her older sister," Grandma said distinctly to Grandpa as they were sitting at the kitchen table. "That girl needs to learn some consideration for others."

Nothing was said directly to me and I was beginning to understand that it never would be.

There was a hedge tree in the O'Bryans' side yard. Like the ones in Grandma East's yard, it always dropped the useless apples and thorn-tipped branches on the ground that had to be cleared away. The tree stretched up and out well enough for a room-sized treehouse that Grandpa had built for Una from cedar wood. Una no longer used the treehouse and reluctantly granted me access in exchange for a promise not to smoke inside. I enjoyed climbing up there to lie on the floor and inhale the cedar as I pretended to be someone else, someone smarter, prettier, and blessed with unconstrained talent for song, dance, and stage.

The bed in my room was full-sized with a wrought iron frame. I could tell that it was old and that my mother might have slept in it, knowing better than to ask by now. The desk and dresser were spare, well-made

Shaker models from Grandpa's workshop that I was warned to take good care of since they'd belonged to my uncle Ian.

A box tucked in a back corner on the floor of my bedroom closet yielded a collection of paperbacks, most of them leftovers from Una's high school summer reading lists. Some of them I'd already heard of, like *The Prime of Miss Jean Brodie* and *The Great Gatsby*. I dug through the rest quickly and cautiously, knowing Una must have forgotten them and would probably move them out of my reach if I drew her attention to them. A small feast of fat things that would be easy to finish by the end of the school year if I could manage to not disappear again.

The O'Bryans' driveway was so long that the house couldn't be seen from the road if it was corn year for the field sitting in front of it. I wondered if they felt safe being so isolated, even if Grandpa O'Bryan did have his small collection of shotguns and pistols, along with a 1950 Winchester that he knew how to use. Katie John meowed and followed me halfway down the driveway on the first day of school before losing interest and turning back.

I wore my favorite shirt, a faded blue cotton button-down with long sleeves and my first pair of straight-legged jeans, which suited me better than the outdated bell bottoms most of us had worn at the Home. Loafer-style moccasins and my single braid of regrown hair completed the approach I'd settled on. A little bit of makeup would have helped but I didn't have any and I was afraid that buying some at K-mart in front of Grandma O'Bryan would have led to a lively after-dinner discussion between her and Grandpa about my fast and shallow concerns. Una never wore makeup unless it was a special occasion.

The bus driver was irate when she saw me grinding out my cigarette on the road just before climbing onto her bus. "Do your parents know you smoke?" she asked.

"Yes."

"And aren't they furious?"

"Not a bit."

"Well, I'd be if it were my daughter."

I already knew from Grandma O'Bryan that the driver's name was Abby and that Abby's daughter was none other than the lovely Anita from the guidance counselors' office. Anita's conception had taken place with the help of a Mexican migrant worker from one of the orchards who was attacked and killed outside a bar in Hamilton one month before he and Abby were to be married and eight months before Anita was born. Abby would live the life of a *True Story* heroine, the determined single mother disowned by family and friends, gamely raising a twenty-four karat child on her own and leaving all of Piqua County no choice but to acknowledge her considerable worth.

Once satisfied that I was hip to her views on teen smoking, Abby backed off and asked me about myself since I was new to the route she'd been driving for fifteen years. She also told me to carry a flashlight during the winter months or I might not be visible from the road, something Una had always done. "I remember your aunt Una," Abby said. "The boys used to say she'd mow them down with no mercy when they played soccer in gym class."

Inside the square-shaped high school, the sea of bouncing teenaged bodies dressed in new clothes chosen directly from the pages of *The Official Preppy Handbook* felt like a carousel. Shawnee's students numbered a bit over a thousand, more than three times the size of the entire Home from preschool to twelfth grade. This meant possibilities and choices, assuming any of the shiny, confident alien beings swirling by would actually admit me into their ranks. Or if I would even want to be admitted; false friends were worse than no friends and my plan was to be circumspect.

My first class was in room G, which I didn't see on any of the classroom doors. After coughing up the nerve to ask for directions, I learned that room G was the greenhouse in the courtyard and could only be reached by walking through a chemistry lab where another class was already starting. A tunneled pathway led from the entrance of the greenhouse to the classroom section. The pathway was lined on both sides with plant-covered tables, rows and boxes of chrysanthemum plants and seedlings that filled the humid air with their bitter-fresh smell, along with several other plants that were recognizable even though I couldn't name them. Deciding to stay, I handed my schedule to the man sitting at the single table parked at the opposite end of the greenhouse.

"Welcome to Shawnee, Miss Sintz," he said as he scribbled my name in his grade book. "I'm Mr. Zaninovich and I hope you like plants."

Instead of individual desks, there were four rows of long tables facing the teacher. I sat in the most isolated empty seat I could find at the edge of the last row. The other kids acknowledged me with quick looks or frank stares; a few of them smiled. I tried not to let anyone catch my eye, just in case they turned out to be the shit-stirring type who accused people of giving them a dirty look and then tried to start a fight.

Most of the girls were color-coordinated. One even had coral pink sneakers to match her jogging suit, which made me blink hard. Others wore straight skirts and knee socks, a combination I'd never imagined. At the Home each girl over the age of thirteen was given a new pair of pantyhose each month and only at gunpoint would any of us have worn knee socks with a skirt. The skirts were always long and A-line, usually only seen in chapel or on special occasions. A skirt that revealed our knees when we sat down would have made any one of us a laughingstock.

The boys at Shawnee were partial to Lacoste polo shirts with the ubiquitous alligator emblem that looked like a scout badge. Their haircuts were shorter and fussier than what I was used to seeing on boys and some even looked like they might be using hairspray. Almost all of them had the same docile, unassuming faces but one exception was a boy with dark brown hair reaching his collar who wore a resigned smile, as if he knew better than most that the world was a strange place and there was no point in dwelling on it.

Mr. Zaninovich introduced himself to the rest of the class and drew our attention to a rectangular fish tank on his table-desk that was filled with water and occupied by a single frog. "I want you all to watch what happens when I put this glass over Kermit here, even though he's amphibian and can breathe in the water." He pulled a kitchen timer from his briefcase and wound it. "We'll leave the glass in there for five minutes and see."

Then Mr. Zaninovich remembered something he'd left in the principal's office and went to fetch it, warning us not to touch the glass until he returned. When the frog began to panic and thrash, some of the girls were almost crying. The boy with the long hair casually stood up and lifted the glass long enough to offer relief to the frog, quickly replacing it when we heard the outer door of the greenhouse opening. Mr. Zaninovich didn't seem surprised or unhappy to find the frog mildly restless instead of being ready to explode. For whatever reason we'd been put to a test and either passed by letting the frog live or failed by not letting it die.

Lunchtime came at twelve-thirty and I found the cafeteria, a dollar in my back pocket from the seven received from Grandma the night before with the explanation that it was both my allowance and my lunch money. The plate lunch was fifty cents and looked almost as bad as what they served at the Home. I grabbed a cup of strawberry yogurt for the same price. There were other things like fresh fruit and sandwiches but I could see that they were going to be beyond my means if the money was going to last me the entire week. The freedom to choose partially made up for the limited choices.

A dark, fine-faced Indian boy accidentally broke into the line in front of me and apologized with the prettiest accent I'd ever heard in real life. No one else spoke to me in the cafeteria until a boy sitting at the table next to mine threw an overripe banana at my back to get my attention. "Hey, Tennessee Tits, you must be new here," he said. "I'd remember seeing a set like yours."

I marched over to where the thrower was sitting with his friends and showed my thanks by whacking him on the head with his gift. Then I unpeeled it and mashed it into the front of his shirt before he could think of a suitable putdown for me since Shawnee's unwritten rules only allowed boys to strike at girls verbally if there were witnesses. Then I unscrewed the lid on the pepper shaker, emptied it into his vegetable soup, and walked out of the cafeteria. No one followed me.

From the cafeteria I went outside to the smoking area. It was full of boys with long, uncombed hair and girls who were all wearing Levi's or Wranglers. There were no Calvin Kleins or alligators to be seen anywhere and I relaxed. No one spoke to me so I sat back and listened mutely like Chief Broom in *One Flew over the Cuckoo's Nest*.

"*God, I hate being back in the fucking school again/Did you see what Carla did to her hair???/Could you spot me a dime bag till Saturday?/Can I get a light?/Oh my God, did you see Brian, his dad beat the shit out of him again/Who's that blond chick over there?/Did you get Mrs. Messmore for math?/I never saw her before, do you think she's deaf, she's not saying anything/Guess what stuck-up little bitch had to go stay with her grandmother in Florida/Have you heard the new Foghat album yet, it's fucking decent.*"

What stood out most for me was the variety and quantity of activities. I smoked a second cigarette and continued to listen, careful again not to make too much eye contact. Twenty minutes later I left for my next class with enough information to make or break a few reputations, along with a hunch that any friends I made at Shawnee were probably going to be like these kids or the boy who saved the frog.

French class finally arrived at fifth period. The teacher's name was Lamar Johnson-Mills and he insisted on being addressed as Monsieur Johnson-Mills. He was a cheery former nerd with five years of living in France on his CV and a slight Georgia accent that was only noticeable when he spoke English. M. Johnson-Mills told everyone to choose a French name for the classroom and I scanned the list of options in our textbook, eventually settling on Yves.

"Mais ma chére, Yves is a name for les garçons, the boys," Monsieur Johnson-Mills said.

"It sounds just like Eve," I said. The truth was I liked the spelling more than anything else.

"C'est un pays libre," Monsieur Johnson-Mills said as he nodded and wrote 'Yves' next to my name in his grade book. I assumed by his affable tone of voice that whatever he'd said was in my favor.

Social studies ended the day. The frog-rescuing boy—Hatton, Seth, according to roll call—was in the seat next to me. "Could I copy your notes at the end of class?" he asked me. "I left my notebook in my locker."

"I guess so," I said reluctantly, not having planned to take to take any notes. If I was confused, which I usually was, notes never seemed to help but I did my best to scribble out some lines during class.

Seth groaned when he saw my handwriting. "Geez, it looks like a bunch of dead spiders."

"Well, next time you can take your own notes and you can write them on your hand or your foot or your dick, for all I care." I shoved my pencil in my folder and hurried to catch the bus. Seth stared after me, surprised by my touchiness.

"How'd your day go?" Abby asked me as soon as I climbed on the bus and fell into the first empty seat.

I did a quick tally. A class inside a greenhouse, I could do as I pleased during the co-ed gym class since the teacher only wanted to play football with the boys, and I'd gotten the better of the only two people who tried to rattle my cage. Beautifully, in other words.

"Not too shitty," I said.

"What kind of language is that for a girl your age?" Abby laughed anyway, happy for my success.

Grandpa was out in the barn with his chickens when I got home and Grandma was still at her part-time job in town at St. Elizabeth's Hospital. Hungry but unsure of what I was allowed to eat, if anything, I went to my room for a nap. Katie John climbed up to join me.

Chapter Twenty

Seth and I began the process of becoming best friends after he offered me a Hershey bar and a believable apology for being mean about my handwriting on the first day of school. Never able to get enough chocolate, I accepted both peace offerings. Seth lived with his mother in a small house just outside of town. His parents were divorced but still friendly enough to eat their holiday dinners together. Seth's mother Glenda had a boyfriend who was old enough to be her father, a man named Bert whom Seth wasn't crazy about but could live with in measured doses. Bert owned the house that Seth and his mother lived in but fortunately for both of them, he made his own home elsewhere.

"He's got a big house he lives in with his two screwed-up grandkids," Seth explained. "He adopted them because their mother's supposed to be a drinker who never looked after them."

"Is he their father's father or their mother's father?"

"Mother's."

"You think he might have driven her to drink when she was growing up?" I asked.

"Probably," Seth said. "He's kind of mental."

I thought it was funny that Seth wasn't more concerned about his mother keeping company with someone who was kind of mental but as we became better acquainted I saw that he wasn't one to lose sleep over the things he couldn't change, big or small. I envied Seth's ability to get along with practically everyone and the way he allowed acts of petty meanness to bounce off his back, wishing I could be the same way.

"It's our first Friday," Seth said at the end of the first week after social studies was over. "We should celebrate and go to Baskin Robbins."

"Okay," I agreed, even though I had no way to get home. We walked up to Main Street, near Garfield's main campus. Most of the student-geared businesses were in that neighborhood, including the co-op bookstore that carried textbooks for Garfield students and required a college ID to enter, much to my disappointment. There was also a health food store, a head shop called the Gingko Berry, two movie theaters, the scenic public library made of red, auburn, and brown bricks, a pet shop, two record and tape stores— one for new, one for used—and three beauty salons. Everything the main street of a college town in God's country ought to have.

After having to let six people ahead of us at Baskin Robbins while I made up my mind, Seth suggested we try ordering not the best combinations we could think of, but the worst. I walked out the door carrying a scoop of licorice with daiquiri ice on a sugar cone. Seth chose lemon and peppermint. We called it a draw and went to a park across the street to eat. My last pack of cigarettes would have to last until Monday, when I got my allowance from Grandma O'Bryan. The ice cream literally took my last penny but I'd been too proud and too greedy for the experience not to accept the invitation.

Seth finished his ice cream and threw his napkin in a trash can near the full-sized sweetgum tree that we were sitting under. "So how about you?" he asked.

"How about me?"

"I told you my deep darks, now you tell me yours."

I told Seth about my mother and her trees, my father and Trilby, Grandma East, the Holmes, the Home, and Willow Lake. He listened mostly without comment except for a small whistle of astonishment when I told him about being left behind at summer camp while the Holmeses went to Texas without me. I didn't tell him about my aborted trip to Dallas the previous spring. Another time, when he knew me better and might not judge me too harshly.

"So your dad left for Florida without telling you and that family just took off for Texas without telling you?"

"Yep."

"What a shitty thing to do."

I agreed but trying to talk about it to anyone in my family always led to accusations of self-pity that made me want to rip the skin off my face. Both of us were in choir and Seth told me about show choir, a class open to sophomores, juniors, and seniors that taught song and dance routines. I tried to see myself dancing on a stage and being watched by an admiring audience like one of the kids from *Fame*.

When it was time to go home, Seth said good-bye and walked to his own house, which was only two miles outside of town. I went in the opposite direction and hitched a ride with a farmer in a pickup truck who dropped me off at the end of the driveway. It was almost six o'clock and I could smell cod frying when I walked in the house. Una, Grandma and Grandpa were sitting at the kitchen table drinking RC. The three of them turned to me at the same time, the better to make me ask myself what the hell I'd done now.

"Where have you been for the last three hours?" Grandma asked.

"I went to the park with a friend," I said, proud of how normal I sounded. "Can I have an RC?"

"Who said you could go out after school?" Una asked in what was probably the same voice she used on students who offended her with wilted excuses for unfinished assignments.

"Well shit, who said I couldn't?" It wasn't as if I'd asked any of them for a ride home.

"You went out somewhere without asking first and didn't even call to tell us you were going to be late," Grandma said. "Then you come home and use foul language. That's real charming."

"Can I have an RC?"

"No, what you can do is go to your room and get started on your homework," Grandma said. "I'll call you when supper's ready."

My books made an uncomfortable heap on the floor of the otherwise tidy bedroom. I flipped through them, trying to decide which subject to start with. It all looked so muddling that I gave up and looked through the paperbacks in the closet. Nothing appealed to me there either. Standing on a chair, I looked on the high shelves to see what else might turn up. Among the photo albums and yearbooks, I found a homemade Raggedy Ann doll. Taking her down for a better look, I discovered the initials E.O'B. carefully stitched into the white fabric directly under the embroidered red heart.

Una stuck her head in the door just then to tell me that supper was on the table and did a double take when she saw what I was holding. "The only way you could have found that doll was to be snooping through the closet," she said. "Who told you to do that?"

"It's my room, isn't it?" I got up and tried to put the doll back on the shelf but Una pulled it away from me.

"It's a guest bedroom and guests have obligations not to be nosy," she said. "And Eleanor made this doll herself so you'd better keep your hands off it. It means a lot to Mom."

We all sat down to eat supper and Una wasted no time letting her parents know about my faux pas. "I caught her messing with Eleanor's doll," Una said. "I told her to leave it alone so now she's going to be sulking and trying to give us all a guilt trip."

"She was my mother," I said. "Why shouldn't I see her things?"

Grandma set her fork down in a careful, deliberate way, as if it were loaded. "You drove Eleanor to distraction around the clock and you couldn't stop pestering her to save your life, even when she was expecting your brother and needing to take it easy. How's that for a why-not?" Her voice had its usual matter-of-fact tone but it was still an open challenge instead of the usual joke or complaint being made behind my back.

"Aren't most little kids like that?" I asked, not quite believing what I'd managed to start.

"Mine weren't," Grandma said.

I knew this was probably the truth. With their usual tenacity, my grandparents had produced three children who were quiet, industrious, and reserved, keeping themselves at a polite arm's length from everyone, just like their parents. The O'Bryans didn't see that a fluke was all it had been. Or they were right and I was a factory second. It wasn't as if there was no evidence to back them up.

Seth and I picked up the habit of meeting after school on Fridays for ice cream, window-shopping, or a trip to the library. Sometimes Seth's mother Glenda drove me home. Far from being the high-strung basket case I'd imagined, Glenda was a friendly woman with a hint of good-natured coarseness that made her more accessible. She gave her blessing when Seth and I began collecting aluminum cans to sell at the recycling center near his house, as did the O'Bryans.

"She's not afraid to get her hands dirty after all," Grandpa said.

Collecting the cans was an activity that placed me and Seth in some disrepute with the preppy crowd at school and led to more competitions between the two of us to see who could come up with the most colorful description of how devastated we were over our lack of social standing.

"Shelly Eversole seems to think I care more about her opinion than I do for that dog shit I just stepped on," Seth might say.

"You'd need a microscope to see how much I care what she thinks," I would volley. Shelly Eversole was a varsity cheerleader who sang in the choir with us, an ice cream blond whose lips were always held in a slight outward curl in preparation for a show of disgust. The snotty-bitch lip curl was one of the latest fashion accessories, more fallout from the Valley Girl craze.

Collecting the cans usually brought me more than three dollars a week, which easily kept me in cigarette money. If I had any extra it usually went for books, pot, or secondhand cassettes from Crazy Cat's next door to the co-op bookstore. I taught Seth how to smoke and we began spending Friday afternoons at his house, getting mildly high and watching *Fraggle Rock* before Glenda came home from work. It was a near idyllic routine and I was lulled into what passed for serenity in my mind, even agreeing when Seth suggested we look for summer jobs in Baumburg.

When one of the managers from K-mart called me at the O'Bryans' house in early May with the offer of a summer job in their greenhouse, I gave a happy squeal that made everyone's eyes roll. "I don't see how you can work at K-mart while you're at your dad's," Grandma said as soon as I hung up the phone. "Once school's out, you're going back to Indiana for the summer. You and Annette will have to learn how to get along."

How stupid I'd been to squeal like that, letting everyone know I had something to be happy about. "Can't I stay here?" I asked, not having expected to be evicted for the summer.

No," Grandma said without pause. I went to my room to cry and self-abase in private.

"She really thinks she's something." Grandpa's voice was indulgent.

"K-mart offers her a job and she's walking around like she just won the Nobel," said Una.

I could hate myself into a pile of dead ashes but it would never be enough to convince the O'Bryans that I was realistic about my true worth.

The next day at school Seth asked me why my face was covered with red marks. I told him I had a rash, not knowing the word for self-mutilation. If anyone in my family noticed, they made no direct comment.

"We meant to tell you last night that you can come back here in the fall," Grandma said the next morning at breakfast. "Just so long as you stay out of trouble and get your grades up."

Why? So I could go to college or do something amazing and incredible with my life? So I could bring honor to my family? Hardy fucking har har.

"I'll miss you," Seth told me on the last Friday of school while we were eating ice cream. "There's never anyone else to talk to."

"What about Lily?" I asked, referring to Bert's dysfunctional granddaughter. Lily was a year older than us but she was still a freshman and always took the remedial classes. She dropped in to join us for *Fraggle Rock* once in a while.

"Lily's not much for conversation," Seth said. "I mean it's one thing to be ignorant but it's like she enjoys not knowing anything. You try talking to her about anything besides beer, pot, or the Go-Go's and her eyes just kind of glaze over and she laughs at you."

My father said no when I asked for permission to join Seth at the annual last-day-of-school party in the park on Main Street, where the high school and junior high kids celebrated each year with a carnival and endless repetitions of Alice Cooper's "School's Out" on an outdoor PA system until everyone else in the neighborhood was ready to start ripping their own fingernails out. Under no circumstances was I going to be running loose in Baumburg until he finished work at seven. Promising to go to Seth's house after the party didn't help.

"You don't need to be messing around going to anyone's house," Dad said. He never said what he thought I did need to be doing. Or why everything had to be a matter of need in the first place.

Chapter Twenty-One

Trilby spent most of the summer playing baseball while Dad spent most of it working and Annette spent most of it talking to her mother on the phone and complaining about the heat. I spent most of it reading the paperbacks I'd found by going through the hallways with Seth after school on the last day to root through whatever the janitors pulled from the unemptied lockers. I would have complained about the heat but there was nobody to hear it.

There would be no summer job. The corn detasslers had already been hired for the summer and Dad and Annette decided that letting me look for a job in Hazelwood was a bad idea since I was liable to start gossiping and telling embarrassing stories about myself and my family. I continued to collect cans and wrote letters of complaint to food companies about one product or another that they sold, which usually brought free samples or coupons in the mail. Annette was pleased enough by the largess to compliment my industry and keep to the ceasefire that we were both under orders to observe.

If I wanted anything from the store, I could either put a request in with Dad in the morning before he went in to work and take the fifty-fifty chance that he'd remember or ride into Hazelwood with Annette on Saturday mornings. I preferred the former, especially since the honeymoon was clearly over and Annette was beginning to use me as a sounding board to complain about my father's shortcomings as a husband. She was adamant that someone with a college education should never use slang or euphemisms for anything sex-related, which made her conversations that much more gruesome.

"Your dad never wants to have oral sex," Annette complained to me on more than one occasion. "I enjoy cunnilingus once in a while, there's nothing wrong with that."

"Okay," I said, willing the subject to change or myself into an oblivion where my stepmother's voice couldn't reach me.

"That's all I ever hear from you," Annette said. "You never care about anything or anyone but your own sweet little self."

Dad was drinking more and I saw that he'd switched from beer to vodka, especially on Sunday mornings. At Annette's urging they joined a Southern Baptist church across the road from the motel and attendance was compulsory for Trilby and me. Annette never talked about sex at church and was managing to give everyone there the impression that I'd been out of control as a preteen but Dad was now coping with her help. The two of them received plenty of sympathy from other members of the congregation and gentle exhortations not to give up on me.

"Don't smile, your face will crack," I was told one Sunday by Joanna Foley, Trilby's Sunday school teacher.

"Vous êtes vous remplir de merde," I said with an acid smirk that appeared to satisfy her. Vive Monsieur Johnson-Mills and first-year French.

"There you go, you can do it." Joanna walked off to boast of her success.

"Honey, you seriously need to be turning to Jesus and beg his pardon for your sins," said Louise Irvin, who was in charge of the youth group that I refused to join and who always spoke to me as if I were half my age. "And remember we're all sinners, but once you reach out to him, you'll be all filled up inside with a warm light and that's how you'll know you've been forgiven."

Instead I turned to Jesus and begged him to make all of them disappear and quickly. Almost everyone who spoke to me at the church made their approach with the idea that I didn't even believe in Jesus and that said belief would have to be exhorted and hand-wrung into me. But if I didn't believe in Jesus, how was he able to talk me out of serving a plate of Ex-Lax brownies to the pack of them at the Fourth of July picnic?

I counted off the days until I could return to Shawnee, Seth, and the drama club, where I could pretend to be like the kids who were going to college.

Annette's metabolism was slow and she gained several pounds due to my father's taste for farm cuisine that went straight to the avoirdupois. A small fortune's worth of diet candy was mostly left to fossilize since it tasted like caramelized Play Doh. Annette continued to buy Twinkies, cupcakes, and Ho-Hos, supposedly for the family but we didn't see much of them.

"What happened to the Oreos?" Trilby asked as we were sitting down to supper. "There was half a bag this morning and now they're all gone."

"Ask your sister," Annette said. "Consideration for the rest of us isn't exactly her strong point."

"If I've been eating them then how come I've lost eight pounds since I got here?" I asked, angry enough to forget that I was playing right into Annette's chubby hands. "While you just about have to turn sideways to get your ass through a door."

My father slapped me on the mouth with the back of his hand. The indifference of the gesture upset me more than anything else. I fled the table and went to hide on the stair landing where I could hear Annette's voice, rich with satisfied contempt: my father had barely touched me and I'd gone bawling my head off. He should have knocked me on my butt and really given me something to cry about. I could hear Trilby excusing himself, a chair being pushed out from the table. This was followed by the clink of a plate being scraped and set in the sink, a courtesy that my father insisted we observe. The scraping noises were slow and sad.

"You ought to send her back to that school," Annette continued. "You know the O'Bryans don't much want her and if they send her back here you'll be stuck. You have to face it that she's been out of your hands for too long and she's just not the same child. She's probably not even a virgin anymore."

My father said nothing but there was a sharp, smacking sound, followed by a surprised wail from Annette. I ran back downstairs to the kitchen, where Annette was crying as she held a wet towel to her face with what I saw as overkill. Trilby looked stricken and my father had the grace to be ashamed until he noticed me standing behind my brother.

"Sometimes I think you should never have been born," Dad said. "Something's just not right with you." He ordered me out of the kitchen. When Trilby tried to follow me upstairs he was told to stay and help wash the dishes.

I went to my room and lay on my bed, taking no pleasure in the idea of my so-called virtue since from everything I'd heard on the subject, a hymen was something that would have to be disposed of eventually, like a wisdom tooth or an appendix. I wished it was something I could simply expel on my own since losing it the traditional way sounded painful, not to mention awkward.

As for my father wishing I'd never been born, that made two of us.

Later that night I snuck downstairs for a Pepsi and almost fell over a Slinky left lying on the kitchen floor. Picking it up at the ends, I made a loop and shook the Slinky up and down in the air for a few seconds until it became boring. Then I tiptoed into Dad and Annette's bedroom and carefully set the Slinky in the center of their bed before hurrying back to my own room, where a copy of *Flowers for Algernon* was waiting for me.

"What the hell is this thing doing on the bed?" Annette's voice carried down the hall. "Are you trying to be funny or something?"

Fifty points for me.

"I don't know what it's doing there," my father yelled back. "What's the big deal anyway? It's just a stupid toy."

"You put that there just to get my goat, didn't you?"

"Why would I do that? I don't know why it gets your goat in the first place." A dresser drawer slammed shut.

Annette knocked the screen loose and threw the Slinky out the window, along with a trousseau of alluring lingerie she'd bought for her honeymoon. "Damned if I need these for anything."

"I've been looking for this," Trilby said the next morning when he found the Slinky among the lace and nylon debris in the front yard. I held up a rose-colored nightie, liberally trimmed with fluffy cream lace. It came down to my knees and wasn't sheer. Lying nearby was the matching robe. I gathered them up and shook them off. Trilby asked what we should do with everything.

"Nothing," I said. "Just leave it where it is."

"But what if somebody comes by and sees it all?" he asked. "People'll think Annette's lost her mind."

"She had to have one first," I said. Just the same I helped Trilby gather everything up in a Hefty bag and put it in the garage, reasoning that Annette could do as she pleased with it from there. The rose-colored nightie and robe I retrieved later that day when my conscience-ridden brother wasn't looking and they came back to Baumburg in my footlocker. I was more than ready for some crisp, apple-scented autumn days.

Chapter Twenty-Two

For the first day of sophomore year I wore my Jack Daniels t-shirt and brought my collection of Beatles tapes to show Mrs. Kerkovich, the music teacher. My hope was that some of their songs might lend themselves to a decent dance turn for the show choir. It wasn't a strong hope; the Beatles didn't do dance music although it was possible to shake and rattle after a fashion to "Everybody's Got Something to Hide Except Me and My Monkey." Such a song would never make it onto Mrs. Kerkovich's list of suitables, even if the sheet music could be found for it.

"Maybe some kind of polka for "Obla Di, Obla Da?" Mrs. Kerkovich suggested without enthusiasm. "Charity, do you really think that's an appropriate shirt for someone your age to be wearing?"

While my t-shirt bothered the adults, my taste in music raised disapproving eyebrows among the young, as always. "Why do you like music like that?" asked Courtney Blessner, a mediocre second soprano who was looking through my tapes. "You should listen to Culture Club and Michael Jackson. This stuff is old." She twirled the string of pearls draped over her sleeveless apricot sweater and favored me and Seth with a patronizing smile, the lesser god's children too sadly ignorant to realize how unfavored we were.

Seth laughed. "You should see your face, Charity Eleanor. I bet you're having that pickaxe between the eyes fantasy again."

"Silly bitch," I said of Courtney at lunchtime when everyone from the drama club was gathered at our favorite table in the cafeteria.

"You know it's not nice to talk that way," Becca D'Angelo said. Her father was a history teacher at Shawnee and through him Becca had picked up a few rumors about my shady past and irregular present. Sometimes she took it on herself to offer constructive criticism of my speech and deportment.

"I wasn't trying to sound nice," I told Becca. "And while I'm at it, kiss my ass."

A potential showdown was averted when Will Payton began pelting us with crackers from the next table, the same boy who'd thrown a banana at me on the first day of freshman year. I returned his hail with a flung spoonful of yogurt that landed on his sleeve and Becca's face showed something like admiration for a second before she caught herself. Becca was a natural as the well-heeled schoolteacher's daughter in her plaid skirts with the matching sweaters or blouses. Pretty and boring. I believed Becca wanted everyone and everything to be pretty and boring to ensure that she'd never feel out of place or in the wrong.

Danny Schaedel was one of the newest members of the drama club to sit at our table. Although his parents were American, Danny was returning from twelve years in Haifa, Israel, with trips to Europe, Japan, and Australia under his belt. He had a smooth baritone voice that went unnoticed since he politely refused to join the choir and spoke perfect colloquial English with a trace of an accent I assumed was Hebrew.

Like me, Danny scorned MTV and considered the Beatles patron saints. He appeared at school each day with his unfashionably long, dark red hair bundled into a ponytail, always wearing distressed khaki pants or boot-cut jeans, oversized t-shirts, and an open vest that was loaded down with buttons identifying his pet causes. Danny's parents often did volunteer work at school and I noticed that they always smiled whenever they looked at him. Danny looked as if he could be an ambassador from one of those alternative universes that I was always hoping to stumble into.

The drama club advisor was a senior-year theatre major from the university named Geraldine whom Una remembered seeing four years earlier as Tilly in Shawnee's production of *The Effects of Gamma Rays On Man-In-the-Moon Marigolds*. Getting a new advisor each year was an advantage for the drama club since the quick turnover meant there was no time for politics to develop and the plays were always well done. It was entertaining to watch the tryouts for the fall plays, when the cheerleaders and other members of the top shelf crowd would arrive to audition for a part, assuming their reputations meant success was assured.

When they failed to get so much as a walk-on, their newfound interest in theatre was quick to dissolve.

Seth wasn't able to come to the first drama club meeting and Geraldine gave me a ride home when she saw me standing with my thumb out two blocks from school.

"You shouldn't hitchhike," she said as I opened the door of her ancient Thunderbird.

"Or smoke pot and play Russian roulette at the same time," I said as I slid into the car.

"Now that's a conversation stopper."

I gave Geraldine the directions to my grandparents' house and we drove outside of town. I stared at her hands as they held the steering wheel, admiring her sensibly short nails that were filed into neat ovals and the coral ring on her right pinky. I wondered how I might get Geraldine to touch me. It was easy to imagine her as Tilly, softly delivering the ethereal closing speech in *Marigolds*.

"What's your favorite Neil Simon play?" Geraldine asked as we turned from the state route onto Kaiser Road, where the O'Bryans lived.

"*Barefoot in the Park*," I said. "Or maybe *The Star-Spangled Girl*"

"How about *Little Me?*"

"I thought it was stupid when I read it."

"Plays are meant to be seen, not read," Geraldine said.

"So where am I supposed to see it?" I asked.

"Good question."

Grandpa was sitting in the rocking chair on the front porch when we got to the house. "How do," he said to Geraldine as he got up and walked towards us. "Your right front tire's pretty low. Miss Piglet here must have put too much weight on it."

"That's quite a driveway you've got," Geraldine said. Grandpa put air in the tire and gave her the name of a friend who sold used ones and could be trusted not to fleece her.

"She seems like a nice gal," Grandpa said as we watched Geraldine drive away.

"Yeah."

"I didn't hear you tell her thank you for giving you a ride home."

"I did," I said. "Before I got out the car."

"Well, you should have said something right when she left, too," Grandpa said. "It was on account of you that her tire went flat." He smiled when he said this, another one of those jokes that wasn't.

I dropped my book bag in the living room and went to the basement for an empty Mason jar to collect a pond water sample for biology class. There was a small fishing pond less than a quarter mile from the house, directly in back of an old barn that Grandpa no longer used. I found a jar and walked to the pond. Squatting at the edge of the water, I scooped up a half quart of the murky matter and held it up to the fading sun for a closer look at the nonstop activity of the miniscule life forms now in my captivity. I watched the pond as if it were a crystal ball, knowing it was no more than fifteen or twenty feet deep in the center. Could drinking from it be fatal? Then I tossed in a pebble. It didn't skim but I wasn't expecting it to.

Square Pegs was on TV after dinner that night and in a role reversal, I excused myself to do homework while Una curled up on the living room couch. "Don't you like this show?" she asked, her voice needling as I came into the living room to find my book bag. "It's all about Young Adults, just like you."

One day Una would be told to go shit in her hat and if I was lucky, I'd be there to see it.

I opened my world cultures book and tried to focus on the electoral process of the Soviet Union. Instead of a punch card or a fill-in-the-blank, everyone was handed a slip of paper with the name of the official candidate sponsored by the Communist party. Simply dropping the slip into a ballot box was the way to vote for the official candidate. There were private voting booths available but they were rarely used since it meant the voter was planning to cross off the name of the official candidate and do a write-in. Between that, the weather, and having to stand in line all day to buy bread, I knew I was too much of a wimp to ever be Russian or anything else that called for exceptional fortitude. I closed the book and picked up the script for *The Importance of Being Ernest*.

Seth and I went to the auditions together. He was cast as Lane, the smartass butler. I didn't get a part but Geraldine made me the stage manager.

"You read really well," she explained to me at the first rehearsal. "Your delivery is really smooth but your voice is sort of, well, I'm not sure how to put it." Geraldine floundered for an adequate description of my monotone. "And you tend to swallow your words. It's really hard to hear you sometimes."

My pleasure in being the stage manager was dulled by the kind words. Geraldine clearly felt that I needed a salve. I took my copy of the script and stood next to her in a circle with everyone in the cast for vocal warmups.

"*To sit in solemn silence on a dull, dark dock in a pestilential prison with a lifelong lock, awaiting the sensation of a short, sharp shock from a cheap and chippy chopper on a big black block,*" we chanted like occultists.

In bed that night I dreamed that I was being led to the guillotine for unspecified offenses. A man in a black mask who sounded like Mr. Travenski, the vice principal at Shawnee, was explaining to me in a bored voice that my head was going to be surgically detached from my body for the purpose of ending my life.

"But I haven't done anything wrong," I cried. The people in the crowd were irritated and contemptuous of my inability to be proud and silent.

"It'll just work out better for everyone this way." The man in the mask was getting impatient. "You're always thinking about yourself."

"You were screaming in your sleep last night," Grandma said at breakfast. "Pretty loud, too. What's up with that?"

"Don't know," I said. "There must have been a ghost in the room or something."

Grandma rolled her eyes an eighth of an inch. "How can you have a ghost in a house that nobody's even died in yet?"

A poltergeist, what else? A troublesome, destructive spirit that arrived or was accidentally conjured in a house where someone might be in emotional turmoil, especially if the someone was in puberty. Forgetting that my remark about the ghost had been a complete fib, I began to imagine a possible future with a poltergeist in residence as if it were a new pet under consideration that I was going to name Poindexter. Would it be possible for me to channel energy to Poindexter or withdraw it at will? Maybe I could train Poindexter to do things like sweep the dishes off the table when the O'Bryans were giving me another one of their pep talks on my attitude problem, slovenliness, pathetic grades, or lack of industry and imagination over supper.

There was a rehearsal after school. I sat next to Geraldine again and tried to focus on Oscar Wilde's tap-dancing dialogue. Maryam Jalili, a freshman from Iran, was chosen to play Lady Bracknell, the part I'd hoped for. Scanning Nick Lucas up and down with an exaggerated air of genteel derision, Maryam practiced the speech of refusal that Lady B would deliver to Jack aka Ernest Worthing after he asked for the hand of her daughter, the Honorable Tight-Arsed Gwendolyn Fairfax. I liked watching Maryam perform her caricature of the drawling, skin-deep English gentlewoman of the Gilded Age. She even had a natural English accent from her years at a British-run elementary school in Tehran that was closed in 1979

"To lose one parent, Mr. Worthing, may be regarded as a misfortune; to lose both looks like carelessness."

It certainly did.

There wasn't much that Seth and I didn't talk about. I even told him about Lindy Albertson from before Camp Willow Lake, before the Home, before my first blow job or hand job or even before the pervert who spied on me and Carrie Holmes at the county fair when we were taking a piss the summer before sixth grade. Clean, sweet Lindy from another lifetime who would probably want nothing to do with me now and I'd be the first to understand.

"I guess it's not normal, is it?" I asked.

"Maybe you'll outgrow it," Seth said.

"Maybe," I said, taking comfort in my admiration of Danny Schaedel, even though I wanted to be him more than have him.

At Seth's urging, I asked Danny Schaedel to the Sadie Hawkins dance and was politely turned down. "My grandparents are flying in that day from Tel Aviv," he said regretfully.

"Sure, I understand," I said as quickly as I could and fled the scene. The first and hopefully last time I would approach a boy was gotten out of the way. In the future they would have to come to me or wait for someone more aggressive.

Becca D'Angelo was late getting to our table the next day at lunchtime. She sat down in the chair next to Nick Lucas, her face rosy. "I just asked Danny to the Sadie Hawkins and he said yes."

I stared into my strawberry yogurt, refusing to meet Seth's eyes.

Five minutes later Danny arrived at our table, hesitating when he saw Becca and me well within spitting and hissing distance of one another. "How are you, Charity?" Danny asked me with elaborate courtesy as he settled into the chair next to Becca.

As well as anyone could be with a name like mine, he must have thought. I ignored Danny, shame crawling on me like lice. Who had I thought I was, expecting to become cohorts with someone like him? Danny's family traveled around the world and took him with them; that alone put him out of my league. I went straight home after school instead of going to Seth's; his commiseration would have been more than I could endure. Sitting in the basement with a copy of *Trinity*, I chain-smoked and read until Una came down to tell me dinner was ready.

"You need to do something besides sitting down here like a chimney," she complained, waving the air.

"Does Grandpa keep those guns loaded?" I asked, gesturing to the rack hanging on the wall where the shotguns were displayed.

"I don't think so, why?"

"Just wondering."

"Well, maybe Dad could teach you how to shoot." Una turned and headed back up the stairs. "You could use a hobby."

Seth and I now had enough points in theatre activities for membership in the Thespian Society. On Thespian Initiation Day I went to school as Eliza Doolittle in a long, ratty black dress and a black boater hat that I actually liked, singing "Just You Wait, 'Enry 'Iggins" on command from any Thespian or teacher, who would then sign a paper that I was required to carry with me. A minimum of twelve signatures was required. Seth was Puff the Magic Dragon. Everyone agreed that his singing was the best.

At lunchtime the initiates had to take the stage in the cafeteria and perform their pieces for the crowd, followed by a group rendition of "That's Entertainment." Will Payton threw an apple at me. Seth caught the apple and ate it. Mr. Travenski caught Will and gave him a week's detention. Danny joined us on the stage dressed as Shakespeare and nervous about singing "What is a Youth?" Seth and I agreed to let bygones be bygones and sang it with him.

"*Caper the caper, sing me the song, death will come soon to hush us along . . .*" the three of us cried merrily. Our trio went over well and some of the kids even threw pennies instead of food.

Seth and I went to Plato's Pizza after school to share a singles' deep-dish, though we could easily have eaten two. While we were eating, he showed me a pair of tickets to the university's production of *Pippin*, freebies from one of his mother's clients. "It's the same night as Sadie Hawkins," Seth said. "We could go see it instead."

"Hell, yes," I said immediately. A musical at the university was worth a hundred school dances. I grabbed Seth's hand and kissed it.

"My mom always said I knew how to cheer a girl up."

The atmosphere felt more gelled than usual when I walked into the house that night. Una looked up from the book she was reading to grace me with an ambiguous lift of her eyebrows. Grandma and Grandpa were nowhere in sight until I went to my room and found both of them waiting for me. It was all very well-staged.

"I never thought I'd say such a thing but I'm glad Eleanor isn't here to see this," Grandma said as she held up a plastic sandwich bag. A nickel bag that was tucked inside the toe of an old pair of sneakers handed down from Una that I used for walking in the woods when it was muddy. Grandma was looking for something in the closet and noticed the smell of pot immediately. Now I knew the source of my own sensitive nose.

"I reckon you're going to say it belongs to a friend," Grandpa said, as if disappointed in advance that I couldn't be more original. Once again they were deciding what my thoughts were, what words and deeds I was planning. It was too much, the two of them waiting for me to cringe and prevaricate for their self-satisfied amusement. I snatched the bag from Grandma and stuffed it in my back pocket.

"It's mine."

"We can't be having this in our home," Grandma said. "Once school is out you're going back to your dad's, or back to that place up north, or wherever."

I'd had the time of my life on Thespian Initiation Day and now the bill was due.

"It looks like I'm out on my ass again," I told Seth the next day over a lunch I didn't eat. He helped himself to my peanut butter sandwich and listened while I told him about my grandparents finding the pot. He was silent at first, carefully chewing my sandwich as if there might be a prize in the peanut butter. Then he unexpectedly stood up and excused himself to make a phone call. Fifteen minutes later Seth joined me out in the smoking lounge, looking pleased.

"My mom said to come over to the shop after school and we'll all talk about you staying with us." He could have knocked me over with a French fry.

After school was out we walked up to Main Street, where Seth's mother Glenda ran a typing service that catered mainly to students from Garfield who were too busy or too lazy to type their own papers. Glenda's typing speed was an astonishing seventy words a minute on her Smith Corona. I wondered if she could teach me.

"Hey, troops." Glenda nodded to us without breaking her rhythm. "Have a seat while I finish this page." Another minute went by before she pulled the sheet of paper from the roller and placed it face down on top of a stack. "So, Charity, I hear your grandparents are putting you out. What gives?"

"They found out I've been smoking," I minimized.

"Smoking what?" she asked, deadpan. Seth laughed and I gave him a quick kick in the shin. "Okay, I'm not here to judge." Glenda said as she reached for a clean piece of paper. "Whether you were smoking Virginia Slims, mary jane, or banana skins, that doesn't make it right to throw a fifteen-year-old out on the street. I just want the facts."

"It was pot," I sighed.

"Okay, that's better."

"It's not like she's a drug addict," Seth put in.

"I never said she was, little man."

I called Dad for permission to move in with Seth and Glenda. Having been briefed by Grandma and Grandpa, he was already in a foul mood that wasn't helped by the sound of my voice. In the background I could hear Annette yelling instructions that Dad tried to ignore as he told me that I was behaving like someone without an ounce of decency, using marijuana and moving in with my boyfriend.

"He's not my boyfriend, he's just a friend," I said, sidestepping the cannabis issue. "I can see the thought of someone offering me a home just because they like me really screws up your world."

"I just want to make sure you're in a place where you can't get in any trouble."

"And I want to make sure that little bitch gives back that nightgown and robe she stole from me," Annette yelled.

Dad hung up and didn't call back that night, which seemed like a good sign. Instead he came to visit three days later looking exhausted and sheepish, as if the fight between him and Annette hadn't let up since the phone call. His skin was getting red even though it was too early in the year for sunburn.

"Just act decent while you're there," my father said as he capitulated on the living arrangements. "I don't want people thinking you were raised in a barn. And Annette keeps saying she wants her nightgown and robe back."

"I don't have her stupid nightgown and robe." This was now the truth. I'd almost forgotten that they weren't really mine and Annette's reminder had spoiled my pleasure in wearing them. I dropped them off at the Goodwill bin outside Garfield's administration building, a good excuse to take a walk on the park-like campus.

The health teacher was running late the next morning and Will Payton was holding court in the classroom. "I got a week's detention just because of Tennessee Tits here," he complained loudly enough for everyone to hear when I entered the room. Some of the girls consoled him and a few disapproving looks were thrown my way. I snapped like a popcorn kernel.

"Now, isn't that just crying-ass sad?" I asked everyone in the room as I walked to my desk, my voice as loud and deep as I could make it. "Poor little Willie boy here has to stay after school just because he tried to put my eye out with his apple like a fucking chimpanzee and he was stupid-ass enough to do it right in front of Mr. Travenski. I'm just making his life so sad, I think I'll cry me a goddamned Lake Michigan."

The evil spell worked. Will immediately tried to pretend I wasn't in the room as his friends laughed at him and called him Poor Little Preacher Boy Willie— his father was a minister. Every time during class when Will checked to see if I was looking at him—and I always was—I would pretend to play the violin, mime-crying melodramatically with my mouth wide open. Will never bothered anyone from the drama club again, which worried me a little since I wasn't used to things going my way.

Chapter Twenty-Three

Seth and Glenda's house was a three-bedroom cottage with gray aluminum siding. It looked small but felt roomy enough on the inside. The single bathroom had no lock on the door and everyone was scrupulous about knocking first. The yard was small and Glenda was indifferent to furbelows like shrubbery, flowers, or grass that was cut on a regular basis.

Bert came to visit a few times a week, always using his own key to get in. Seth warned me that Bert enjoyed snooping, which I discovered for myself after coming home from school two days after the move-in to find Bert in my bedroom. He lacked the decency to be embarrassed even though we'd caught him rooting through my closet.

"Glenda told me about you coming to stay here." Bert's voice was self-assured and I could see he was the type who saw himself as above reproach in all things. "I was just looking to see if you were all moved in."

"Sure you were," Seth laughed, which he had the luxury of doing since he was his mother's son. I only stood mute, too immobilized by stunned outrage to do anything else.

Sometimes Bert brought Lily with him on visits and other times she came on her own to join us for *Fraggle Rock* and share an occasional bottle of wine or ale filched from the shelf at Kroger's. Lily was small for her age and cute, with an amoral set of ethics. Glenda and Seth liked her even though they worried about her occasional brushes with the law that Bert was always quick to soft-pedal. Lily's aura of neglect reminded me of the girls at the Home but at the same time she was spoiled and overindulged by Bert, whom she manipulated without shame. The contradiction made it hard for me to decide whether to offer Lily my friendship or maintain a safe distance.

Seth and I found summer jobs through a program run by the state that paired teenagers with elderly shut-ins to do a few chores or errands for minimum wage. Most of them lived in the senior apartment complex in town near the Kroger store. My favorite client was Mr. Berenski, a blind man whose daughter-in-law did his shopping, laundry, and heavy cleaning, leaving me with little more than a few dirty dishes to wash, the mail to read, and the man himself to entertain a bit. An avid moviegoer in his youth, Mr. Berenski was surprised by how many of his favorite films I knew from watching the Saturday and Sunday afternoon reruns on TV over the years since there was usually never anything else to do on the weekends.

"Fifteen years old and she knows who Norma Shearer was," I heard Mr. Berenski telling his son over the phone one day. "I wish they'd make a few more kids like her."

I decided on the spot that if any of the Berenskis needed a kidney or some plasma, they should call me first and if they wanted to adopt me, that was fine too.

Sometimes I went for walks with Lily if Seth wasn't around, usually into town or by a river that ran near the house. Lily asked me questions about the Home, something no one besides Seth had ever done. My father didn't want to hear anything about it and my brother was only curious about the trappings of the place, as if a swimming pool could cancel out any multitude of sins.

"Did any of the girls at that place get tinkerish?" Lily asked me on one of our walks to the river. We were trying out a new pipe that she'd stolen from the Gingko Berry and I gave a startled, angry cough; it was my turn at the stem.

"That's a stupid-ass word," I said as soon as I could talk again.

"Did any of them ever touch your tits? They're so huge." Lily gave me a quick poke in my left breast and I slapped at her small, freckled hand. "Grandpa says the same thing."

"What?"

"You heard me." Lily tried to blow a smoke ring. "He said you've got huge tits and a great ass. And he said you're probably a tramp too, but who cares? He's a fucking asshole."

"Yeah, well, no argument there. I don't know what the hell Glenda sees in him."

Lily handed me the pipe and stretched out in the grass. "He used to be nicer to her. He always stops being nice to his girlfriends after a while because by then he's calling all the shots. Grandpa could put her and Seth out of that house any time he wanted to. That's how he got custody of me and my brother. He kicked our mom out of the house we were living in and then he went and told children's services she didn't have a place to live and couldn't take care of us. She started drinking again after they took us away. I hate him for that." Lily gave a short laugh, as if hating her grandfather was fun.

"You two are the best," Glenda said when she came home late from work the next night and found me and Seth in the kitchen cooking smoked sausage, fried potatoes, and green beans. "Is there enough for four? Bert's here."

Bert walked into the kitchen as she spoke. "Hi ho, lads and lassies," he said to me and Seth.

"Hi ho," Seth replied.

"Aren't you going to say hi ho?" Bert asked me.

"No." I busied myself stirring the potatoes to avoid him.

"Come on, say hi ho for me like a good girl."

Why couldn't I just say hi ho like Seth and forget about it? Because giving in to such a request always made me feel more like a whore than when I'd actually been one, especially with that 'be a good girl' business. Infantilizing and objectifying at the same time.

The evening began politely enough but immediately soured without warning while Seth and I were clearing the table. Bert stretched back contentedly in his chair and reached out to smack my ass when I walked past him, hard enough to hurt. "That's for being a bad girl," he said triumphantly.

"What the hell do you think you're doing?" Glenda cried.

As for myself, I dropped the stack of plates I was carrying into the sink and spun around, ready to decapitate Bert with anything handy but Seth grabbed me from behind and carried me out to the back porch, where we could hear Bert and Glenda arguing. From the sound of it, Bert either believed that Glenda was fooling around or he was pretending to in order to distract her from his behavior towards me since no one was laughing it off as expected.

"What would the kids say if I asked them?" Bert's voice was smarmy.

"The same damn thing that I just told you." Glenda's voice was rising the way it always did when she became upset.

"Yeah, I bet they would lie for you. Especially that little tramp."

"Don't talk about her like that, she's just a kid. And you keep your hands off her."

"If they're big enough they're old enough. Girls who bloom early always want to get started early."

"How would you feel if someone said things like that about Lily?" Glenda asked.

"Lily would never give anyone cause to," Bert said.

I knew this was true at least; whatever her other shortcomings, Lily didn't have a promiscuous reputation at school. Her mannerisms and clothes were too tomboyish and she wasn't the type to flirt any more than I was. It was tempting to speculate on Lily's preferences but I resisted the urge. Speculation would lead to temptation and temptation would lead to fiasco, one way or another. Even I had that much sense.

Everyone at school was asking questions about my living arrangements with Seth and the two of us started a rumor that we were fraternal twins separated at birth. He'd been sent to a research laboratory at Proctor & Gamble while I'd been stolen by gypsies. I wished. We stuck to the story until people got tired of hearing it and stopped asking.

Even though I knew Geraldine wouldn't be back, I was still disappointed to see her replacement, another Garfield theatre major named Marcus who had everyone recite the Solemn Silence poem five times to warm up our tongues. When that was finished he talked about his ideas for the drama club and the fall play, which was to be a seventeenth-century comedy by Molière, née Jean-Baptiste Poquelin, called *The Imaginary Invalid*.

"In those days European doctors were pretty backward and they recommended leeching, purging, and enemas for just about anything," said Marcus. "Molière couldn't stand doctors, as you'll see when you read this script. And the harlequin clown that you see on those romance novels is a symbol for a standard character in French comedies from the seventeenth century, a troublesome old man who drives everyone crazy, like Argan the invalid."

Scripts were passed out and we divided into groups and pairs to practice reading the scenes. I decided almost immediately to try for the part of Béline, the gold-digging young wife. And since M. Johnson-Mills was always praising my French accent—which sounded good mostly because of my monotone—I used it liberally.

"Oh Madame, the dear departed is deceased," Jennifer Marnetti wailed as she read the part of Toinette, the clever and loyal housemaid.

"May heaven be praised," I said, pretending that I was hearing the news about Bert. "I am finally free from a terrible burden."

"Hah!" Nick Lucas sat bolt upright, the dead husband no longer dead. I gave a short scream.

"The dear departed is not deceased," Jennifer cackled joyfully as Nick advanced upon me to deliver a piece of his mind.

The next day I went with Seth to look at the audition results on the drama club bulletin board next to the trophy case. He immediately spotted his name, having been cast as Dr. Purgon, a small but decent part. Nick Lucas had the lead, which surprised no one.

I jockeyed around people, trying to see past the boys. Argan: Nick Lucas, Toinette: Jennifer Marnetti,

Angelique: Julie Onaitis, Béline: Charity Sintz, Cléante: Brian Sayres, Dr. Diaphorus: Danny Schaedel, Thomas Diaphorus: John Supasnik, Dr. Purgon: Seth Hatton, Louison: Amy Sasaki. And so on. I left the group and went to my locker to get my French book. I hadn't studied for a week and there was a quiz. Monsieur Johnson-Mills was a martyr where I was concerned; I loved the class but was hopeless at focusing.

Halfway to French class I came skidding to a halt and ran back to the bulletin board. Everyone was gone now and it was three minutes to the bell. There it was, Béline: Charity Sintz. Could our new director have me confused with someone else? I saw Donna Supasnik walking down the hallway towards me. She was the rehearsal assistant and could tell me if a mistake had been made with the audition results.

"Why would you think that?" Donna asked. "You were really good. Your voice is so much stronger than last year and you have a great French accent."

I ran to French class and even got a B on the quiz.

Rehearsals for the Shawnee High School Players' production of *The Imaginary Invalid* ran into overtime when Brian Sayres aka Cléante fell from the scaffolding where he was hanging stage lights, literally breaking a leg. Once the paramedics arrived, we all piled into whatever cars we had access to and followed them to Saint Elizabeth's without changing out of our costumes. I was wearing a lavender dress that showed most of my cleavage and was liberally garnished with chartreuse lace per Marcus's request. It looked hideous but Marcus promised that the chartreuse would be muted to a yellowish ivory under the stage lights.

Since Brian had to keep his cast on for two months, Marcus decided to use it in the story, wedging in a couple of well-placed lines about Cléante hurting his ankle during his fight with the punk who insulted Angelique, an incident that took place offstage anyway. It worked so well that Brian would receive several compliments from audience members about the authentic look of his cast and crutches.

In the first scene I was required to make a fuss over Argan the hypochondriac invalid as he moaned and whined about his lot in life, with me crooning empty endearments after each complaint. Trying to keep them all straight seemed impossible and I worried about being replaced in the part until Marcus pointed out that since Beline was only pretending to care about Argan, it really didn't matter much if I said, "Oh, my poor chèri," when I was supposed to say, "There there, my lamb."

"Everybody except Argan knows you don't mean a word of it anyway," Marcus added. "Be a little creative."

I was. Sometimes during rehearsals I would ad-lib a few pet names to Nick of my own invention like my poor scrubble bubble or my sweet little pickle pie. Marcus loved it and for a few minutes here and there I even liked myself.

Seth faced a similar challenge in the third act as the quack Dr. Purgon. Insulted by Monsieur Argan's hesitation to follow traditional medical procedures, Seth was required to show up at Argan's home in an egotistical rage, hexing Argan susceptible to every internal disease known to man that ended with an 'itis' suffix. Unlike me, Seth couldn't ad-lib since he ran the risk of forgetting the names of the diseases and spoiling the comic effect if he were to say measles instead of colitis. We practiced our lines as we walked down the road at night.

"And from peritonitis into hepatitis!" Seth called out, holding one finger in the air the way Marcus wanted him to.

"Dr. Purgon!" I clasped my hands imploringly, filling in for Nick.

"And from hepatitis into colitis!" he continued.

"Dr. Purgon!"

"And from colitis into bursitis!"

"That's not in the script."

"And from bursitis into hideositis!"

"Dr. Purgon!"

"And from hideositis into jackoffitis, which will be the final result of your folly!" We did the diabolical laugh together as we walked into the house.

"You two are going to scare the neighbors," Glenda said from behind the battered copy of *Wifey* that she was reading.

The opening night of the play felt like my wedding night and it didn't matter that I had no one to marry. I did my makeup the way Marcus wanted, with distinct triangles of pale violet greasepaint over the base coat of pancake, followed by generous applications of eyeliner and mascara. My impossible hair was neatly tucked under a white house cap with a ribbon that matched my lavender dress. Julie Onaitis wore a pink dress and matching ribbon in her cap, as did Amy Sasaki, who played younger sister Louison. Jennifer's cap had a black ribbon to go with her maid's costume. Seth wore a black pancake hat and a long black robe, an old graduation gown with a decorative front made to conceal the zipper.

I nearly lost my nerve in the first act after seeing Grandma and Grandpa O'Bryan in the audience. Then I remembered that they were probably still on the drama club's mailing list. I wondered why they'd come, given that sentiment was hardly their forte.

"Hello," I said to Grandma and Grandpa during intermission, hoping they couldn't hear my voice shaking. "What brings you here?"

"We got a card in the mail and thought we'd come," Grandpa said flatly, his tone of voice effectively killing any last hope I might have that their sentiments towards me had changed and that I was no longer going to be known as the girl whose family couldn't stand her.

"We forgot you were in the drama club," Grandma said. "I see they finally let you be in a play. I guess they needed a girl that looked mature."

Seth and Nick Lucas stood back as if to catch me when I fainted but I picked up my trailing lavender skirt and walked away without saying another word. I did the second act with a scowl on my face and by act three I was only too happy to run screaming offstage after being tricked by Jennifer/Toinette into revealing my true colors, just as my grandparents had tricked me by showing up unannounced to remind me of my true value and reduce my stage debut to the level of a preschool Bible verse recital. The O'Bryans stayed for the short cookie and punch reception that was held after the curtain call as well, mostly keeping to themselves and watching while other people came up to me and told me how good I'd been in the show.

"You looked so pretty up there," Mrs. Schaedel said to me with her arm around Danny. "And that look on your face when Argan came back to life was priceless."

The O'Bryans snickered quietly at Mrs. Schaedel's naivety as they drank the punch and nibbled on the cookies being served.

But my mood lifted at Julie Onaitis's cast party when the prerequisite Mad Libs books were produced, with Becca filling in the blanks since she could never come up with any words. "I need an adjective, somebody," she said.

"Insipid," I suggested.

"How do you spell that?" Becca asked. I spelled it for her, slowly and carefully.

"That was mean," Seth said later that night when we were in our pajamas.

"How often do you get a chance like that?" I asked.

"Not too often."

Glenda and Bert came to the closing night show. Glenda enthused over our efforts while Bert stood a pace behind her and stared at me, smiling as if he and I shared a secret. Lily hadn't come, which was no surprise. We hadn't been seeing much of her lately.

"You kids were so terrific," Glenda said. "I nearly peed my pants laughing."

"Don't be so vulgar," Bert said.

"Don't be so tight-assed," Glenda replied.

"How about if we stop at King Kwik for a Pepsi?" I asked quickly.

"Or a Coke," Seth added. "Which one do you think is better, Pepsi or Coke?"

The next morning Seth and I had to drag ourselves out of bed like constipated slugs. Post-production letdown—we'd been forewarned by Marcus. It didn't seem possible that the physical and emotional energy we'd blown for the past few weeks was for something now finished and with no tangible evidence that it ever existed in the first place. We missed the bus and walked to school since Glenda's truck was missing its carburetor; Bert was still mad at her. Seth's father took him out to dinner that night for his aunt's birthday, leaving me to wallow in post-production letdown on my own, and Glenda put a frozen pizza in the oven for our dinner to cheer me up.

"Do you think we could get a kitten?" I asked Glenda while we were eating. "They've got a sign out for free ones at that little red brick house on the corner of White Birch and Matthews Fork."

"Bert doesn't like cats," Glenda said. "He's kind of afraid of them."

"Pissant," I said, even though I knew I had no right to complain since my place in the house was due in part to Bert's grace and favor. Grace and favor was a new expression I'd learned in English class during a lesson about Charles Dickens, *David Copperfield*, and social norms for the Victorian era. If something wasn't yours by right, but extended to you as a courtesy subject to change or withdrawal, it was something you had by the giver's grace and favor. Fall into disfavor and you were up shit creek.

Seth came home from the birthday dinner in good spirits, needling my chronic jealousy. When he tried to tell me about his evening I cut him off and went out to the garage to smoke a roach. Outside I saw Bert crouching beneath the living room windowsill, where he could easily see Glenda.

"Don't tell her I'm out here," Bert ordered, confident of my obedience for reasons I couldn't imagine.

I didn't tell Glenda. Instead I told Seth since he was the first one I ran into after beating a cheetah back into the house. Seth told Glenda, who only sighed.

"God, he's so off the wall sometimes." Glenda closed her book and got up from the couch. "Well kids, I think I'm going to hit the hay and I suggest you do the same. There's school tomorrow."

"What about the Herbert?" I pointed to the living room window, not sure if Glenda realized that Bert was literally and not figuratively hiding outside.

"He doesn't have school, he can stay up as late as he wants to." Glenda yawned.

"Don't worry about it," Seth said. "He's always doing weird shit like that."

I didn't ask what I was supposed to worry about if a crazy man hiding outside the house didn't qualify. I took two towels from the bathroom closet and draped them over the lower curtain rod on my bedroom window. Then I opened the window a few inches and sat down to smoke. Rustling noises came from outside.

"Glenda's in bed," I called out the window. "You know this isn't her room." There was a sound of rapid footsteps outside as Bert scurried off like a rat. I allowed the roach to kick in and smooth over my desire to run him down with his own truck.

Chapter Twenty-Four

The township police paid a visit to Bert near the end of the school year, acting on a tip that Lily was responsible for the robbery of a house in their neighborhood. The police chief in Baumburg felt sorry for Lily and Bert because of Lily's mother and offered to smooth things over if some stolen jewelry that had sentimental value to the owner was returned. In this event, no charges would be filed.

Bert responded by going into one of his usual rampages against the police for even hinting that his grandchild might have stolen anything and ordered them to leave, which they politely did, only to return two hours later with a search warrant. The jewelry was found under Lily's bed and she was whisked off to Juvenile Hall in Anderson, the Piqua County seat. Glenda had the unenviable task of placating Bert, who kept insisting that the police chief had stolen the jewelry himself and planted it in Lily's bedroom.

"Bert would drink a bucket of piss if Lily told him it was lemonade," I said to Seth as I reached for a pair of scissors. We were sitting on the living room floor with Nick Lucas and Danny Schaedel, rooting through a pile of old magazines for pictures to put in a collage about mental health that we were making for extra credit. My best find was a close-up of someone's eye that took up half a page.

"Decent," Danny said. "We'll put that in the center with a caption: 'Is Big Brother Watching You?'"

Our health teacher took the class to the city park on the last day of school. Most of the kids grouped up to throw Frisbees or play softball. I wandered off on my own and came to a stream that was hidden from the rest of the park by a thick row of sycamore trees. Without hesitating, I slipped off my shoes and socks and waded in. The bottom was covered with smooth, mossy rocks and the water was sweetly chilly. I waded upstream several yards where there was a visible bend. After getting around the bend I took off my shirt and bra.

A shrill whistle came from above. I looked up and saw Nick and Danny leering down from the trees they were perched in at the edge of the stream like little boys playing Robin Hood, for shit's sake. I slapped my arms over my chest.

"Take it off, Charity!" Nick cheered.

"Yeah, don't be enslaved to bourgeois hang-ups," Danny added from his tree.

"I'll hang you up by your balls in a minute," I said as I replaced my clothes, pleased with my comeback. The boys made loud, disappointed sounds as they climbed down to join me and we stayed in the water until everyone was rounded up for the return to school. Our collage got a B-plus.

Seth and I waited until no one was left at school except the janitors and began our annual custom of searching through the hallways for anything useful from the emptied lockers. As usual we didn't leave empty-handed and as usual I couldn't believe how many of our schoolmates came from families that could afford to throw away scarcely touched school supplies or perfectly good clothes and shoes. My best finds were a pair of barely worn boy's Adidas that fit me well enough and a paperback copy of *The Bell Jar*.

As soon as we got home there was a call from the manager at Baskin Robbins where Seth had a new summer job, asking him to fill in for someone who was sick or at least pretending to be. Seth changed his clothes and walked back into town while I settled down to have a closer look at our haul from school. *The Bell Jar* was begging to be read but I wanted to wait until after supper before starting it to avoid any interruptions.

Bert's truck pulled into the driveway a few minutes after Seth left. It was only two o'clock and he knew that Glenda never made it home before six or even seven if it was term-paper season, which it was. He'd probably forgotten that it was the last day of school since Lily was still in Anderson.

"Hey, girlie," Bert said as he came through the door. "What are you doing, skipping school?"

"We only had a half day today. It was the last day."

"Sure it was," he said, settling himself on the couch. He flipped through some of the dissected magazines and newspapers from the day before. "So where's the boy at?"

"He just left for work," I said, slow-witted as usual. Mrs. Kelly had warned us back at the Home about dealing with situations like this one. First try to slip out of the house as quickly as possible to avoid the degenerate in question if you saw him coming up the path. And never admit that you were alone if you didn't have to.

"And what are you doing with yourself besides playing hooky?" Bert asked with a vacant grin on his face.

"We only had a half day today," I repeated.

"Well, you've probably skipped other days," he said. "So what else do you do then, besides live in my house and eat up all of Glenda's food?"

"I don't eat up all the food." My voice shook; like most sixteen-year-old girls, I would have more easily forgiven someone for shooting me than for implying that I overindulged and took up more space than I was entitled to as a result.

"Well, you probably eat a lot of it." Bert didn't seem to have much interest in what he was saying. "Not like my Lil. She's a toothpick."

That was true; Lily was built like a bobby pin.

"She doesn't have them big bosoms like you do."

My back was to Bert but I sensed that he'd shifted from his seat to move closer to me. I moved out of his reach and went to the kitchen for a Coke, stalling the showdown as I wondered what form it would take. The idea that I could inure myself to the unpleasant surprises was a joke fit for the gallows.

"Come back in here a minute, I want a word with you," Bert called from the living room.

I walked out of the kitchen, standing stiffly at the doorway.

"Now damn it, come all the way in." I'd never heard Bert swear before. "There's some important things you need to understand and I'm going to try and help you here so you can just wipe that snotty look off your face when I'm talking to you." He was amused and reproachful at the same time, sure of his role. "You need to know about men."

"I know about men," I tried to joke. "You can't live with them and you can't flush them down the john without killing your pipes."

"You need to know how to behave with men," Bert continued, oblivious. "You need to learn to like men instead of trying to mess with other girls like Lily." He unbarred the last hold. "It's on account of you she went to jail."

And so it emerged that during Bert's most recent visit to Juvenile Hall, Lily had shed a lake's worth of tears after confessing to him that the diamond ring she'd stolen was to be a present for me. Following this sad news was Lily's report that I had seduced her the previous summer and now held her in emotional captivity, exhorting her to commit actions that she would have otherwise dreamed not of. It was classic Lily and would have been hilarious if not for Bert standing in front of me and proposing to save me from my deviant self by screwing me. Screwing was the right word; it had the sound of orthopedic devices.

"What about Glenda?" I pushed Bert's hand away once more, hoping to shame him into backing off.

"Glenda doesn't need to be bothered with this. None of this is her fault." Bert and I had somehow become accomplices while the rest of the world was an innocent bystander. "Let's go to your room now."

Bert stepped closer and put his hand on my ass in a way that left no room for misinterpretation. He had a faint smell of mothballs; who used mothballs for everyday clothes? I ducked away from him and went to my room to get my book bag. If I was fast I could get out of the house and away from the senile possum in heat roaming inside it. But Bert followed me to my room, where I was pacing and considering my nonexistent options. I was tempted to slam the door in his face but there was no lock on it and I was afraid that any dramatic action on my part would be followed with an equal and opposite one on his.

I came out of the bedroom with my book bag and Bert nonchalantly grabbed my elbow as if I were a kitten trying to escape. That was probably what spurred me into using more force than was necessary when I rammed my elbow into his ribcage and followed up with an evil and satisfying crack to his shin with my new Adidas. Bert made noises like a newborn donkey.

"You're a sick-ass billy goat and you've got a sack of fish shit for a mind!" I yelled over his whimpering. "You should be castrated and have your hands chopped off!" The beau geste was even more satisfying than kicking Jerry Corbett into the drainage ditch back in sixth grade.

"Honey, I am so sorry," Glenda cried the next day while I packed. "I know Lily's full of it but this house does belong to Bert and I have to do what he says. Seth and I have to have a place to live."

"You could get an apartment," I said to Glenda. "And I could give you some money from my job this summer, to help pay the rent. I could ask my father to give you some money too, for my food and stuff."

Glenda wouldn't look me in the eye, which meant my cause was lost. I wondered how my family was dealing with the prospect of having me around their necks once more and considered the possibility of asking to return to the Home for all of two seconds. Better to stand at the side of the road with my thumb out and something sharp within easy reach.

Seth stuck his head in the doorway of the bedroom that wasn't mine anymore. "Need any help?"

I flung *The Bell Jar* at him, knowing I was being hateful but knowing it only made me uglier. My patience with good but futile intentions was used up. Seth withdrew.

Bert decided to make himself available when my father arrived to pick me up and I came outside with my footlocker to find him speaking to Dad with a fake expression of pious concern on his face. It made me want to use something sharp right then and there, though a bludgeon would have done just as well. My father quickly turned to look at me as if I were the last person in the world he expected to see. Then he immediately swung back to Bert, fists balled. I had the pleasure of seeing Bert step back, hands raised placatingly.

"No need to be that way, son," Bert said. "I'm just telling you so you can get her some help. There's places you can send her."

"She doesn't need any help," my father said in the voice that Trilby and I knew as Red Alert. I opened the passenger door of Dad's truck and got in. He said nothing to me during the ride, glaring at the road in front of him. When we got home he retired to his bedroom with a bottle of Smirnoff's and refused to come out for supper. Annette flung the pot roast, potatoes, and carrots on the table for the rest of us, a meal prepared with the aim of putting Dad in a good mood, or at least a sober one. Instead it was only me and Trilby at the table to appreciate her efforts.

"Bless, O Lord, this food to our use and us to thy service. In Jesus' name, amen," Annette said with head bowed and hands folded. Trilby and I had barely finished our own amens before she turned to me. "Well, your dad's drinking himself stupid so I hope you're happy."

I braced myself for a verbal barrage but Annette wasn't up to it. Trilby gamely tried to hold up a decent table conversation by asking me about school. I answered in monosyllables and ignored his descriptions of the sports he was involved in. Annette ate in silence and mopped sweat off her face with a paper towel.

"Why didn't you just fix sandwiches instead of having the oven on half the day for a roast?" I asked.

Annette slammed her butter knife down. "If I want your opinion on my cooking or my anything I will damn well ask for it and I promise you this won't be happening anytime soon."

In this respect Annette kept her word and spoke to me only when it was necessary from that point on, which meant there was yet a balm in Gilead.

Chapter Twenty-Five

A *Hindu belief regarding horoscopes: anyone born when Mars is in the first, second, fourth, seventh, eighth, or twelfth house of the astrology ascendant chart is known as a manglik, someone whose first marriage will end in death or divorce. Some mangliks will remove the stigma from their horoscope by taking part in a marriage ceremony to a peepal or banana tree. In some cases the tree is burned down at the end of the ceremony to guarantee that the manglik is a true widow or widower who can now be safely wed to a member of their own species.*

I was the only senior in the first period gym class at Hazelwood High School. The others were all freshman girls who immediately made bids for my friendship when it became known that Trilby was my brother. I'd failed to notice that he was growing into what most of the girls liked to call a hunk, an expression I found too stupid to even complain about, while the bolder ones referred to him as a bitching fox. Trilby was equally polite to each of these girls, never flirting with anyone unless he had true designs. His Quakerish sense of honor only added to his appeal.

One of my few friends at Hazelwood High was Lucy, a girl who worked with me in the school library. Lucy and I sang in the school choir together and usually got rides to and from the concerts with Lucy's mother Cleo or her older brother Jaime since my father and Annette refused to take me anywhere that wasn't strictly necessary. I had an Ohio driver's license acquired with Seth's help but asking to borrow Dad's truck or Annette's Nova would have been treated like a bad joke.

Lucy was friendly with a reasonable sense of humor and circumspect habits even though she had more freedom to come and go than most girls. Lucy's father was out of the picture and Cleo worked long hours at a tire factory near Cincinnati. She also had high blood pressure and spent most of her free time sleeping or in front of the TV. Cleo kept skillets full of used grease in her oven.

I sent repentant postcards to Seth, which he answered sporadically. From one of his responses I learned of Lily's release from Juvenile Hall shortly before Halloween and her confession that she'd lied about me seducing her—Lily was having no end of fun tormenting Bert with how she'd managed to bullshit him, Seth wrote—but no one apologized or suggested that I be reinstated. The people I needed didn't need me, what a surprise.

I showed Seth's letter to my father but he only gave it a superficial scan before putting it to one side, refusing to discuss the subject. He must not have even told Annette, who would have gloried in such queer and evil tidings for me. She was already trying to convince Dad that I should be sent to the state hospital in Madison and his strongest inclination these days was to keep me from drawing attention to myself. I didn't even have to go to church anymore.

Lucy's brother Jaime was nineteen, an unpretentious country boy who liked painting and drawing. When Lucy called me at his request to suggest a date between the two of us, I agreed and we spent the evening getting high in his bedroom. Jaime did a sketch of me as I lay on the floor and sang Simon and Garfunkel songs. We impressed each other minimally well.

"Do you think I'm any good?" Jaime asked shyly as he held up the finished product, which bore a resemblance to me and at least a million other girls.

"It's pretty," I said truthfully.

"You think so?" He looked tenderly pleased. "Do you think I could like, draw you in the nude? With no clothes on? Just sometime?"

"Well, you couldn't draw me in the nude with clothes on," I replied, approximating the level of coyness that respectable girls were supposed to assume at such times. My response was part of the courtship ritual; when Jaime had suggested drawing me nude, he meant he hoped we could have sex one day relatively soon. The connotation of my reply was that hoping was reasonable.

Jaime was flattered to learn about my intact hymen, which made no sense to me at all. After a one-month courtship period that we agreed was long enough to keep me from looking cheap, he arranged for a time when Cleo and Lucy would be out of the house. On the appointed evening we sat on the floor of his bedroom discussing how best to get started.

"Are you on the pill?" Jaime asked me.

"No." There was no place in Hazelwood to get the pill without a doctor's prescription and no way to see the doctor without insurance or Medicaid. And any high school girl who tried to fill a prescription for them at one of the two drugstores in town was sure to be reported to her parents and possibly even to Mr. Donnell, the high school principal.

"I don't think I have any rubbers. Is it ok if I pull out in time?"

"I guess that'll be all right." I was getting impatient, not having expected the occasion to be so cut-rate.

Jaime went slowly, which helped, and it seemed to take a long time. I didn't have an orgasm, which I wasn't expecting anyway, and I didn't bleed, which I was expecting since it hurt like hell. Jaime was surprised too.

"It's weird that you didn't bleed," he said. "You were as tight as a square knot down there."

Jaime and I began spending Friday and Saturday nights together, sometimes doubling with Lucy and her boyfriend Johnny, a smoking buddy of Jaime's who worked at the tire factory with Cleo. Jaime didn't have a job, although Cleo gave him spending money from time to time in return for doing household chores and keeping the car running. Most of the time we stayed home and watched TV.

I met Jaime's father Roy only once when he stopped by to visit one evening shortly before Easter. Roy was accompanied by his second wife, a woman with hair bleached the color of Swiss cheese going bad and skin like a dirty, overused towel. Roy himself was the kind of man that Clint Eastwood or Charles Bronson would have cheerfully thrashed eight ways to Sunday and I would have enjoyed watching it.

"Well, it's about time you two made an appearance," Roy said when Jaime and I came downstairs after giving up hope that his father might leave before propriety dictated that we show ourselves. "I would of come upstairs to say hey but I thought you might be bumping and grinding."

"Why the hell didn't you tell him to eat shit and die where he stood?" I demanded when Jaime and I were safely back in his bedroom.

"This is the eighties," he said defensively. "Girls are supposed to be strong and fight their own battles while they're out having so much fun."

"And what'll you do while I turn a fire hose on your dad? Run around looking for a tit to suck?"

"Hell, yes."

We fought and made up, which took the rest of the evening, and Jaime drove me home at one in the morning. Since it was Friday and the school year was nearly over for the seniors anyway, I didn't think it was important, especially since I didn't even have an official curfew. Annette was in the mood to see it differently on that particular evening.

"If you think you're such a bigshot just because you're a senior then you can just move on out of here," Annette said, fairly smacking her lips in anticipation of a showdown. I looked at my father, who drained his glass and said nothing. "You're not going to go out sleeping with your boyfriend and then come back here like it's some kind of flophouse for tramps."

In the assumed privacy of their bedroom, Annette urged Dad to send me to Madison before I got pregnant. He was still saying no, it would make the family look bad and what if they gave me shock treatments or a lobotomy and turned me into a zombie? Annette insisted that it would be an improvement but my father held firm, for the moment at least. I decided to keep my footlocker packed and ready to go in case he faltered.

But an escape route was soon to present itself. "Mom wants to move to Cincinnati," Jaime told me on a Saturday afternoon while we were parked on Green Creek Road and debating on whether or not it was warm enough to go skinny-dipping.

"Shit, when?" I asked, reaching for a cigarette.

"As soon as school's out and Lucy graduates. You and Lucy."

I tried to take stock. Once school was out, any legal obligations to me that my father and Annette felt bound to observe would be out the door and most likely so would I, in or out of a straitjacket. There were no jobs in the area except farm work, which was seasonal. Even if a job could have been found, I still had no car and there weren't any buses or taxis in Hazelwood. There were almost no apartments either, only houses, trailers, and shacks. And going to college was no more viable an option than sailing the outer rings of Saturn as far as I knew. College was for kids who were allowed to know how to make things happen.

Cleo gave her permission for me to join the family in Cincinnati. She knew about Dad and Annette and often expressed her pity for my situation to Lucy, which felt like barrel scrapings, but I was in no position to be stuck-up. I finished packing my footlocker and told Trilby that it was filled with old books I hoped to sell at one of the secondhand stores in the city.

The house Cleo chose was an older, two-story frame with dark brown vinyl clapboard siding in a quieter corner of the Westwood neighborhood. The idea of neighborhoods was something I'd only known about in theory and now I saw several that could have made a bite-sized meal of Mount Olive. It was like the first day of high school again. Numbers meant prospects and possibilities if I could ever learn to negotiate my way through the crowds.

On our first morning in the new house I went out to explore and job-hunt, climbing aboard my first metro bus and paying the sixty-five cent fare—soon to go up a dime—as if it were the visitors' entrance to the Statue of Liberty. As I carefully dropped the necessary coins into a contraption that resembled an empty gumball machine, the bus driver must have noticed the shamrock-green color of my horns. He handed me a bus schedule.

"You new to the area?"

"Yeah," I said as I unfolded the schedule and tried to figure it out. "I'm looking for a job."

"South Vine's a good place to start if you want to try the fast food joints," he said. "But stay away from Over-the-Rhine. It's dangerous there."

I made a note to visit Over-the-Rhine as soon as possible and got off the bus at Third and Vine, stepping onto the sidewalk and into a swift current of humanity that had no compunctions about laying hands on me or anyone else to nudge us along if we were standing in their paths. As I eased my way in like a car at an intersection, I noticed that my view was mostly of chests, shoulders, and necks, which meant at five foot four I was short and hadn't even known it. An elderly, crimson-skinned man wearing a wool plaid jacket in spite of the heat asked me for a quarter, the first of many.

"Can't you go to a church or someplace to get some food?" I asked, wanting to cry at the sight of him.

"Stupid twat," he said in a dry, tired voice.

"Would you like to buy a rose, miss?" a voice at my elbow asked. "Picked fresh off the bush this morning." A round-bellied man wearing only a beard and a bedsheet was holding a bucketful of red, pink, and yellow roses. I turned him down; roses smelled too sweet for me and they had thorns.

None of the fast-food restaurants were hiring and I was afraid to try any of the nicer places in my M*A*S*H t-shirt, everyday jeans, and grubby Adidas. The next day I tried some of the malls but quickly realized they were out of my reach. The mall shops wanted girls who smiled all the time—or at least a part of it—and who could chatter with the customers in the Valley Girl sub-dialect, which would mean having to use expressions like 'truly outrageous' and 'that's so gay.' After three nerve-wracking weeks, the only place desperate enough to take me on was the Ho Ho Wok, a new Chinese restaurant fifteen minutes from Cleo's house by bus.

"The Ho Ho Wok. Sounds like the name of a dance step," I heard Lucy telling Cleo that night while they were watching the late show in the living room and I was in the kitchen looking for a Sominex.

"Now if only Jaime would find some work," Cleo continued.

"Yeah, right."

Lucy's sarcasm was well-founded since Jaime had no interest in looking for a job or exploring the city with me. His habits of staying in his room, drawing, and getting high were easy enough to transplant from Roosevelt County to Cincinnati. At the end of the summer I started pushing for us to get a place of our own, hoping it might give Jaime some motivation.

"Why do we need to move when Mom said we could stay here?" he asked.

"Because I'm going to be eighteen soon and I'd like to celebrate in a home that doesn't have skillets of stale grease sitting inside the oven," I said.

"How am I supposed to concentrate on drawing if I'm spending most of the day flipping burgers to pay for an apartment?"

My conscience bit. "I'll find a cheap place," I promised. "And maybe I could find another job too."

"Another restaurant might be nice," Jaime said. "Everybody loves those leftovers you bring home."

Jaime, Cleo, and Lucy were at first suspicious of the stir-fry and spring rolls that I brought home from work, just like my Grandma East confronting her first pizza back in 1973. Chinese food was still a novelty in Cincinnati but the aromas were breaking down the cultural barriers. It wasn't long before someone in the house was asking me to bring home their favorite dishes at least once a week.

Tian Tsai, the owner of the Ho Ho Wok, did most of the cooking himself. He was a dour, conscientious man whose English was nominal. Since his arrival from Taiwan at the age of eighteen, most of Tian Tsai's time was spent standing over a wok or a cutting board and doing his father or his older brother's bidding. The Ho Ho meant financial and psychological freedom but left Tian Tsai with no time or energy for cozy nighttime ESL classes.

Tian Tsai communicated to me through his wife Hsiu Ching, who spoke more fluent English even though she hadn't been in the U.S. as long. Seven years after her arrival from Taipei as Tian Tsai's bride-to-be, Hsiu Ching was a quick-tempered young suburbanite with a porcelain doll face, a charge account at Lazarus, and two beautiful children who would grow up to be twice the sizes of their parents. Hsiu Ching was the excitable type and under duress she became a screamer, screaming at me to hurry up, slow down, ask fewer questions, smile more, and find some shoes to wear that didn't make my size nine feet look so big, preferably all at once. Hsiu Ching would never be able to pronounce my name and at first never called me anything besides stupid girl. She had trouble pronouncing that too.

"Stupid girl, what's wrong with you? I say twenty times, don't give customers too much noodles, we lose money."

"Stupid girl, you give house-fried rice to table twelve, not plain-fried rice. What the hell you thinking?"

Sarah, the only other full-time employee, was Hsiu Ching's antithesis: a tall, wide-shouldered woman with thick, chestnut brown hair that reached her waist and bovine hazel eyes. A defector from one of the Amish communities in northern Indiana, Sarah had eloped with an outsider and was subsequently disowned by her family. She talked about her husband Ben and their four children when she wasn't waiting on customers or trying to undo a disaster of my making. Ben was a stay-at-home father who did freelance carpentry in their basement, a skill he'd learned in part from volunteering at a barn-raising and cozying up to Sarah's father and brother, both of whom were master craftsmen.

"That was before he stole me from them," Sarah said. She made no attempt to conceal her pride at having been stolen, which meant she was acclimated to modern life even though her voice still had a whisper of a German accent.

I found a one-bedroom apartment not far from Cleo's house for two hundred and fifty dollars a month. It was next door to a small, privately owned grocery store just like the one in Mount Olive where I'd once stolen Marlboros and candy bars, right down to the heavy pneumatic door that eased itself shut. The best part was the old-fashioned deli case to the right of the entrance that held ground beef and cold cuts. The owner made sandwiches to order and I had a bologna on white with mayo. The bread was Butternut and the bologna was Eckrich, both my favorites. The apartment was clearly meant to be.

It was a small place, with only one large closet in the bedroom. The kitchen was the size of a bathroom and the bathroom the size of a walk-in closet. Sliding glass doors in the living room led to a postage stamp balcony. I chose bamboo blinds and a papa-san couch from Pier One. We were on the third floor, with a quartet of Mormon missionaries below us who served as an occasional audience for my hausfrau act. I was completely in the dark as to how a proper couple should be perceived by those around them and acting naturally never occurred to me.

Soon I discovered that without Jaime's family to serve as a distraction, everything up to and including his breathing began to irritate me. He also wanted to have sex every night, regardless of my schedule. If I was too tired, he complained about being the one who did all the work.

"It doesn't matter who's doing the work, I can't sleep if it's being done," I said, wanting to hit him.

Jaime also liked to sleep with one arm under my shoulders and the other lying across my stomach in a way that made his elbow poke into my bladder, which meant having to get up and use the bathroom at least once after getting into bed. No one in a soap opera, liquor ad, or MTV music video ever had to use the bathroom. And when climaxing took Jaime more than half an hour—admittedly I wasn't much help—he became hurt when I nodded off.

"I've got to be at work in six hours," I said. "Why can't you just leave me alone? I'm so fucking tired all the time and you won't do a damn thing to help so why can't you at least let me sleep?"

"I'm trying to help now." Jaime looked sad and sounded ridiculous. "I'm trying to address your sexual needs, aren't I?" He sounded like he was quoting one of the more pretentious articles they sometimes ran in *Penthouse*. If a gun had been handy I might have used it. On myself or on Jaime but not both of us. One way or another, I wanted to be alone. Old prayers to be wanted and needed tossed back in my face.

Sometimes I couldn't sleep anyway, no matter how tired I was. Wide awake at two in the morning, I'd sit in the living room, polishing off one Marlboro after the other. While the air filled with blue smoke, I went through my collection of mental pictures, taking another look at my brother's christening at the Presbyterian church or Lindy Albertson on the school playground making chicken noises. Or Kenny the truck driver teaching me how to smoke pot after I serviced him, me and Seth practicing lines from *The Imaginary Invalid* as we walked down the road to his house. Everything had inexplicably led me to a small, spick and span apartment in the sauerkraut and Oktoberfest capitol of southern Ohio, complete with a pseudo-spouse whose genitilia met the required specs.

Everything I had belonged to me for no other reason than chance.

Sometimes I would shake off my melancholy by focusing on Hsiu Ching's most recent tirade or the latest mini-feast prepared by Tian Tsai for everyone's late afternoon lunch. I liked thinking about the restaurant; it was almost like being inside a foreign country where the rules were different and it was possible to recreate myself with people who expected strange behavior from me because I was an *adoka* girl, which Sarah said was a Taiwanese slang word for foreigner that literally meant 'big nose.' Proud of my sense of smell, I refused to be offended by it.

I started keeping red wine in the apartment and sometimes had two or three glasses in the evening. Jaime didn't like it; I was a lightweight and it didn't take more than that for me to become tipsy. Observing his displeasure, I began to drink more, hoping to turn him off with my stupors and vomiting.

"Stop guzzling that shit, you know it makes you puke," he said once, grabbing the carafe of Paul Masson from me.

"It's life that's making me puke, not wine," I said with a drunk's laugh. "Life and sauerkraut."

Jaime never hit me but sometimes he shook me until I blacked out, which happened easily with my low blood pressure. He always offered tearful apologies after each incident and blamed them on artistic temperament. Since I saw no future for the two of us, I made no demands for Jaime to change his ways. My failure to lay down any laws led him to assume that all was well and he returned to his pastels and watercolors, maybe even getting a small charge from the incidents.

The restaurant was closed on Mondays, which left me free to stay up late on Sunday nights. Sometimes I left the apartment and wandered through the streets in the dark for hours at a time, conjecturing on the lives of the people inside the houses behind the drawn curtains and shutters who were peacefully asleep and unaware of the ghoul standing outside their fenced yards. Everything was black, white, or gray under the streetlights, like an old TV show with characters who were blissfully ignorant of anything that took place after 1962.

Chapter Twenty-Six

Jaime came back to the apartment late one night after a visit to his mother's and became suspicious at the sight of the empty carafe of Paul Masson and an equally empty Sominex bottle. He drove me to the hospital, where a young-looking doctor administered ipecac and berated me for wasting his time. At his age he could easily have been an intern or resident working 36-hour shifts who was one step away from divorce court and possibly attempting to smoke a peace pipe with his wife before being called in to see about me. It was equally possible that he'd been about to score with a nurse in the on-call room.

"You know you can go to jail in the state of New York for this," the doctor said.

"Can I smoke in here?" Jaime asked.

"Only if you want to blow us all to hell and back." The doctor jerked his thumb toward the oxygen tank sitting three feet away from us.

"You know, maybe your stepmother wasn't totally wrong about you belonging in a nuthouse," Jaime said to me when the doctor was out of the room. He took me back to the apartment and went to Cleo's to spend the night. Finding myself alone was at first startling, then blissful, even with the prune taste of the ipecac in the back of my throat and my stomach violently sore and still threatening to erupt at odd intervals.

One week later I left the house for a late-night walk and didn't come home, though not by design. Prowling until my knees gave out, I sat on a fire escape to rest and my eyes closed without warning. When they opened again it was daylight, my purse was gone, and I was late for work, a first for me. Hsiu Ching was spoiling to pitch a fit when I arrived, partly for my tardiness and partly because Jaime, for whom she had no liking, had been calling the restaurant looking for me.

"You tell him no more calling here," Hsiu Ching said. "He always talk stupid on the phone, tell me 'sayonara.' What the hell for he say sayonara? He want to talk Japanese, he can call Samurai Garden downtown and say sayonara all day. I got too much work to do, no time to play Japanese for him."

It was another one of Jaime's irritating habits that he always ignored me when I tried to share what I learned at work, like the fact that China and Japan were about as much alike as America and Russia, never minding the variables of Taiwan and Hong Kong.

"They're all the same," Jaime would laugh. "How about if you pretend to be a geisha for me tonight?"

"I'll break up with him," I said to Hsiu Ching as if the idea had only just occurred to me. She was cheerful for the rest of the day, pleased that I was minding her opinion so respectfully.

My chance to leave came soon after that when Jaime went with Lucy and Cleo to visit his grandmother in Middletown for the weekend. Our lease was about to expire on the apartment and I called the landlord to explain that I'd be forfeiting the security deposit and moving out. It would give Jaime a month to decide whether to find a job or return to Cleo's nest.

The downtown YWCA rented rooms on a monthly basis for thirty percent of the renter's income, with no full-time students, children, or pets allowed. A communal kitchen was on the premises and single-user bathrooms were in the halls. Since relying on tips made my income unpredictable, a figure of five hundred dollars a month was determined to be a fair claim and I handed over a hundred and fifty dollars in cash for the first month's rent.

My first morning at the Y began when I heard a girl down the hall complaining to someone about how dry the air was and how she hoped the Salvation Army would be serving pancakes for breakfast. The clock said quarter till six; breakfast at the SA would be served until 6:45 a.m. and everyone had to be finished and out the door by seven.

My resident's card from the Y gave me the option of eating breakfast there but I went to the Dunkin Donuts across the street from the Ho Ho instead. Every day I walked by women who slept in stairwells and lined up at the back door of McDonald's at closing time. Sometimes I was tempted to join them; it was ages since I'd had a Big Mac. I held off out of guilt since food was one commodity I had no trouble acquiring. Tian Tsai never failed to set a good table for all of us, especially now that Sarah was pregnant again.

The restaurant was subjected to a blitzkrieg of hysterical phone calls from Jaime. When his threats of suicide by phone failed to move me, he came to the restaurant in person after closing time and waved a butcher knife for everyone to see. Though I knew he was intending to hurt himself—or at least make me think he was—the others assumed he meant to use the knife on me and Sarah called the police, who sent a male/female team out to investigate. Jaime was sent to the hospital for evaluation and I was questioned about my part in the incident.

"You know, if you were just using this guy to get a place to live, that was a really cruel thing to do," the male police officer said. "You can't treat someone like that and not expect them to react badly."

Hsiu Ching piped up indignantly. "That boy, he's plenty stupid, can't do nothing. This girl, she always work hard and pay the rent for them, pay for everything."

I allowed Hsiu Ching to continue without interfering, basking in the support instead of acknowledging the truth that I had in fact used Jaime, having been in love with nothing more than the idea of staying out of a padded cell and moving to a place where I could find a job. And for this reason I cried, piling on the hypocrisy by allowing everyone to assume it was because my feelings were injured by the curt manners of the Queen City's finest. I took a temporary vow of celibacy.

Tian Tsai's older brother Chung came to help out at the restaurant for a month while Hsiu Ching was visiting her family in Taiwan. Chung insisted that I call him Uncle and as Uncle Chung he was a mixed blessing. Sometimes he brought a box of candy or a half-gallon of Cookies n' Cream for me and Sarah and we were expected to repay the favors by pretending to respect him.

"Hey Sarah, you got a big belly," Uncle Chung laughed. Sarah was seven months along by now.

"You have a big butt," Sarah replied.

"Hey, that's not nice," Uncle Chung said. "Why don't you be sweet, like Cherry?"

"Up yours," I said in a friendly way. I didn't like being called Cherry but I knew it was the best Uncle Chung could do.

"You need spanking, little girl."

"You need to get out of my face unless you want to make these wontons yourself."

Tian Tsai was becoming better disposed towards me, possibly because of our similar natures. Like mine, his expression was usually one of grim determination, regardless of mood, and our social skills were equally deficient. The customers preferred Sarah, who never forgot people's names and had no trouble making conversations with perfect strangers. In my favor I was punctual, conscientious, and trustworthy, lacking the imagination to be otherwise without feeling guilty about it. For these reasons my uninviting countenance was partially forgiven.

Although I was too self-conscious to try learning Mandarin or the Taiwanese dialect like Sarah, Tian Tsai and I developed a system of gestures that were used for communicating pertinent information. If I stood in the kitchen doorway and jerked my head to the right it meant I was going next door to the video store to buy a Pepsi or rent a movie. If there was no objection on his part, Tian Tsai would nod. Sometimes he came out and gave me money from the cash register; depending on how much it was, I was able to tell if he wanted a movie or an Orange Crush. Tian Tsai always allowed me to choose the film and always seemed happy with my picks, which were usually something with Chuck Norris or Bruce Lee.

Someone always drove me home from work after the incident with Jaime. I liked riding with Sarah's family in their boxy green cargo van with its full-sized mattress in the back for stretching out on and a cooler that was used for longer trips since the van had no air conditioning. I always sat in the back with the kids, flopping onto the mattress if we'd had a busy night at work. Levy, Jerusha, and Thaddeus, the three youngest, would flop down with me and tell me stories, happily competing with each other for my attention. Elizabeth, the oldest, was a sophisticate of eight who would sit back and urge her siblings not to get on my nerves until we could coax her into joining us.

"How old are you, Charity?" Elizabeth asked me one night.

"I'll be nineteen next month."

"Do you have any brothers or sisters?" Thad asked.

"I have a brother. His name's Trilby."

"That's a weird name," Levy said. "Is it in the Bible?"

"You're such a geek," Elizabeth said to her brother.

Sarah broke in to ask for the definition of geek. Ben suggested that it was perhaps a synonym for nerd but Elizabeth said no, it was way more bad, almost like a bad word. In that case, Sarah didn't want to hear it again. No almost-bad words from her children. I bribed everyone into the peace process by offering to tell a story.

"Now once upon a time there were two brothers," I began. "One of them was very rich and one of them was very poor. And one day—"

"How come one brother was rich and one was poor?" Thad asked. "Why didn't the rich brother share?"

"Because he was selfish," I continued. "So anyway, the poor brother and his wife were really hungry and couldn't get any food from anywhere—"

"Why didn't he go to the church pantry?"

Sarah told Thad to stop interrupting and that went for everyone else too.

"So the poor brother went to his rich brother one day and asked him for some food. And the rich brother was a real jerk who never liked to share so he said, 'Okay,

I'll give you a little something but only if you promise never to ask me for anything ever again.' And the poor brother promised, because he really didn't have any other options. So the rich brother gave him a loaf of bread, a candle, and some bacon and sent him on his way."

"How come the rich brother didn't give him any milk?" Levy wanted to know.

"Because people didn't drink milk as much in those days," I said quickly, not wanting Sarah to get angry with him. "They didn't know how to pasteurize it and it like shi—really nasty. So the poor brother was walking home with the stuff when he met an old man dressed in rags who said, 'Please sir, I'm very hungry, could you give me something to eat?' And the poor brother said, 'Well, I'm poor myself but I have a little food here.' And he gave the old man half the loaf of bread and the candle and he was going to give him some bacon too but the old man said, 'No, no, you've given me enough. Now I want to give something to you.' And the old man told the poor brother to walk down the road a ways until he came to a cave in the side of a mountain. If the poor brother was to go inside this cave and down a flight of stone steps, he'd find a magic world underground filled with gnomes."

"What's a gnome?" Levy asked.

"A little person," I said.

"You mean a kid?" Jerusha asked.

"No, like someone who gets older but doesn't get bigger."

"How come?"

"I don't know, maybe a birth defect," I said thoughtlessly.

"Mommy, is our new baby going to be a gnome?" Levy asked.

"No, he will be a mechanic," Sarah said without hesitation, as if she'd already considered both options. "Or she will. Every family should have one."

Ben pulled into the Dunkin Donuts parking lot and ran inside to get a mixed box of twelve while Sarah and the children listened to me explain that the gnomes in question had a magic mill capable of spitting out anything in the world except bacon, so naturally when they saw the poor brother's bacon, the gnomes were wild to get their hands on it, just as the old man had promised. The poor brother traded the bacon for the mill and went on to become a rich, happy man.

After producing enough to keep himself and his family out of want in perpetuity, the no longer poor brother gave the mill to a sea captain who was looking for an alternative to his long voyages for salt-mining. The sea captain placed the mill on the deck of his ship and ordered it to produce salt, which it did, but unfortunately the sea captain had forgotten how to turn the mill off. When it produced so much salt that the ship was in danger of sinking under its weight, the captain and his crew threw it overboard, where it continued spewing salt, saturating the world's oceans.

"How come it's bad luck to spill salt?" Elizabeth asked.

"I've heard it's supposed to mean you'll be spilling tears soon." Sarah yawned; it was getting late. "Maybe when you throw some salt over your shoulder, you're throwing away the reason for the tears."

Chapter Twenty-Seven

The ancient Celts used a Zodiac chart in which a person's astrological sign was not an animal or mythical beast, but a tree. In The Celtic Tree Calendar, Michael Vescoli writes that, "the Celts associated the strength to be oneself, which is latent in every person, with the oak. The truly strong man is he who has traveled a long way on the road to himself. Utterly dedicated, of his own free will he serves mankind, a cause, an art, responsible only to himself and full of the joy of living."

The oak sign is a rare one, given only to those born on the vernal equinox.

I still went for walks late at night, although insomnia wasn't much of a problem anymore now that I was working full time at the Ho-Ho and enjoying my own bed without anyone digging their elbow into my stomach. Being able to go out for a walk whenever and wherever I wanted still felt like a privilege. If I heard or saw other people coming I ducked into an alley or behind a garbage bin. Mostly I saw the standard issue down and outers whose emotional or chemical incapacitation made them unresponsive to everything, even the three-dimensional painting of Cincinnatus that covered the north side of the Kroger building on Central Parkway. I watched them all like an observer from outer space who was taking notes on the behavior patterns of nocturnal bipeds.

It was on one of these nights that I heard the noise of a fight coming from near the front of a building on the west side of town. At first I tried to ignore it as a spat between drunks but there were a handful of voices and only one of them was crying out in pain, following each crunch of knuckles pounding flesh. I crept closer; reaching for the butterfly knife I kept tucked in my pocket.

"Fucking nigger fag." A voice, slow and cold like sewage in the winter. "We ought to cut your balls off like they did in the old days."

From the light of the street lamp I was able to make out two white men holding a black one while a third did the punching. I also realized that I was standing just outside of Oscar's, one of the city's very few gay bars.

Oscar's clientele was mostly male and the three had probably been lying in wait for someone to walk out of there alone. What would a girl scout do? I could hear the voice of Nurse Lakota from Camp Willow Lake in my head, telling me in her cool, sagacious way to get to the front door of Oscar's, make a noisy fool of myself to distract the evildoers, and run inside for help.

The first part of the job was accomplished by slamming a trashcan lid against the front of the building and yelling, "Earthquake!" loud enough to leave me with a sore throat the next day. Then I ran inside Oscar's, where the surly-faced bouncer refused to call the police. "Any time we have trouble, they use it as an excuse to try and take our license. Besides, the cops give us more shit than the rednecks. They arrested two guys last week just for holding hands in a parked car."

"Just say they're beating him up because he's black," I demanded, backing my way towards the door.

"Like that would help? No can do, little fish."

"Asshole." I ran back outside to find a pay phone but the attackers were gone and the injured man was trying to stand up.

"Are you okay?" I asked inanely as I tried to help him stand, just like in the movies.

"Well, I've been worse, but not any time recently," the man said, gingerly touching his bloody nose. He was tall and built like a panther, with a melodious accent I couldn't place and a high, sloping forehead. Under normal circumstances his nose was firmly Romanesque, although it was swollen into a potato at the moment. He didn't seem surprised when I told him about the bouncer. Then he asked if I could drive.

"Is it an automatic?" I hesitated.

"Of course. I'm much too nelly to handle a stick. My name's Abdi, by the way."

I didn't know enough gay humor to laugh. I accepted the keys to Abdi's rickety Ford Fiesta and drove him to the nearest hospital. St. Sophia's was just outside of the downtown area in Blue Lake, a neighborhood full of old Victorian mansions and newer mock Tudor houses that could usually count on peaceful nights for the ER unless the city and county hospitals were full up and ready to blow. It was quiet when we walked in; only three people were waiting and none of them appeared to be in agony. The gray-haired receptionist jumped out of her chair with a look of alarm when she saw Abdi, who was leaning on my shoulder as we walked into the room. But instead of running to see where he was hurt, she remained standing at her desk.

"Mister, you have to go to the city hospital, we only take insured patients unless it's a matter of life and death and if someone's standing up it obviously isn't." Her name pin said "Mitzi" and her voice was rapid and bellicose, as if the sooner she got her words out and claiming the air, the sooner we would disappear and she could forget that we existed. Mitzi's chest heaved as she prepared for battle in the event that we got lippy with her.

"Not to worry, I come prepared to deal," Abdi said as he tried to reach into his back pocket without moving his ribs. He produced an insurance card for Mitzi and she turned red and defensive, the blame on us for not meeting expectations and provoking her worst side for the world to see. Once accommodated, Abdi accepted the attentions of the medical staff and refused to make a police report.

"So where are you from?" I asked while we waited for the X-rays, curious to know the source of his distinctive speech and profile.

"Somalia." Abdi's bloody, swollen lips barely allowed the word to leave his mouth.

"Oh, that's nice," said the nurse who was wiping down his face. "That's an African country, isn't it? Is it pretty there?"

"The best thing about Somalia is that I don't live there anymore," Abdi said as the anesthetic kicked in for him.

"Don't say that," she scolded him. "It's your motherland and I'm sure it's a beautiful place."

"Well, if you mean beautiful as in Keats' beauty is truth and so forth," Abdi said. "Although the truth is there is nothing less aesthetically pleasing than the sight of people being shot or hacked to pieces or starving to death. Would you ask me to dance if my stomach were feeding on its own walls until the muscles collapsed and gave me a nice pot belly?"

"Probably not," I said.

"That's some attitude you've got," the nurse said coldly. I wasn't sure if she meant me, Abdi, or both of us. In her own way she was as outraged as Mitzi.

Unmet expectations had a way of bringing out someone's inner hanging judge.

Once his patch-up job for the cracked ribs, cracked nose, and ripped skin was finished, I drove Abdi back to his apartment building in Walnut Hills, a restored Victorian mansion converted into smartly remodeled two-bedroom units. Abdi's living room walls were a deep cream and the woodwork trim was cherry or mahogany, like golden vanilla ice cream with deep red strawberries. There wasn't much furniture, a fact Abdi was in the process of remedying a bit at a time since he'd only recently graduated from UC with his master's degree in the new field of computer engineering. Although he had a good job already at Belcan, Abdi sent money to his mother and sisters in Cairo and didn't like buying with credit if it wasn't necessary.

"People think they need everything right away," Abdi said. "No single person needs much to start with. A bed, a table with a chair or two. A desk to work at. I have a computer here at home too, you'd be surprised at how useful they are. And I like a TV for company sometimes but I found a nice used one for twenty dollars."

"Sounds good to me," I agreed, thinking of my room at the Y and how happy I'd been to have some space of my own, no matter how Spartan. "I better get going now so you can go to bed."

"Here, drive my car home." Abdi held out the keys once again and I shook my head.

"There's no place to park at the Y."

"You live at the Y?" Abdi was surprised. "You have such nice skin." Seeing my blank face, he quickly added, "I mean, I thought it was mostly recovering junkies who lived there. And they almost always have bad complexions."

"Really?"

"Yes, really. It's mostly because they get constipated, if I'm not mistaken. And then they love to eat sweets once they're off the drugs or the drink."

There was no judgment in Abdi's voice, only sympathy, which might have been the reason why I suddenly started crying and couldn't stop, or even try to. Caught unaware, Abdi recovered quickly and made a bizarre picture of concern with his swollen eye, stitched mouth, and taped nose as he gently pushed me into a brown leather club chair and handed me a box of tissues before limping into his kitchen. He returned with a glass of wine and held it out to me.

"I've never been a very good Muslim."

"Thanks," I hiccupped as I accepted the glass, something warm, red, and much tastier than Paul Masson.

"So, why the tears?" Abdi asked.

"I don't know," I said as the wine unthawed me. "I guess because people are so ugly."

Abdi waited patiently for me to explain further, which I was unable to do with any coherency. I'd been on a slow burn all evening, stewing about the men who hurt Abdi, the bouncer at Oscar's, Mitzi the Duchess of Bitchness, and the self-righteous nurse who thought she had the right to tell someone how they were supposed to feel about their own damn country. I wanted to round them all up at gunpoint and ask them who the hell they thought they were and why their worthless asses were even taking up space on God's blue and green earth.

As for Abdi, he barely referred to any of the evening's unhappy events after we left the hospital. It would take me a while to understand his attitude towards American racism; though he was never happy to be a victim of it, there was no penetrating emotional damage for him. As an immigrant, Abdi hadn't anticipated one hundred percent heartfelt acceptance from everyone in his adopted country—which he loved to distraction just the same—any more than I would have expected it in Somalia. Abdi could shake his head and sometimes even laugh at the traditional native prejudices and then have a good night's sleep. It was rejection from a mother-in-law, not a mother.

When I refused to take his car, Abdi suggested a cab, his treat. When I turned that down as well, he insisted that I would either ride a cab home or he would drive me himself. I accepted the ten-dollar bill he offered and we sipped another glass of wine together while we waited for the cab.

"Do you have a boyfriend?" Abdi asked. "I have a coworker from Vietnam who's just about your height and he wants to meet someone nice. He's very good-looking, too."

"Pass," I said as I took another gulp of Abdi's very good wine, even though I did prefer short men for dancing.

"But he'd be a good catch," Abdi said. "He's nice, he's had a good education and he makes good money. Why don't you let me fix you up with him after all you've done for me tonight?"

"Nope."

The finality in my voice made Abdi take a second look at me. "Ah, so that's how it is."

"That's how what is?" I asked.

"You prefer the ladies," he said.

"I do not."

"Sure you do," Abdi insisted in a friendly way. "Why not admit it? It's a free country and just think how much easier life is when you're gay. You don't have to worry about getting pregnant and you can check people out in the locker room before you make a move on them."

What about the people who were responsible for Abdi's wrapped ribs and stitched lips? This I didn't ask. "What about AIDS?"

Abdi's face fell slightly. "That's true," he owned. "But in a very cruel way, AIDS is an equalizer. For years gay men have lived like kites or balloons, just floating. Now they have to face their own mortality, just like girls who grow up knowing that they'll get married and very possibly die in childbirth or be killed by their husbands or the younger men here when they have to register with the SSS. And straight men usually don't have as much freedom to experiment as gay men because women are the gatekeepers. They have to find a woman who says yes and any woman worth having is liable to have a price, like marriage or some kind of commitment."

"I don't." I lit a cigarette. "I'd rather die than be married."

"Like I said, you prefer the ladies."

The taxi came and I said good-bye. Abdi gave me his phone number and asked for mine but I had none. He promised to take me out to dinner soon to thank me, a promise I assumed he only meant as a polite gesture. Once the painkillers wore off, Abdi would remember that I was a waitress with nothing to wear besides a handful of jeans and shirts from the Salvation Army and my aprons from the restaurant.

Back at the Y, I collapsed in my bed but couldn't fall asleep in spite of the busy evening, the late hour, or the wine. Abdi's voice floated in my head, alternately crying for help and chuckling as he insisted that I preferred the ladies. When sleep finally came, I dreamed about Lindy Albertson and her chocolate brown eyes.

The next day I tried putting Abdi's claim to the test. Focusing hard on Sarah as she wiped down tables, I felt nothing. Then I turned my attention to Hsiu Ching as she put a new roll of tape in the register. Still nothing. Abdi didn't know his ass from his jawbone.

I spent the next week people-watching and trying to get a reaction from myself but most of the women who ate at the restaurant were suburban broody hens whose voices made my teeth hurt. I tried ignoring them in favor of the more intelligent-looking ones I saw in the library but nothing happened. Then I tried the same thing with men and got the same results. Whichever part of me did my preferring was switched off or inoperable, at least for the time being. I decided I didn't care, also for the time being.

Chapter Twenty-Eight

Abdi came to the Ho Ho for dinner two weeks after our meeting in front of Oscar's. His appearance was unexpected, partly because I'd assumed his promise to visit was only an empty gesture and partly because his face was completely healed and I saw his features clearly for the first time, which were fit to be displayed on a coin. Seeing him made me wonder how two men would make love, if it hurt, and if they took turns.

"Can you recommend something good?" Abdi asked as he scanned the menu.

I suggested the hot sliced pork, a spicy dish with green and white onions that Tian Tsai made with hoisin sauce. Abdi apologetically refused, saying he couldn't eat pork. "Call it my last taboo."

He agreed to try the Governor's chicken, my favorite, and also ordered some butterfly shrimps for an appetizer. I forgot that they came wrapped in bacon, which he politely picked off and gave me to munch on when Hsiu Ching wasn't looking since she'd already had a near-seizure when Abdi asked if I might sit down with him. It was embarrassing but Hsiu Ching and Tian Tsai had been keeping an eye out for me since the incident with Jaime and the police so I let it ride. Abdi and I talked while I cleaned up the dining room.

"So how have you been?" he asked as he sipped his tea.

"All right I guess."

"Is that all?" Abdi took me literally, or pretended to. "That sucks."

"How'd you learn such good English?" I asked him. "I could barely get through French in high school."

"I don't know," Abdi said. "I like talking with people in English. I like listening to it, too. It's a fun language."

"Fun?" Hsiu Ching walked out of the restroom in time to hear his words. "What fun? English makes me crazy. How come you say mouse and mice but not house and hice, huh? And my kids, I ask them if they want fish for dinner, they don't say yes, mama, no mama. They say is pope Catholic or no way José. All the time, talking crazy. Today I have a carryout customer who says I'm a dirty lady because I ask her son if he wants a fork."

Alas, Hsiu Ching always had trouble with the letter 'r' if it came in the middle of a word.

"Why would they think you're dirty because you offer them a fork?" Abdi asked politely.

"How the hell I know?" Hsiu Ching threw her kitten paw hands in the air as she walked to the kitchen. "Americans are too much mixed up."

"Sarah and I don't know how to tell her," I said when Hsiu Ching was safely out of earshot.

"That's too bad. Listen, once you're through here I was hoping you'd let me take you out for a drink at that new nightclub down the street," he said. "Tonight's the night they have the lady strippers."

"As opposed to the slutty strippers?"

"So what do you say?"

"Why would you want to watch women stripping?" I asked. "Are you bi?"

"Not for me," Abdi said. "For you. I've heard a lot of them are actually lesbians."

"Are you still going on about that shit?"

He was, and in the end he won. Curiosity, like cancer, killed without regard for demographics. It wasn't necessary to be a cat.

Brothers' Nightclub offered female strippers on Sunday nights and male strippers on Mondays. On Fridays and Saturdays they opened the dance floor to the customers and a live band cranked out top forty selections like "Our House" or "Sledgehammer." A novice when it came to such places, I assumed that Brothers knew where it was at with their rotating disco ball suspended from the ceiling and blinking pastel spotlights that were used to highlight the strippers as they did their routines.

The girls were introduced before they came out by a male emcee who gave first names only and made a few Gong Show-style witticisms about the act itself before yielding the floor to the dancer. Though I wasn't to know it then, Brothers ran a fairly tasteful show. The girls were all young, pretty, and good dancers. No fireman's pole for anyone to coil herself around and none of the girls sat at the bar waiting for someone to buy them a Screwdriver that was only orange juice.

"Tell me which ones you like," Abdi said. "I'll tip them for you."

"Tip them?"

"Yes, tip them. That's what you do if you really like the girl's dancing. It's how they make most of their money."

The first girl to perform was Sheila, a golden blonde Playboy bunny brand in a cheerleader costume who bumped, ground, and peeled as Cindy Lauper trilled that girls wanted only to have fun. Though Sheila danced well, her Barbie doll looks and kitschy style made me yawn. Abdi poked my arm to remind me that it was contagious.

I excused myself to use the bathroom and when I came back the second act had already begun, a girl making slow, graceful moves to an equally slow and sinuous tune, belying the Georgian-period costume and powdered wig she was wearing. I wondered if she was supposed to be Dolly Madison. As the music unexpectedly gained speed and slammed into the aggression of Styx's "The Queen of Spades," Abdi managed to shout to me that the girl was supposed to be Marie Antoinette. She stripped down to a black G-string with a knife sewn to the front and I admired her ability to negotiate such a costume but nothing more. Maybe I was frigid.

A few girls and a few Long Island Ice Teas later, Abdi decided that desperate measures were in order and he tried to bribe a brunette in an angel costume into doing a lap dance for me as she twirled and broke to J. Geils' "Centerfold." Abdi made his point by politely tucking a dollar bill into her T-bar and offering her a five with a note attached. Brothers made their point by ejecting us from the premises as theatrically as possible.

"Sick fags," the bouncer snarled at our backs as he and the equally self-important doorman watched us leave.

I steered Abdi to the car. "Smooth, we nearly got lynched."

"I never thought a woman who'd undress in front of a roomful of strange men would be so uptight."

"What difference does it make?" I asked as I tried to get the car keys from him. Abdi wasn't refusing to give them to me so much as he was refusing to hold still, gesticulating high above my head as he made his points. "What woman's going to fall for me?"

"Why wouldn't a woman fall for you?" Abdi brought his arms down and dropped the keys into my hand without warning. "You're as cute as can be, you're smart, you work hard, and you have courage."

"Courage?" My voice went up a key. "I have about as much courage as a clam."

"What about when we first met? What about you running up to help me the way you did? That took a lot of courage."

I busied myself with tucking Abdi into the passenger seat and starting the car to avoid answering. What he called courage I called animal instinct coupled with adrenaline that could easily misfire. But I had no wish to explain this to my new friend. Being told that I had courage was a compliment I wanted to savor a little before Abdi had a chance to reconsider it.

We went to Friendly's for sundaes and I ordered my favorite Jim Dandy combo, three parts cookies and cream, one part vanilla, and one part orange sherbet with both hot fudge and strawberry topping. Abdi's eyes grew as the waitress placed the fishbowl-sized concoction in front of me. He was having a more conservative banana split.

As we ate, Abdi talked about himself for the first time since our night at the ER. In Somalia his father had been a legally certified camel herder; I wondered if this might correspond to being a cowhand in America. Abdi's parents had sent him to a secular school for boys where he learned Arabic and English, along with several of the more popular Beatles songs. "Hey Jude" was his personal favorite.

Abdi left his village at the age of seventeen to work in a luxury hotel compound in Riyadh that specialized in catering to visiting Europeans and Americans. Finding a job in Saudi Arabia was easy since the population contained an unusually high percentage of rich people who, to quote Abdi, would break out in boils and shit cement blocks at the thought of getting their hands dirty and I didn't even want to know how they treated women there.

One of the regular guests at the hotel had been a married American diplomat who was too cautious to seek out the gay circuit in Saudi Arabia. The diplomat struck up a friendship with Abdi and they had a discreet affair that picked up whenever the man was in Riyadh and didn't exist when he wasn't. To show his gratitude, the diplomat had helped Abdi get a student visa to the United States and after graduating from UC with a degree in a lucrative new industry, Abdi was able to get a green card. He and his diplomat friend limited their relationship to the occasional Christmas card.

"He has a wife and children here," Abdi said. "And he didn't want me to feel like I owed him because he helped me get the visa."

In spite of this generous portrait, I was goaded. "I hate people like that," I said. "They just go around taking what they want. It's guys like that who spread AIDS. Do you think if his wife was doing the same thing he'd just sit on his ass singing Peter, Paul, and Mary songs about it?"

"Maybe not," Abdi plucked a strawberry out of his dish. "But my dear, it sounds like you hate a lot of people."

"Because there's so many assholes out there," I said defensively, caught off guard.

"Yes, there are." Abdi shivered and rubbed his arms, the ice cream and Friendly's air conditioner giving him an unexpected chill. He spooned up his banana split in silence until I was beginning to think that I'd either offended or bored him stupid. Just as I was about to apologize for being a pill, Abdi asked me, "Do you ever wonder about your death?"

"Endlessly."

"No, not like that," Abdi said. "I mean, do you ever wonder about how it will happen? Have you ever tried to find out, by going to a fortune teller or something?"

"I'd rather be surprised," I said as I looked around the dining room for a waitress and hoped there was fresh coffee. "This is a weird thing to be talking about over ice cream."

"I just happened to think of it. Three years ago I got caught in this snowstorm in the middle of the night and my hands got frostbite because my car died and I had to walk. And it all happened in just a couple of hours while I was inside Denny's eating a late dinner. I come outside and I'm like, shit, it's supposed to be almost April. I was reading at Denny's until three in the morning, it was spring when I went inside and the middle of January when I came out. I swear there were three inches of snow on the ground and it was dumping more every minute. This soft, heavy snow, floating down like coconut flakes."

Abdi's car broke down on the highway, twelve miles from his apartment. Since the car's heater didn't work, he decided to try walking. A few other cars were on the road in spite of the weather but who was going to stop and give a black man a ride at three in the morning? And since it was warm when he went out to Denny's, he was only wearing a t-shirt and a windbreaker. When Abdi's hands became numb, he took off his windbreaker and wrapped it around them. Finally a semi driver stopped and drove him to the nearest hospital, where his hands were treated for frostbite.

"Holy shit," I said. Even that took some effort.

"But the kicker is that when I was growing up, me and my friends were always talking about how death might come to each of us," Abdi said. "Some of us would marry, have children, and live past our thirtieth birthdays but we knew at least half of us wouldn't. A fatal disease, starvation from a drought, being killed by guerillas or one of those insane groups that wants sharia law, no end of options. But never once did freezing to death ever cross our minds as a possibility."

I supposed the moral of Abdi's story was that what we feared most rarely came to pass. But rarely and never weren't synonyms. I didn't even know what it was I feared the most since I was too afraid to think about it.

Chapter Twenty-Nine

Sometimes Abdi took me out to meet his friends at their favorite bars. After two or three Rolling Rocks Abdi would start bragging to everyone that I'd saved his life and after three or four he was loudly sharing my unfortunate situation as a virgin dyke in need of prospects. We were having drinks at the Hitching Post on a Friday night when Abdi's friend Bruce promised to ask his hag if she knew anyone who might like me.

"Your what?" I asked, certain that I'd misheard.

"Hag. My fag hag."

"Just what in the hell is a fag hag?" I asked as I gulped the last of my Molson ale.

Abdi stepped in to explain that a fag hag was usually a straight person who enjoyed the company of gay people. "Some men are very choosy about their hags. They might only pick someone who's rich or likes modern art or something like that."

"So how's a straight chick who can't get a date going to be able to find me a girlfriend?" I asked

"Oh, she's not straight," Bruce said. "She's a solid Kinsey six."

"So why is she the fag hag and not you?" I asked.

"Only women can be fag hags."

"Says who?" My level of intoxication was at the early belligerent stage and I was all set for countdown.

"Well . . ." Bruce's eyes slid towards Abdi, had I had all my shots? "That's just the way it's always been."

"Well, shit, I guess I can't argue with that kind of logic." I ordered another ale and Bruce made himself scarce.

"You catch more flies with honey," Abdi said.

"And you keep more fleas away with vinegar." I took a swig from my bottle as soon as it was placed in front of me. "And the first person who calls me a fish is going to experience pain, I shit you not."

"I'll keep that in mind." Without gratitude to propel him, Abdi probably would have given up.

Abdi's friend Schroeder owned a house near Hueston Woods in Oxford that was equipped with an indoor swimming pool and a Jacuzzi. Schroeder's real name was Jason but everyone called him Schroeder since he was blond and played the piano for a hobby. When Schroeder decided to have a weekend house party, Abdi managed to wangle an invitation for me after learning that Schroeder's friend Valerie was coming and by chance she'd recently broken up with her girlfriend.

"You'll like her," Abdi promised. "She's been hoping to meet someone nice."

"So why are you bringing me?"

"Very funny. Just relax and let your hair down, like you do when you're with me. She'll love you."

I wondered if I might love her.

Schroeder's house sat on a one-acre lot, far from prying eyes unless a good pair of binoculars was being used. His neighbors might have done well to invest in a few pairs, according to Abdi. Schroeder's parties had a reputation for being stranger than fiction and it wasn't unheard of for four or five couples to arrive on Friday night, only to leave on Sunday night with a complete reshuffle.

Things began awkwardly when Valerie showed up with Sybil, her supposedly ex-girlfriend. Schroeder wasn't expecting an extra guest and there weren't enough bedrooms for him to put me by myself. A single-size futon was produced and laid on the floor in the women's bedroom, which I immediately offered to take. It wasn't mere altruism on my part; I knew the sloshing of a waterbed would keep me awake all night.

Valerie was a soft butch, though I was only beginning to learn about such distinctions. She was thin and stood at what I thought was a statuesque five foot seven. Valerie's dark brown hair was just long enough for her to pass, as everyone said, but only because she worked as a pediatric nurse at Good Sam and could explain her do as being hygienic and convenient.

Sybil was a grease monkey at Jiffy Lube. She was blond like me but her hair was so short that she occasionally got threatened in public, a situation she dealt with by packing a set of nunchucks. Her eyes were green, like peridots. It was obvious that there was unspoken tension between her and Valerie and I wondered why they weren't being more affectionate if they were supposed to be reconciling. They both ignored me as politely as possible.

After drinking a hard lemonade, I decided to put on my suit and go swimming. Abdi and three other men were already in the pool, splashing, sharing drinks, and yanking each other's Speedos down. They all shrieked and pretended to be embarrassed when I stepped in. My white bikini appealed to everyone's aesthetic sense, if nothing else.

"Lord have mercy, you got some cajones, girl," said Jeffrey, a senior at UC who was studying theatre.

"How nice of you to notice," I said before ducking and doing an underwater somersault. I followed up with some slow laps. When laps became boring I decided to try the Jacuzzi and leave the boys to pants each other in peace.

Just as I was settled into the hot, bubbling water, Valerie and Sybil came out to join me. Valerie had on a one-piece black suit while Sybil was wearing a pair of gym shorts and nothing else. Sybil's build was on the stocky side and she was muscle-bound all over, like I thought a soccer player might be. Her breasts were small and shaped like the wide, shallow champagne glasses that were usually seen in America, although I knew from reading trashy novels that proper champagne glasses were long and narrow to keep the bubbles below the surface and the drink from going flat. How could I know so many things like that and almost nothing else?

Valerie began to ask me about myself, where I worked, if I went to school, and where my family was.

Sybil took out a joint and lit it with a cigarette lighter that looked like a small Derringer. I wanted one like it.

"Schroeder will spaz if you get ashes in the tub," Valerie said.

"Not to worry," Sybil slid up to sit on the edge. She held the joint out to me, her first friendly gesture of the evening. I accepted it, even if I was still depressed over my blind date falling flat. At the same time there was some relief in knowing that I wouldn't be making a debut in front of a houseful of boisterous, intoxicated queens.

Sybil asked me about the Ho Ho, a favorite with her coworkers. This led the discussion to what arrangements should be made for dinner. Schroeder always kept a full larder and it was customary for him and his guests to fix a meal at home instead of ordering out after a pizza delivery driver once called the vice squad when he saw Schroeder's date walking naked through the front living room. Dinner might be casual and individual, with people munching on fresh fruit, toasted bagels, and cheese, or communal and formal with one person overseeing the preparation of a roast pork tenderloin with asparagus and wild rice while everyone else served as minions who scrubbed vegetables and washed dishes.

"I think there's some ground beef in the freezer," Valerie said. "We could nuke it and make burgers and fries."

"Let the boys worry about it; that's what they're best at." Sybil pinched out the roach and carefully laid it to one side.

"Worrying or cooking?" I'd found my tongue, courtesy of the pot.

"Both, I guess," Valerie said, trying not to cough. "They've got to be good for something besides hogging the bathroom and getting babies started."

My laugh was bigger than the joke merited; it was my first pot in nearly a year. Then the magic click that Tennessee Williams spoke of in *Cat on a Hot Tin Roof* came to me and I felt peaceful, my initial trepidation and subsequent letdown dissolving like sugar in coffee. I relaxed and stared at Sybil's breasts without reserve, never dreaming that she'd notice.

I also decided that with access to Schroeder's kitchen, I was going to cook a meal to knock everyone's condoms off. Without a word I climbed out of the tub and went back inside to see what the options were. Sybil and Valerie followed, imagining that they'd said something to offend me when the fact was that hardly a word of their conversation even reached me once I'd determined a course of action.

I didn't see any ground beef in the freezer but there were two bags of frozen chicken parts, thighs and legs that only needed to be defrosted and seasoned. I hunted for the ingredients needed to make a decent batch of fried chicken, which took me a while since I was looking in the closets and bathrooms as well as the kitchen cabinets. At the prospect of cooking, Sybil held up her hand to ward off the evil eye and promised to wash dishes before making her escape. Valerie tried to lend a hand, or at least watch out for me and keep the damage under control since I was suddenly behaving very single-mindedly and not at all like the limp and reticent thing she'd shaken hands with two hours earlier.

"Where the hell does Schroeder keep his rice cooker?" I asked as I dug through the cabinets, shoving pots, pans, and Tupperware into the center of the kitchen floor.

"I don't think he has one," Valerie said from behind me.

"It must be around here somewhere."

Jeffrey, Abdi, and Schroeder took a peek in the kitchen to see what the noise was. As they watched me mixing up chicken breading with flour, black pepper, garlic powder, and sugar—a trick I'd learned from Tian Tsai—Valerie mimed to them that I should be humored, but protected. Jeffrey peeled potatoes for mashing since I couldn't find a rice cooker or even any rice. Schroeder insisted that he didn't own one but I spent several minutes combing the house anyway, convinced that he must have simply misplaced it.

A meal was somehow produced as I sang "Season of the Witch" to keep myself focused. When we sat down to eat in Schroeder's dining room I realized the gravy for the potatoes was runny from over-stirring but everyone was quick to insist that it tasted good. It was the first meal I'd ever prepared for anyone besides Jaime or myself.

"A dyke who can cook," said Sal, who worked for a wedding planner. "I do believe the end is near." I was too content to react but Sybil flung a spoonful of gravy at him.

After dinner I had my second hard lemonade. Sybil brought out a hookah pipe and everyone shared a few bowls. After watching me lie inert for several minutes with my back on the floor and my feet resting on a dining chair, Abdi decided it was time for me to call it a night. He carried me up to the ladies' bedroom and dumped me on the waterbed, ignoring my protests. Sybil and Valerie came in a few minutes later to find me still lying on the bed and showing no signs of budging from it. They disappeared into the bathroom together and came out dressed for bed, Valerie in a short nightgown, her glasses off, and Sybil in a plain white t-shirt and gym shorts.

"You think she's ready?" Valerie asked.

"Hell, yes," Sybil said.

The two of them climbed onto the bed with me, one on each side, and my swimsuit was gone in less than five minutes. Working as a team, they touched me everywhere with their lips and fingertips, speaking in soft voices, bathing me with compliments on the condition of my skin and everything it was covering. My mind wasn't on the clichés about dying and going to heaven. The earth was more than enough just then.

Valerie climbed off the bed and began rummaging in her suitcase. "We've got a little surprise for you, Charity," Sybil said. "And I think you're going to like it."

"Whassat?"

I'd never seen a dildo in the flesh, so to speak, although they were a staple in some of Jaime's favorite magazines. My yelling brought Abdi to the bedroom door to save me but he stayed outside and listened just long enough to determine that I wasn't in need of rescuing. Reason and coherence were no longer at my command.

"Do you think we're hurting her?" Valerie asked.

"No way, she wants to be fucked hard," Sybil said.

After I collapsed, Valerie and Sybil attended to each other. When they were finished the three of us lay in a sweaty pile and listened to each other's breathing until it was broken up by a sharp, smacking sound followed by a yell, noises that were coming from downstairs.

"Someone's getting a spanking," Valerie said. The three of us went downstairs to investigate after Valerie turned back once to grab a robe for me since I forgot I was naked, or forgot that it mattered. A stranger in an even stranger land. We didn't find the yeller or the smacker but we did find Jeffrey lying on his back on the den floor and Abdi kneeling over him, both of them jaybird.

"Do you bitches mind?" Jeffrey yelled.

Sybil's Polaroid was sitting on the loveseat where she'd dropped it earlier in the evening. She snatched it up. "Say yogurt."

"Wait, it's too dark in here." Valerie reached for the track light control on the wall. The Polaroid flashed repeatedly while Jeffrey threatened to drown the three of us in the swimming pool. As Valerie and Sybil taunted him with orders to show his good side, Abdi and I laughed, the only ones in the room with nothing to say.

Chapter Thirty

Sybil stopped by the restaurant to see me four days after Schroeder's party. Mindful of Hsiu Ching and Sarah, she sat down to order a meal. It was a slow night, giving us plenty of time to talk. She invited me to go to the movies with her after I got off.

"What about Valerie?" I asked.

"She and I are just friends now."

We saw *Good Morning, Vietnam* at the mall Showcase. Three nights later Sybil invited me to her home, a duplex in Clifton near the university that she shared with her two kittens, a brother and sister named Laurence and Patty after the two girls from *Square Pegs*. It was a show that Sybil remembered more fondly than I did.

"What was wrong with *Square Pegs*?" Sybil asked while we were eating carry-in from LaRosa's.

"A stupid girl chasing after the so-called fashionable cliques at school and dragging her smarter best friend along for the idiot ride," I said. Sybil complimented my wit and rewarded me with a massage that started inside out.

Since I was still living at the Y and my expenses were relatively few, I frequently bought gifts for Sybil. When I arrived at the duplex with a set of pots and pans found on clearance at the Lazarus basement, she protested that it was too much but I waved off her objections by saying I needed things to work with when I used her kitchen since I was now coming over to her house three or four nights a week to fix dinner for the two of us. Sometimes Abdi and Jeffrey joined us, having become something of a pair after Schroeder's party.

"You two look so cute together," Jeffrey said one night in the early fall as the four of us sat down to spaghetti and meatballs.

"We feel so cute together," I said complacently. It was my favorite time of year, Sybil was playing footsie under the table, and I'd been obvious enough to pop a John Denver cassette in the stereo for our dinner music and stare lovingly into her eyes as I sang along with "Annie's Song."

"That's quite a song," Sybil said. "A lot for anyone to live up to."

Within a week of our first date I'd been waiting for Sybil to ask me to move in with her. Not even at gunpoint would I ask first but I didn't expect the wait to be a long one. I forgot about Valerie, even though Sybil's home was full of knickknacks, books, and other small personal touches that were gifts from her. Falling in love with love and lust was occupying the better part of my brain space.

I was also making more money at work since my happiness spilled over there and made me more cheerful with the customers, beefing up my tips. The overload of good karma left me spinning and indiscreet. Sybil sometimes had to caution me when I grabbed her around the waist or kissed her in public. Late one Saturday evening we indulged in a stolen grope at Thriftway behind a display of two-liter Coke bottles and were seen by one of the stockers, a girl near my age whose gold-brown hair was carefully styled to resemble an enormous shrub. She watched us silently until we turned and saw her.

"Are you two, like, gay?" The girl was one of those unfortunates who had perfected her Valley Girl patois so well by junior high that she'd forgotten how to talk like a real person. Her expression was both wary and hopeful.

"Why do you ask, chickie?" Sybil tilted her head and smiled at her, making me slightly jealous.

"Well, I just wondered. I mean, like, aren't you afraid of getting AIDS or something?" The girl backed away slightly, making me and Sybil laugh almost hard enough to knock her down. She walked off sideways to make sure we didn't follow her and the incident became a favorite running joke between Sybil and me.

"Like, aren't you afraid of getting AIDS?" I would ask when Sybil drank milk out of the carton.

"Like, aren't you afraid of getting AIDS?" Sybil would demand if she caught me nibbling raw cookie dough.

The jokes didn't last long. A friend of Jeffrey's from UC was fired from his waiter's job at one of the five-star hotels by Fountain Square after testing positive for

HIV and though he was rehired when the other waiters lodged a group protest, management watched him like a hawk for any mistakes that could be used as an excuse for kicking him back to the curb. Rumors circulated that the hotel owners were planning to fire all of the gay men who worked there or pressure them into quitting.

"It's a nightmare," Jeffrey said as he, Sybil, and I were eating hamburgers at Friendly's. "If this guy so much as drops a fork he's out the door."

"Then if he drops a fork everyone else should do the same thing right away," I said.

"Yeah, like Spartacus," Sybil agreed.

"Well, not exactly." I tried to determine if the principle was the same but Jeffrey moved on ahead of me.

"That's an awesome idea." He immediately went to work building on my suggestion with other possible acts of solidarity.

Later that night Sybil and I held hands and went walking through Clifton. A Ford Pinto pulled up alongside of us with a screech and Sybil immediately reached for the nunchucks in her pocket. Two teenaged boys and their sycophant girlfriends were in the car.

"Fucking dykes!" the boy driving the car christened us.

"You play with yourselves and sleep with dogs!" the girl in the backseat added.

"Scumbags!" said the boy sitting next to her.

"You lick each other's pussies!" The girl in the front seat didn't want to be left out.

The house we were standing in front of had a circle of decorative rocks the size of hedge apples lining a small flowerbed around the mailbox. I grabbed one and threw it at the Pinto but it only bounced on the hood. Sybil's aim was better from playing baseball in high school and she threw a knuckleball that shattered the windshield. The girls began to scream and the car tore away from us in a frantic retreat. The bumper sticker on the back said "Christians Aren't Perfect, Just Forgiven." Sybil and I ran back to her apartment and collapsed on the couch, not wanting to chance it that Jerry Falwell's junior fan club might go to the police.

"Straight people tend to hate gay women more than gay men," I said to Sybil as we caught our breath. "Even with AIDS."

"How do you figure that?"

"Because women aren't supposed to admit that they want sex until a man comes along to seduce them," I explained. "And then they have to become all passionate and acrobatic at a minute's notice or people say they're frigid."

"You think?" Sybil asked. "I've never really dated a guy."

"Haven't you ever noticed that the female lead in the movies is usually some ice princess who has no interest in sex until the leading man warms her up? Any woman who goes around saying she wants good sex and she likes having her private parts touched might as well be a farm animal."

"I'll be dipped in turkey shit," Sybil said. "It's kind of weird to hear you say it all like that but I guess it's true."

Sybil had dinner at the restaurant once or twice a week; on the other nights we ate somewhere else or I cooked at her place. We hung out at the Tri-County mall or Fountain Square, making a game out of things like being the first to spot someone carrying a red suitcase or wearing blue shoes. In the afternoons when I got off work we went to Dunkin Donuts and read the *Cincinnati Enquirer* over coffee and a plate of munchkins. The owners of the place were a couple from Bangalore; the husband worked in the back making the donuts while the wife screamed at the employees and served customers in the front, just like Tian Tsai and Hsiu Ching. It made me think of my own family and what they might have been like as newcomers from their hamlets in northern Germany and southern Ireland.

Part of my afternoons with Sybil were spent reading the wedding announcements in the paper and choosing the prettiest and ugliest brides. Then we made up stories about each of the couples, how they were likely to have met, what their honeymoon would turn out to be like, and whether the marriage would last. If we suspected it wouldn't then it became necessary to provide a probable scenario for the divorce as well. After the weddings we skimmed through the birth announcements; one of the local hospitals always put pictures of the new babies in the paper two weeks after they were born and we kept an eye out for twins or triplets. Why this mattered I never knew. It could have been a superstition with roots in both evolution and religion; surplus offspring meant wealth and longevity for the tribe.

There were no twins in the paper on the day Sybil called me at work and told me not to expect her that evening. "Val just showed up out of the blue and she's really upset about some stuff at work. She needs someone to talk to who knows what it's like for her at the hospital." It was a time-honored excuse, doubly effective in this case since Valerie was a nurse.

"Why don't you bring her here to eat?" I suggested, more suspicious than benevolent.

But Valerie was too upset to go out and eat. She was too upset to do anything except stay in Sybil's duplex and raid the toy box with her, as she would explain to me in a vindictive letter that I received five days later, five days of radio silence from Sybil. Not knowing where I lived, Valerie had sent the letter in the restaurant's care. I read it just before opening time at eleven, which meant the rest of my day was spent running to and from the restroom to cry or throw up.

"Maybe you have the flu," Sarah said as she reached for my forehead.

"I wish it was the plague."

Being a nurse must have made taught Valerie exactly where to find someone's jugular. Her letter criticized me for being clueless about satisfying someone and concluded with a paragraph about being willing to fight for the one you loved. Maybe I would find someone willing to fight for me in the future; I was young. In the meantime, Sybil wouldn't be calling me and I was not to call her.

Sarah convinced Hsiu Ching that I should be sent home early. Uncle Chung was visiting that evening and volunteered to take me downtown. When we pulled up outside the Y, he put the van in park and held on to my left arm to keep me from getting out.

"You need someone to take care of you, little girl, teach you lessons," Uncle Chung said as he touched my face. I snorted, though not without briefly considering his offer. If I was a failure with women, perhaps it would be wise to try making a life that accommodated men.

Then I remembered that there was a paperback copy of *The Little Drummer Girl* waiting for me upstairs on my bed and a king-sized Hershey bar in my desk drawer. With a pack of cigarettes and a can of Mountain Dew from the pop machine in the lounge, I'd be able to drive Sybil and Valerie from my thoughts for a while. Uncle Chung's gonads would have to keep. I patted his hand before removing it from my upper thigh, thanked him for the ride, and slipped into the building.

I was joined in the smoking lounge by Helen, a woman in her forties undergoing treatment for schizophrenia, a graphic example of nature's frailty. It was bad enough when the body turned on itself, developing leukemia or multiple sclerosis, but when the mind revolted simply because a few of the brain's natural chemicals were coughing or seizing up at the wrong instant and making someone like Helen believe that we were being tracked by the KGB through our toothbrushes, the unfairness rang hard and shrill. Giving someone an illness that not only disabled them but made them socially unattractive and provoking seemed like an act of indifferent cruelty. If God's idea was to use Helen as an instrument to teach the rest of us, I hoped He was going to make it up to her afterwards.

"Hey, Faith, what's cooking?" Helen said with a wave. She was reading *Sports Illustrated*, a good sign. If her medication wasn't working she embroidered pictures of insects.

"Charity," I corrected as I lit a Benson & Hedges.

"Sorry about that." Helen said. "I don't suppose you have a sister named Hope?"

"No." I opened *The Little Drummer Girl* and got comfortable.

"Well, excuse the flying fuck out of me," Helen said serenely as she turned a page.

My sentiments exactly.

Chapter Thirty-One

Abdi waited patiently while days turned into weeks after Sybil broke up with me that I spent crying and insisting that God hated me with my usual lack of stoicism before he suggested, ever so kindly, that I try to move on.

"I know this has been a nightmare for you but my dear, these things happen to the best of us," Abdi said as we watched Eddie Murphy in *Coming to America* at the Showcase.

"And good things happen to the worst of us," I blubbered into my Mountain Dew.

I engaged in the usual self-abuse rituals. First on the agenda was going out to a few bars and underground parties on my own to meet someone new but it appeared that I was on a blacklist, courtesy of Valerie. According to the news on a circuit I hadn't even known about, I was not only a girlfriend stealer but not much between the sheets in the bargain.

One Saturday evening I took a ferry across the river to Newport and got punched in my beer-laden stomach at an underground bar called Libby's after asking an attached girl to dance. I ran outside and methodically puked off the edge of the sidewalk to keep anyone from stepping in it and the sound of applause made me look up. A group of shit-faced fraternity boys from UC who were passing by on their way to or from one of the neighborhood's many B-joints had stopped to observe me.

"What's wrong, blondie?" I heard one of them ask. "Too much pussy for you?"

"Want us to fix that?" another one offered.

The boys came closer and stood a few feet away from me, shifting their feet like horses, deciding. Staggering up from my knees, I exaggerated my drunk-and-puking state to try and repel them or at least gain a tactical advantage. With my eyes locked on theirs, I walked backwards and slid back inside Libby's. They were gone when I came back out fifteen minutes later.

Instead of being frightened back to the Y, I started walking late at night again, slipping through the alleys and side streets as usual to avoid being seen by anyone. The Kroger building was always a required pit stop where I studied the Cincinnatus mural and tried to remember which windows on the building were real and which ones were painted. Even in the daytime it was hard to tell.

An invitation to Thanksgiving dinner came from Ben and Sarah, which freed Abdi and Jeffrey to do their own thing without saddling themselves with me for the day. At eight months Sarah was trotting around her house with inconceivable speed and her maternity leave was set to begin in two more weeks, barring any acts of God.

Ben and the children acted happy to see me and I worried a little about disappointing them, as if they might have mistaken me for someone else.

"Charity, look at me," Elizabeth said as she performed a cartwheel. Jerusha tried to do the same but fell sidewise instead.

"I bet you can do a somersault," I suggested.

"Sure I can," Jerusha said. She rolled across the floor like a wheel. Then Levi and the girls did their version of a dance they'd seen on *Kids Incorporated*.

Thad, four years old and not coordinated enough to join in, watched unhappily from the side until inspiration struck. "You want to see our new kitty?" Thad asked me. "His name's Max."

"I would be delighted to meet Max," I said.

Thad disappeared into the next room and returned with a shell-shocked black and gray tabby kitten hanging over his chubby arm. I assumed that Max would allow himself to be petted once or twice before scarpering off to play but once in my lap he immediately curled into a ball and went to sleep, a privilege he probably didn't enjoy often. Max chose to remain in my lap for the rest of the day when I wasn't up helping Sarah.

After Sarah's pumpkin pie and my devil's food cake with white marshmallow frosting were cut and partially consumed, the kids asked me to retell the story about the salt in the sea. I suggested something new instead and they asked for options. "Well, I know a story about a little pink house that was built out in the country and wound up in the city," I said.

"Was it pretty?" Jerusha asked. "I've never seen a pink house."

"I guess it was pretty," I said. "Just not for everyone, you know. So anyway, this house was built out in the country for a young bride and her groom and they planted a ring of apple trees around the yard because the blossoms would match the color of the house in the spring. And the little house liked to watch the sun rise in the morning and the moon rise in the evening. And if it was clear enough at night she liked to count the stars. And it usually was unless it was raining or snowing. But that was okay too because the rain smelled good and the snow made a nice white blanket over the mud and the bare trees."

Levi wanted to know why the house was a girl; Elizabeth shushed him.

"So anyway, the little house was very happy just sitting there, watching the children of the bride and groom playing in her yard and the horses pulling their wagons and carriages on the road that ran past every so often."

"This was before they invented cars," Elizabeth explained to the younger ones.

I complimented Elizabeth on her astuteness and resumed my showcase of the little pink house's idyllic existence. But things began to change. Other houses were built right next to her but they weren't so well-crafted and most of them collapsed or burnt down, only to be replaced with bigger houses and buildings. After a while the little house wasn't in the country anymore because a full-blown city had grown around her. All the pollution from the city made her color faded and ugly. Some mean kids broke her windows and no one replaced them. No one lived in her or took care of her anymore so she was very sad.

"So what did the house do?" Jerusha looked worried; Sarah said she always took things too seriously.

"Well, after some years she was all botched up and covered with graffiti and everything but then something really strange happened," I said, pausing for dramatic effect. It also bought me a couple of minutes to come up with a good plot twist.

"What happened?" Jerusha asked as she rocked on the floor and hugged her knees.

"It turned out that the little house was actually built on a spot where there used to be a hedge tree, which some people call Osage orange trees. Now the funny thing about hedge trees is that it's hard to cut them down and if you leave the roots in the ground, the tree tends to grow right back. And whoever cut down this particular hedge tree didn't dig up the roots so what do you think happened then?"

"What?" four small voices cried. Even Ben and Sarah were watching me with anticipation.

It turned out that the tree's roots were still intact and recently contaminated with mercury from a broken thermometer or something that made it grow to be giant-sized in only a few days. The tree became a behemoth to rival Jack's beanstalk, growing so big that it lifted the little house off the ground and then higher and higher into the air until she was towering over the buildings that once surrounded and smothered her.

"That's neat," Levi said. "The little house turned into a tree house."

"Exactly," I said. "And that tree got bigger and bigger until the little house could see for miles around. And if anyone tried to cut it down, that tree just dropped big giant hedge apples on them until they ran away."

The kids cheered. For my big finish I told how the tree grew so high that it nearly reached heaven. The angels cleaned it up inside and used it as a lookout post, sometimes rescuing alien spaceships that were about to crash.

"You know, that book was laying around our house when I was a kid and that's not quite the ending I remember," Ben said with a sleepy laugh.

Sarah said there was no way of knowing what angels got up to.

I thought my version of the story was more realistic; finding a new resource was more likely than being rescued out of nowhere and turned back into your old self.

Abdi opened his guest bedroom for me after the Y gave me the boot for stumbling home with Merlot on my breath one night too many. "Stay as long as you want," he said, handing me a spare key. "You saved my ass once."

"What about the rest of you?" I hugged him, taking us both by surprise. I wasn't a toucher.

Sometimes I thought about calling my father. That would mean swallowing my pride, which was supposed to be pointless if it stood between me and what I wanted. I finally dialed his number after tracking down some pot and smoking a little for fortification. Number no longer in service. I called the only other number I could remember in Mount Olive that was liable to still be up and running.

"Yallo."

"Hi, is this Mount Olive Feed & Seed?"

"Yeah."

"Is this Luther Sintz?" Damned if I was calling him uncle anymore.

"Yeah," he grunted.

"This is Charity."

"What charity?"

"Charity Sintz, your cousin." Jackass.

"Oh. Well, what do you want?"

I asked for Dad's new phone number and Luther immediately wanted to know my reasons for needing it. "Your dad went through a lot of grief on account of you," he said. "I honestly don't know if I'd be doing him any favors by putting you in touch with him."

There was no genuine reproach or censor in Luther's voice. He was behaving like a prick because he thought it was fun and he wasn't smart enough to think of anything better to do. I told Luther to give me the number or take a flying leap straight to hell.

"There's no need to get smart," he said. The pin in the balloon that held my tolerance for the chuckleheaded.

"Do you think you could stop being an asshole for about two seconds and give me the number or do I have to come all the way from Cincinnati to knock you down in front of God and everybody?" I asked, ready to give up.

"You're sure being a grouch. Hang on a second . . ."

Handling Luther wasn't much of a challenge and probably never had been, if I'd only known. I got Dad's new phone number and his new address, which was inside Hazelwood instead of out in the township. I'd always wanted to live in town when I was small.

Abdi came in from the mailbox with a handful of letters and a copy of *Playgirl*. "Bills, a solicitation from Greenpeace, a letter from my sister in Cairo, and some cute boys, yum yum. You should get your mail sent here; it would make more sense."

"That's all right," I said, not wanting him to think I was going to make myself too much to home.

"Well, it's your choice. Besides, with you here, the mailman isn't going to call the vice squad on me," Abdi said, holding up the *Playgirl*. Greg Evigan was on the cover.

"Why don't I heat up those pot stickers and we can watch *China Beach*," I suggested. "They're vegetarian."

"No thanks, I'm getting a little burnt out on Chinese food," Abdi dropped the mail on the table and headed to the bathroom.

I suddenly felt cold inside and my right hand hurt. Bringing home free food, washing the dishes, and scrubbing the bathroom religiously every week wasn't going to keep my welcome fresh forever. I wanted my own place that no one could take, turn, or wish me out of and where I'd be the one to do the welcoming or the evicting. Abdi's lovely home wasn't mine; I hadn't earned it. I wanted my own humble flat with my own kitchen, bathroom, and a fridge filled with food that I liked. No roommates or lovers, only a cat and not one from the pet shop or the shelters. I'd check the alleys behind the restaurants for whichever one followed me home first and that would be the one I was meant to have.

I also wanted Sybil back, to sit with her again at the Hitching Post, holding hands and feet under the table. I imagined walking in there, coming upon her and Valerie at the bar having a beer and me chasing Valerie away with a pool stick. I would then claim the empty stool next to Sybil and the barmaid would bring us each a glass of red without having to ask. Sybil and I would drain our glasses in one gulp, hop off our stools in sync, and dance while Paul Simon sang "You Can Call Me Al" on the jukebox. As fantasies went it was pretty sad. I was hardly the type to chase someone with a pool stick and "You Can Call Me Al" wasn't even a love song.

It wasn't long before I gave in and called the number Luther had given me.

My brother answered after four rings. "Well gosh, where have you been all this time?" Trilby asked. "Still in Cincinnati? Are you going to UC?"

"I don't think I'm the college type," I said.

Trilby went on to tell me about his own plans to attend IU and study sports medicine if he could win enough scholarships and get a Pell grant. His guidance counselor and gym teacher were assuring him of success; his GPA had never been less than 3.9 and he excelled at football and baseball. Though I'd sometimes heard people making references to financial aid for college students, I assumed it was only for honor-roll types like my brother. Neither of us spoke for a moment until I realized I was running up Abdi's phone bill for no reason. I asked Trilby about Annette.

"She moved out just a few weeks after you left," Trilby said. "She told me she was hoping things would get better between her and Dad once you were gone but they didn't. I didn't think she was being very fair. But anyway, Dad's getting married again and they bought this house together a few months ago, here in town. It's really nice. It's even got a dishwasher."

When I suggested coming for a visit, my brother hesitated. It would be best, he said, if I spoke with Dad first, who had declared me persona non grata after I ran away. His feelings had been deeply hurt.

"But if you talk to him and maybe kind of apologize for taking off, just explain that it was because of

Annette and not him, he'll understand," Trilby said. "I think he already knows that, deep down."

I said nothing.

"Charity, are you still there?"

The next day I went to K-mart and bought Abdi a new phone to replace the one I'd ripped from his kitchen wall and threw out the window, for which he was characteristically forgiving.

Chapter Thirty-Two

The giant sequoia is the only surviving species of its genus; the others disappeared as the earth cooled and dried itself at the end of the Cretaceous Period. And yet the Sequoiadendron giganteum is able to thrive in a handful of spots in the Sierra Nevada forests that happen to be sitting on a good source of moisture where the sun can't reach. The giant sequoias tend to prefer a non-homogenous environment and can usually be found in a mixed-species group of evergreens.

It was freezing in Kansas and there were no tall buildings, woods, or slopes to divert any of the wind. The unplowed parts of the landscape were as flat as a surfboard and emerald green, a croquet lawn for the gods. I could see the same green and brown quilt for miles in every direction.

The Greyhound driver stopped at a TA Center in Colby to refill his tank and let the rest of us do the same. In addition to the usual gasoline, drinks, and snacks, customers could choose from enough *Wizard of Oz* memorabilia to choke a brigade of flying monkeys. I was tempted by a ruby slipper paper weight but decided to save my money; there was no telling what might happen between Colby and the Golden Gate Bridge.

"I think you're out of your mind," Abdi had told me while I was packing.

"Who said I was in it to begin with? Anyway, you traveled even farther away from home," I reminded him. "All the way from another continent. I'm just going across the country."

"I had good cause."

"Maybe I do too. Just not the same as yours," I said as I debated whether or not to pack my dictionary.

"I never should have given you that copy of *Tales of the City* for your birthday."

But Abdi capitulated and bought me the 1989 Fodor's guide to California for a going-away gift while Ben and Sarah took me to Steak N' Shake for dinner. They brought Jacob with them in a basket since Sarah was nursing him. I sang snatches of songs for Jacob and held his soft, tiny hands, wondering how Sarah and Ben would ever be able to turn him loose in the world outside their family.

Ben gave me his old paperback copy of *On the Road*, which he credited with changing his life when he read it at the age of seventeen. After finishing high school in Phoenix, Ben had caught a bus to Death Valley in California, paid his respects, and then hitchhiked eastward across the country to Lubec, Maine. This was where he saw dawn breaking at two in the morning.

"You haven't lived until you see things like that," Ben said. "It's like proving to yourself that the world really is round instead of just taking someone else's word for it."

Ben's original plan was to turn back and travel northwestward until reaching Alaska but midway through the boundaround, he met Sarah in Elkhart, Indiana, where her family was selling hams and apple butter at a sale barn. Part of Ben's meager funds were spent on a pint of apple butter to get his toe in the door with Sarah, who already resented her parents for denying her a rumspringa and was ripe for the plucking. Ben and Sarah were the first to understand my need to go somewhere of my own choosing and planning.

"Sometimes I feel like the first seventeen years of my life were just a dream," Sarah said as we waited for our burgers to arrive. "All the things I did, what I expected from the world, I might as well have been on another planet." I asked Sarah if she missed the Amish community and she shook her head. "It's a good world but I like my life now. I feel like I have a whole house when I was only expecting a room."

Ben and Sarah's words gave me some reassurance that traveling across the country to find or build my own house wasn't a stupendously terrible idea.

Hsiu Ching called me stupid girl and had fits in eighteen directions when I told her I was leaving, just like old times. Tian Tsai stood in the background and wore his worried look, one of his three expressions. I would miss Tian Tsai and his cooking. Hsiu Ching stopped yelling long enough to give me a sack filled with pink navel oranges and yellow-bean sesame buns, along with a letter of introduction to some of Tian Tsai's relatives in San Francisco who owned an apartment building, a grocery store, and two restaurants in a neighborhood known as the Sunset District. As the bus pulled out of the station, I waved to Abdi, Sarah, Ben, and the children from my window, momentarily certain that I was leaving the only people who would ever like me. My stomach quivered from motion sickness until we were on I-70 and I relaxed enough to begin reading *On the Road*.

A woman went into premature labor on the bus just outside of Colby and we had to turn around. The bus itself broke down for a third time before we could reach Denver and the driver cried uncle. We waited inside a truck stop for the replacement bus to arrive. The air outside was dry and freezing, more like early December than early April to my sensibilities.

"This totally sucks ass," said the woman who'd been occupying the seat behind mine on the bus since St. Louis. Now she was parked next to me at the restaurant counter.

"Shit happens," I replied, too tired to be clever. I didn't know her name but I thought of her as Candy Woman since she was always eating sweets when she wasn't coughing and complaining about her cold.

"Yeah, and I bet you think you're hot shit, don't you? Too busy with your book to give anyone the goddamn time of day," Candy Woman said as she reached into the industrial-sized bag of M&M's that she'd been feeding from like a hog at a trough as she spoke without pause about herself, her cold, and her bodily functions for twelve hours straight. She took offense at my inability to fake an interest in her monologues.

An old but impeccable green AMC Rebel station wagon pulled into the parking lot in front of the general store that joined the truck stop diner and deposited a large group of riders, all of whom were dark-haired and spoke a combination of English and something unknown to me. Sixteen in all, they looked like an extended family. The women all wore long dresses and long hair while the men were in suits, ties, and fedoras. Three small boys in the group were dressed in jeans and sweatshirts but the single, tiny little girl wore a purple raincoat over a rose-colored dress. The group headed to the entrance of the general store but two minutes later most of them were quickly walking right back out again.

"I better not see any more than one of you at a time in here or there's going to be trouble," the store cashier's voice warned. "And I'm not taking my eyes off whichever one of you that is."

"Check out those gypsies," Candy Woman said as she poured a saucer of chopped up M&Ms into her milkshake.

I walked to the front window of the diner and watched the group like a fascinated child who was too young to be tactful. One of the younger men noticed my attention and turned away, politely trying to hide his distaste. "Walk like an Egyptian" was playing loudly on the radio of the Rebel Wagon and the little girl began to dance.

Impulsively I joined in the dancing from my spot at the window, making the girl laugh and wave at me until two of the women in their group came running over to herd her back to the fold, glaring at me for thinking to pollute their beautiful child. It was sweet, in a way. The little girl in the purple raincoat wouldn't be going through life unprotected if her people had anything to say about it.

I went inside the store to get a 7-up and some Sominex or something that could help me sleep through the sound of Candy Woman's voice for part of the ride. When I came back outside the replacement bus was pulling up and I hurried to get a seat on the right-hand side. Candy Woman followed like a run of bad luck, taking her usual place directly behind me.

"I like sitting near you," Candy Woman said. "You're too stupid to be stealing my shit and you make me laugh." Her booming guffaw quickly became a hacking cough. "Shit, this cold is killing me."

"Here." I handed her three blue pills. "Try some Tylenol cold medicine."

"Why, thank you, honey." Candy Woman accepted the pills, washing them down with a swig of Dr Pepper. "And here I was thinking you were just a snotty little cracker bitch."

My evil thoughts were less frequent now, probably because I was too busy trying to look at new things and keep an eye on my purse and duffel bag at the same time. The duffel bag was a trade from Ben, who accepted my Navy footlocker in return. The bag was easier to drag from one spot to another and it gave me a soft place to nap on during the longer layovers.

In less than half an hour Candy Woman was snoring peacefully from the Sominex and I was able to get all the way to chapter eleven in *On the Road*. As with Jack Kerouac aka Sal Paradise, it looked like my trip from Denver to San Francisco was going to be uneventful. And as feckless as I was, it was also possible that I might be dead by the age of forty-seven like Jack Kerouac but unlike my mother, I wasn't destined for sainthood.

xxx

Acknowledgements

Writing is a solitary act but no book could be brought to life in a cocoon. First thanks to David Booth, professor, advisor, and pal extraordinaire, and his good lady Ingrid for their friendship and support. Another round is due to my family in Christ at Dignity San Francisco and Dignity Dayton for the same, along with old friends like Shannon Demaree, Jennette Caden, and the Segal clan of Dayton, who always thought I had something to offer.

More thanks goes to under-appreciated English teachers everywhere like Mark McClane, James Boehnlein, and Charity's godfather Ed Davis, who was there for the birth. Thanks also to newer friends like Ernest Hebrard, Joe Lino, Karl Mettinger, and my long-suffering landlord Jerry Curtis for their many kindnesses. To my family: steps, stairs, and all, for the story that we've all written and are still writing together. To my parents, for the gift of faith.

A Note on the Typeface

The font used in this manuscript is known as Hightower Text, which was chosen for its aesthetics and readability. Hightower Text was designed by Tobias Frere-Jones in 1994 as a modern version of Nicolas Jenson's 1470 Roman type.

www.ingramcontent.com/pod-product-compliance
Lightning Source LLC
Chambersburg PA
CBHW021846020426
42334CB00013B/209